$295

*EARLY
AMERICA*

Bradley Chapin

EARLY AMERICA

The Free Press, New York
Collier-Macmillan Limited, London

To
Nancy Newton Chapin

Preface

*I*n this book I have tried to set out the essential narrative of our colonial history in a compact and precise form. Beyond the narrative, about which there is general agreement, one necessarily becomes involved with interpretations of the significance of events and institutions. Here there has been much disagreement, for example, about the qualities of Puritanism, the constitutional structure of the old empire, the effect of mercantilism on the colonial economy, and the nature of colonial politics. Rather than set out conflicting views, I have presented in the text the interpretations that seem to me to be most sound. The reader is referred to other views in the Bibliography.

The bibliography of early American history is immense. Anyone writing a book such as this stands deeply in debt to the great comprehensive historians such as George Bancroft, Herbert Levi Osgood, and Charles M. Andrews. He is also indebted to the more specialized scholars who continue to produce in large volume the books that give us both a broader and better understanding of the colonial past. I have relied heavily on these historians for both facts and ideas.

I stand in debt especially to Professors John T. Horton of the State University of New York at Buffalo and Curtis P. Nettels of Cornell University. They introduced me to colonial history. Professor Horton put at my disposal extensive materials upon which a part of Chapter Ten is based. I thank him for the help. The opportunity to teach courses and seminars at the University of Buffalo and at The Ohio State University has kept me constantly at work, and the teaching has probably influenced this book more than any other factor.

BRADLEY CHAPIN

Contents

Contents

EARLY
AMERICA

Chapter 1

Opportunity for Empire

*F*or a century after 1450, the Iberian kingdoms of Portugal and Spain monopolized the commercial and colonial opportunities created by the voyages of discovery. Portugal had sailed down the western coast of Africa, around the Cape of Good Hope, and through the Indian Ocean to the wealth of the Orient. Spain had broken the Atlantic barrier and from a first base in the Antilles had gone on to create an empire stretching through the Americas from Florida to Peru. Both powers regarded their areas as exclusive monopolies and had confirmed the idea by treaty and papal sanction. They had, in fact, divided the newly discovered oceans and lands between themselves.

The Intruders: Corsair, Sea Dog, Sea Beggar

Conditions in sixteenth-century Europe guaranteed that the kings of Portugal and Spain would not exercise their monopoly unchallenged. The Hapsburg-Valois rivalry, English Elizabeth's anti-Spanish policy, and the revolt of the Netherlands produced wars that would not be limited to European objectives.

The Reformation and its attendant wars of religion aggravated national differences. New merchant classes sought profitable overseas enterprises. Protestantism, profits, and nationalism furnished the forces that challenged the Iberian princes.

The first course was dictated by the logic, but not the facts, of world geography. Portugal had reached India by sailing south and east. Ferdinand Magellan, in a kind of heroic postscript to Spanish oceanic discovery, had reached the Orient by sailing south and west, and his party had circumnavigated the globe by the time it returned to Spain. If Asia could be reached by rounding Africa and South America, might not the same objective be realized by rounding North America and Europe? Through the sixteenth and early seventeenth centuries, France, England, and the Netherlands sought the northwest and northeast passages. Genoese John Cabot, in the service of Henry VII, made the first two North Atlantic crossings (1497, 1498). A quarter century later Giovanni Verrazano sailed the coast of North America for France (1524). Henry Hudson went out, first for the Dutch, then the English, discovering the great river and bay that bear his name (1609). A score of mariners followed. Jacques Cartier began the penetration of the continent via the St. Lawrence (1534–1542). The idea of a northern water route to the Orient died slowly; in quest of such a route the northern explorers laid the base for the claims of France, England, and the Netherlands to North American territory. Because the heroic voyages that sought the northwest passage produced no profit, Spain protested only formally. England also tried to find the northeast passage, and the voyage of Hugh Willoughby and Richard Chancellor resulted in regular commercial relations with Russia (1553–1554).

Protestant sea power thrust the challenge to the very vitals of the Iberian empires. Portugal's grip on her monopoly began to relax in the second quarter of the sixteenth century. To police the whole west coast of Africa proved an impossible task. Illegal traders regularly visited the Guinea coast, taking off gold, ivory, slaves. After the unification of Portugal and Spain, the Dutch made the main assault in sea campaigns that were the natural incidents of their war for independence. Beginning as mere interlopers, Dutch merchant captains openly challenged Iberian power in the East Indies. At Java, in the Moluccas, Ceylon, and Malaya, they traded with native princes. The Dutch States-General confirmed the *de facto* creation of a great commercial empire by chartering the Universal East India Company (1603).

While the Portuguese power withered, the raiders drove into the area of the Spanish monopoly. The anti-Valois policy of Charles V, King of Spain and Holy Roman Emperor, gave the French their opportunity. From Dieppe, Jean d'Ango let loose his privateers and they quickly found the weak spots in the long Spanish treasure routes. The treacherous passage from Havana to the Atlantic and the waters off the Azores became a galleon master's hell. The French raids took such a toll that Spain adopted a system of convoy, the armada.

Daring Huguenots even tried to establish settlements on the fringe of the treasure routes. In 1562, Admiral Gaspar de Coligny sent out Jean Ribault to establish a settlement; his effort at Charlesfort (South Carolina) failed. Two years later, René de Laudonnière made an attempt in Florida. Bringing Spanish military power to bear, Pedro Menendez annihilated the French party. But all of these acts were mere pinpricks on the edges of Hapsburg power. With the defeat of the Turks at Lepanto (1571) and the unification of the Iberian peninsula (1580), Philip II approached the apogee of his power. The sixteenth century had this far belonged to Spain.

Through two decades, Elizabeth I pursued those devious policies that ultimately committed England to open war with Spain. The complex causes of the Anglo-Spanish conflict can only be summarized here. Since English Protestantism was personified in Elizabeth, Catholic sovereigns could not help but be interested in the tangled conspiracies that sought the queen's death. Real or fancied Spanish backing of anti-Tudor plots continuously aggravated relations. Also, Elizabeth sporadically moved to the support of the embattled Dutch, inevitably alienating Philip. A further cause of war resulted from intrusion of the English into Spain's maritime monopoly.

English commercial penetration of the Spanish American monopoly, a persistent theme of European diplomacy for two and one-half centuries, began because Spain had no source of slaves under her control. The government let limited contracts, *asientos,* to non-Spanish merchants to guarantee an adequate supply. Behind the voyages of John Hawkins, the first fighting trader, was a large scheme. He wanted an *asiento* from Spain and would give in return protection from French corsairs. His first voyage (1562) was uneventful. The African Negroes sold at good prices in New Spain. Out again, Hawkins easily overcame a feigned resistance to the illicit trade. His third voyage drew blood. Having disposed of his wares with some difficulty, bad weather forced him to the port of San Juan de Uloa (Veracruz). The arrival of a Spanish fleet with a new viceroy brought parlay and agreement, which the Spaniard almost immediately violated. At point-blank range, in shoal water, the squadrons fought a murderous action. Only two of five vessels returned to England, bearing with them the news of Spanish perfidy.

After San Juan de Uloa, the greatest of the sea dogs, Francis Drake, dominated the scene. Though Elizabeth pretended friendship with Spain, Drake tore off the mask and did so with the queen's covert encouragement. Ocean marauding had been made hazardous to the extreme by Spanish protective measures. Drake struck at other points. With astounding audacity he stormed and took Nombre de Dios, the bastion at the Caribbean end of the trans-Isthmian treasure route. Frustrated at the very doors of the vault containing the gems and gold (the party had by-passed tons of silver because it was not sufficiently portable), Drake returned to a hidden harbor. Later he twice raided the mule trains that transported the treasure across the Isthmus. The second time he carried off a great booty. With the whole Spanish main on guard, only one soft spot remained—the stretch of Pacific from Peru to Panama. There fat, unarmed galleons laden with precious metals lumbered up the coast. Drake went out again in 1577, destination unknown. He passed through the Strait of Magellan and proceeded up the west coast of South America, where he took several prizes. Knowing that all the power of Spain would concentrate to prevent his return, Drake proceeded north and then struck out due west into the Pacific. Upon his return to England, the Spanish ambassador cried loudly for Drake's head as a pledge of Elizabeth's friendship. However, the queen, who could create those moments of high drama, went aboard the *Golden Hind* and bestowed the accolade of knighthood on Drake.

Spain stood eloquently defied. Through half a decade Anglo-Spanish relations steadily worsened. Then Philip set the ponderous wheels of Spanish power in motion. At Cadiz he constructed a great armada that was to proceed to the Netherlands, take off Parma's army, and invade England. Few doubted a Spanish triumph.

But a revolution, one that would shift the center of sea power to the North Atlantic, was in the making. The instruments of that revolution would be new English naval forces and strategy. Since the reign of Henry VIII the English had been developing a new navy. The great, high-decked galleons were refitted to carry much larger guns. A new class of smaller, swifter, heavily armed galleons were added to the fleet. The new navy concentrated on speed and fire power. The Spanish regarded a naval vessel as a vehicle for infantry. The English used their ships as platforms for high-powered artillery. And the English captains knew how to use them. To a Drake or a Frobisher, English security was not best guaranteed by using the ships as an offshore wall against invasion. In their hands the fleet became an unsheathed sword, striking the enemy in his home waters.

With such forces assembled, Drake proceeded to destroy the first Spanish armada. He sailed into Cadiz harbor in Spain and burned it to the water line. Then he passed into the Azores and took the great galleon *San Felipe*, which yielded a treasure more than adequate for the Cadiz strike. Philip's career was persistence unrewarded. The Spanish armada, reconstructed, put to sea under the command of a landsman, the Duke of Sidonia. The English gave battle in the Narrow Seas. In a three day running action, the armada suffered serious reverses. Outmaneuvered and outgunned, the Spanish sought safety on the Flemish coast, where shoal waters nearly beached them. Gradually the armada struggled into the North Sea. Along the west coast of Ireland, violent storms wrecked many vessels. A remnant limped back to Cadiz. Though the war dragged on for fifteen years, all the rest was anticlimax.

In retrospect one sees that Elizabeth had clear-cut war aims.

She wanted Spanish recognition of free navigation of the seas; of freedom to trade, subject only to regular commercial regulations; of the principle that only actual settlement established valid title to newly discovered lands. As late as 1599 Spain refused to make these concessions. The war outlasted the queen, who died in 1603, so that it was left to her successor, James I, to make the peace.

James approached foreign policy dynastically. As the Stuarts had no quarrel with Spain, he opened negotiations immediately upon his accession. Diplomacy produced the Treaty of London. Because no agreement could be reached on overseas settlements, the matter was omitted. Compared with the French-Spanish treaty of 1598, which specifically endorsed the extreme Spanish claims, the omission was an English victory. In any event, the English interpreted the omission to mean that they were free to settle outside the area of effective Spanish occupation. As to trading rights, the treaty was open to several constructions:

> [W]ithout any safe conduct, or other special or general license, the subjects and vassals of both kings may . . . both by land and by sea and fresh waters . . . approach, enter and sail to the aforesaid kingdoms or dominions . . . to enter any ports in which there was commerce before the war, agreeably and according to the use and observance of the ancient treaties and alliances . . .

Interpretation of this clause was to become a source of constant friction.

By 1604, the limits of the Spanish Empire had been fixed by Protestant sea power. The lesser Antilles, the Guiana coast of South America, and North America above the thirtieth parallel of latitude had been opened to development by the nations of northern Europe. The Dutch had established themselves in the Portuguese empire. In the seventeenth century, England would challenge Dutch supremacy in the Orient and turn to the task of North American and Caribbean settlement.

As sea power opened the opportunity for empire, forces of change—economic, religious, political—worked powerfully to recast English society. The causes of expansion and settlement are found in these complex patterns of change.

Economic Causes of Expansion

The most pervasive forces urging Englishmen to move outward were economic. The general trends of the time, particularly a rapid increase in money supply, favored speculative efforts. Some inflation had occurred as a result of the opening of new silver mines in the Tyrol. A tremendous increase in specie had resulted from the discovery of the mines of Mexico and Peru. With an insufficient domestic economy and a deficit-financed government, Spain had assigned much of her bullion to the bourse at Antwerp to purchase imports and repay Fugger loans. The effect was inflationary. Prices rose and opportunities for profit multiplied. England shared in this upward trend, and her merchants sought opportunities for investment.

During the sixteenth century, English attitudes toward foreign trade changed radically. At the beginning of the Tudor era (1485), foreign factors, particularly the Hanse and Venetian merchants, had practically monopolized English external trade. The Tudors pursued a nationalistic economic policy. Henry VII led off with a Navigation Act requiring traders to use English ships when available. Tangling with the Hanseatic League and Venice, he gained English access to the Baltic and eastern Mediterranean. Through the reign of Henry VIII, the volume of English trade steadily increased. As chief minister to Edward VI, the Duke of Northumberland, ably aided by Thomas Gresham, attempted to give a larger portion of the foreign trade to English factors. Mary defied the Hanse, putting the valuable Flanders' cloth trade into the hands of the native Company of Merchants Adventurers.

These nationalizing tendencies came to fruition in Elizabeth's time. As far-ranging English seamen opened potential trading areas, the government chartered corporations to develop them. The traditional form of corporate organization had been the regulated company. Because it possessed a monopoly of a particular trade, merchants bought membership, much as a seat is purchased on a modern stock exchange. Members conducted their business as individuals. The Merchants Adventurers, enjoying a monopoly of the export of woolen cloth, was such a company. During the latter half of the century, the crown created many new companies. The Muscovy Company (1555) handled the Russian trade. After 1579 the Eastlands Company enjoyed the monopoly of the Baltic trade. The Venice and Turkey Companies became the Levant Company in 1592. The East India Company, a joint stock company created in 1600, challenged emerging Dutch control of the Asian trade.

An early, eloquent prophet of English expansion was Richard Hakluyt. At Sir Walter Raleigh's suggestion he wrote the *Discourse Concerning Westerne Planting* (1584). A straight mercantilist argument, it pointed to the economic advantages that would accrue to England if colonies could be established. Colonies would make the nation less dependent on foreign sources of supply. Commerce, particularly the North Atlantic fishery, would create a reservoir of trained maritime personnel. New settlements would drain off surplus population and create markets for English manufactured goods.

In his *Discourse*, Hakluyt wrote of the need for expanding markets. What created this demand for new markets? A technological revolution, rooted deep in the Middle Ages, bore fruit in Tudor-Stuart times. So long as men had traded, wool dominated the English economy. As an export commodity it went out in two forms—as raw wool or as cloth. The changing export ratio of these two forms was a sure, steady indicator of the emergence of modern England. Raw wool had been the great medieval export. Monopolized by the Merchant Staplers, the trade was rigorously controlled by government. Gradually the export of raw wool declined, and in the seventeenth century was prohibited by law. The domestic manufacture of cloth grew so rapidly in the three centuries before 1600 that an industrial revolution was in fact effected. Though subject to local variations, the main features of the process of change are easily discernible.

The production of cloth was subject to constant technological improvement—for example, the water-driven fulling mill and the replacement of the distaff with the spinning wheel. Mechanical improvements brought greatly increased production and an ever-widening variety of goods. The woolen cloth industry had been organized on a capitalistic basis since the late fourteenth century. Drawn by the need for water power and the desire to escape cramping guild restrictions, enterprising men relocated the industry in the rural countryside. The great clothiers were aptly named "putter outers." Buying raw wool in large quantities, they put it out to households or other small establishments for processing and weaving. The entrepreneur moved the wool from stage to stage, acting ultimately as a wholesale merchant. Thus organized, the woolen industry produced a large surplus for export. Finding the markets or vents for the cloth was an item high on the agenda of Tudor-Stuart statesmen. Any blocking of the vents threatened financial and social catastrophe. Businessmen and politicians, seeking vents around the world, naturally were attracted to the idea of colonies as markets.

As producing units, American colonies appeared to have the potential to make the nation less dependent on foreign sources of supply. England imported large quantities of naval stores, potash, salt, sugar, dyes, fruits, and wines. National security and prosperity urged the development of English-controlled sources of such commodities. What England had formerly purchased from southern Europe she hoped to produce in the Lesser Antilles and the more southerly mainland colonies. The northern colonies would supply those goods previously garnered from trade with the Baltic nations.

The American fishery, promising immediate returns, was particularly valuable to England. There was the example of Dutch prosperity based on control of the European herring fisheries. This near-monopoly galled the English. American waters would supply the English market and provide a valuable commodity for re-export. In addition the fishery acted as a nursery for seamen, creating a permanent, trained reserve to man the ships of the line in time of war.

Hakluyt had argued that colonial development would drain off surplus population. Though statistics of the period are unreliable or nonexistent, the population of England probably remained static throughout the sixteenth and the greater part of the seventeenth century. Yet there is every evidence of large-scale unemployment. The cause is to be found in an agrarian revolution, which effected a ruthless redistribution of the English people. Elizabethan literature is pervaded by two protests—

one against enclosures, the other against the increase in rural rents.

During the medieval period, English agriculture had been organized manorially. The farmer lived in the manor village and worked his allotment, a series of strips in the open field. He enjoyed considerable security. His work and money obligations to the lord were fixed by custom and contract, and at law he was a free man. The enclosure movements seriously dislocated this stable rural pattern. The enclosures, various in kind, broke up the old village-oriented society by consolidating lands. In many cases arable land was enclosed. By abandoning the open-field strip system of cultivation, the efficiency of agriculture was improved considerably. More drastic in its effect was enclosure for sheep pasture. Large acreage that had provided gainful employment for many farmers was enclosed for sheep grazing; a shepherd or two could do the work. "Shepe devour men," wrote Thomas More.

> Sheeps have eate up our medows and downes,
> Our corne, our wood, whole villages and townes.[1]

The sharp inflation of the sixteenth century created more rural unrest. Landlords, particularly merchants who invested in country estates, resented the fixed customary rents. Whenever possible they renewed leases or installed new tenants at greatly increased rents. Many relied on hired labor that could be had for a short term and low wages. Second only to enclosure, the tactics of rack-renting landlords were the subject of the pamphleteers' protests.

In due course expanding industry would absorb the rural unemployed—small comfort for the people set adrift. Throughout the first century of American colonization the vagabonds— rufflers, wild rogues, pryggers of prancers, whipjacks, bawdy baskets—roamed the English countryside.

The economic factors affecting the settlement of America may be summarized as follows: Government policy supported the development of commercial opportunities by Englishmen; inflation and profits made risk capital available; experiments with

1. Richard H. Tawney and Eileen Power (eds.), *Tudor Economic Documents* (3 vols., London: Longmans, Green & Co., 1924), III, 81.

corporate forms accustomed Englishmen to think in terms of large enterprise; colonies appeared as potential markets for the expanding woolen industry and as sources of supply that would undergird national prosperity and security; a dislocated rural population looked West for land and employment. From Elizabeth's time on, economic facts urged government officials, entrepreneurs, and the plain people to colonial ventures.

The English Reformation as a Cause of Colonization

The second most powerful factor affecting English colonization was religious change. Coincident with the opening of the New World, the Protestant Reformation ruptured the religious uniformity of Catholic Europe. The fracturing process begun by Luther continued through the centuries of colonization. Men read the Bible, asked questions, and found different answers; a varied array of churches and sects was created. As the sects fragmented, governments continued to pursue policies of religious uniformity because princes regarded a common spiritual allegiance to be an essential bulwark of their sovereignty. The trend toward religious diversity collided head-on with policies of uniformity. The collision produced intolerance, persecution, war, and a compelling cause for emigration overseas.

The causes of the Reformation in England must be sought elsewhere than in the fertile fields of sixteenth century religious dogma. England withdrew from the Catholic communion for reasons of state. The separation of the English as a result of the desire of Henry VIII to have his marriage to Katherine of Aragon invalidated brought a long historic trend to a logical conclusion. Since the time of William I, English kings had resisted papal pretensions and had preserved a fair degree of autonomy for the English church. Frustrated by the pope's incapacity to deliver his "divorce," Henry moved in Parliament to sever the connection. The First Act of Supremacy (1534), rejected papal authority and made the king the supreme head of the *Anglicana Ecclesia*. But the revolt against Rome was no invitation to Protestant reformers, and The Six Acts prescribing a rigid orthodoxy drove the point home. The Henrician Reformation established the independence of the English church, but in liturgy, doctrine, and internal polity that church remained Catholic.

Through the stormy, short reigns of Henry's first two successors, the English church oscillated violently between the poles of Rome and Geneva. In the reign of the boy-king Edward VI, Somerset and Northumberland pushed the church rapidly in the direction of Protestant doctrine and practice. Acts of Uniformity ordered the use of Thomas Cranmer's magnificent Book of Common Prayer. Edward's Catholic sister, Mary Tudor, pulled the English back to the Roman communion. Because the government enforced conformity by statutes armed with penal sanctions, the English people had been forced for a generation to play a grim kind of religious roulette.

The first order of business for young Elizabeth was to produce a durable church settlement. She approached the problem as one of national policy, without strong religious sentiments. Her first Parliament laid the base for settlement. A new Act of Supremacy cut the nation loose from the pope. Another Act of Uniformity readopted the second Book of Common Prayer. The episcopal system and much of the liturgy of Rome were retained. Having made the effort to construct a Church of England on a broad base somewhere in the middle ground between Geneva and Rome, Elizabeth approached the problem of enforcement in the spirit of moderation. Persecution was alien to her character; she did not wish, she said, to make windows into her subjects' souls. The great majority accepted the settlement, whereas others, with covert reservations, conformed only outwardly. But no compromise could accommodate all. On one side of the settlement, labeled recusants, stood the unreconstructed Roman Catholics. At the other extreme was a diverse group who wanted a more thoroughly Protestant church. The Nonconformists included a large group of Puritans and smaller congregations of Separatists. At different times each of these religious communities provided substantial numbers of emigrants to America.

The nature of the Anglo-Spanish conflict made every Catholic a potential enemy agent. A minority of Catholics, at home and in exile, worked actively for the Counter Reformation. Daring Jesuits filtered through the country, traveling, they said, only for souls. Parliament consistently regarded Catholic activity as high treason and the law officers prosecuted Catholics intermittently. By early Stuart times a permanent, largely unmolested, Catholic minority lived within the nation. At all times they existed under the ban of law. Any crisis, foreign or domestic, tended to whip up a sudden storm of anti-Catholic hysteria. The ingrained prejudice against the Catholic is a permanent fact of seventeenth and eighteenth century English and American history. The hope of toleration attracted many Catholics to America.

The Protestant Nonconformists were more numerous, powerful, and articulate. Puritanism enrolled the majority of the Nonconformists. Though the term *Puritan* covered persons of various opinions, certain common points of view are discernible: they tended toward the theology of John Calvin and regarded the Bible as the sole and adequate spiritual authority; they rejected the episcopal system of church government; they advocated a simpler liturgy, one stripped of Roman panoply.

The Puritans' desire for reform moved through several stages, culminating in armed rebellion. During Elizabeth's time they worried first within the Church of England. In convocation they concentrated on attempts to simplify the form of worship. By the second decade of her reign, they argued openly in Parliament, urging a reform of the prayer book. In the 1580's the stern standardizing tactics of Archbishops John Whitgift and Richard Bancroft forced them to adopt new tactics. The Puritan clergy within the Anglican Church formed the "Classis," a secret synod whose members covenanted secretly to introduce as many reformed practices as possible.

The accession of James I brought renewed hope to the Puritans. As he proceeded toward London, the nonconforming divines presented their program of change in the Millenary Petition. Fancying himself a theologian, James summoned a great convocation of churchmen to Hampton Court. James detected a trend toward king-yoking Presbyterianism in the Puritan demands. With a famous aphorism, "No Bishop, no King," he pricked the balloon of Puritan hope. With the single exception of the new translation of the Bible, the Puritans made no gains during the reign of the first two Stuarts. By the late 1620's many Puritans regarded as impossible the task of reforming the Anglican Church. Surrounded by pomp, Archbishop William Laud forced the acceptance of his High Church ideas. To a Puritan his religious ideas were little different from popery. The great Puritan exodus to New England coincided exactly with the ascendancy of William Laud.

The second major group of nonconforming Protestants was the Separatists. Though they shared many ideas with the Puritans, the major tenet of their belief was the separation of church and state. The Separatist church was a community of like-minded believers, bound together in voluntary association. Government regarded the Separatists as particularly obnoxious. From the monarch's point of view the severing of church from state threatened to undermine all authority.

Politics and the Imperial Opportunity

During the first century of American colonization, the English worked out a constitutional settlement that profoundly affected the development of America. The central fact explaining the development of the English Constitution is a tension between the monarchy and the community. The kings tended constantly to consolidate authority in their hands whereas the community strove to check royal power, affecting the balance of constitutional power in the process. Through the long medieval cycle, the kingly power had been limited by a feudal nobility jealous of its rights. Magna Carta is but the most famous of the many documents that illustrate this role of the barons.

During the early fifteenth century a variety of forces had weakened the feudal nobility. By law when possible, by force if necessary, Henry VII virtually destroyed their power. The Tudors were despots limited largely by conscience and policy. The Tudor genius consisted of their capacity to use royal power for the national advantage, to popularize a despotism. Elizabeth summarized the best of the Tudor effort in her "golden speech":

To be a King and wear a crown is a thing more glorious to

them that see it than it is pleasing to them that bear it: for myself,
I was never so much enticed with the glorious name of a King,
or royal authority of a queen, as delighted that God had made
me his instrument to maintain his truth and glory and to defend
this Kingdome (as I said) from peril, dishonour, tyranny, and
oppression.

There will never queen sit in my seat with more zeal to my
country, care for my subjects, and that sooner with willingness
will venture her life for your good and safety, than myself. . . .
And though you have had, and may have many princes, more
mighty and wise, sitting in this state; yet you never had, or shall
have any that will be more careful and loving![2]

However great the Tudors had been, the Constitution stood
on an unsatisfactory footing when Elizabeth died (1603). Personal reverence for the old queen had kept criticism to a minimum, but immediate political problems faced the new Stuart
dynasty. These included the question of monopolies, the contest
between the common law and prerogative courts, the future of
the Nonconformists, the royal revenue, the rights and privileges
of Parliament. Such an agenda demanded a high level of states-
manship, one too high for the Stuarts. The existing imbalance
of power in favor of the monarchy was aggravated by Stuart
theories of their divine right to rule. The hope of a more satisfactory constitutional settlement lay with Parliament and the
common law courts.

The nation quickly demonstrated its restive mood to James I.
Withholding traditional revenues, the first Parliament won two
victories for the privileges of Commons: the right to be judge
of their own election and freedom from arrest while going to,
attending, and returning from sessions. This first skirmish revealed the Achilles heel of the Stuarts—the poverty of the monarchy. The areas of royal activity had increased rapidly, with
inevitable increase in cost, but the concept of royal revenue remained medieval—that is, that the king should live off his own
income and certain traditional duties except in time of public
emergency.

James's first Parliament set the stage for a classic constitu-

2. William H. Dunham and Stanley Pargellis (eds.), *Complaint and
Reform in England* (New York: Oxford University Press, 1938), p. 347.

tional conflict, a struggle in which Commons used its fiscal competence to wrest concessions from the king. The long uphill fight produced an apparent major victory for Parliament in 1629. Financially embarrassed by the costs of war unsuccessfully waged, Charles I signed the Petition of Right. But within the year, he repudiated the document and launched his experiment in personal government.

Charles's chief ministers of church and state, Strafford and Laud, pushed their policy of "thorough," an attempt to govern England in the king's name without Parliament. That they nearly succeeded was due in large part to the impotence of the common law courts. The judges of these ancient courts held office during the monarch's pleasure. The Tudor-created prerogative courts, especially Star Chamber and the Court of High Commission, further weakened the central courts at Westminster. Here royal justice worked directly without regard to the common law forms that guaranteed the subject's right.

The Stuarts tried to circumvent Parliament by raising a revenue without consent. Though the great justice, Sir Edward Coke, stoutly defended the common law, the majority of judges came to heel. As early as 1607, the Barons of Exchequer upheld the royal right to levy taxes on foreign trade. In the *Five Knights' Case*, the judges approved forced loans. Charles I, violating every precedent, levied ship money on all England and in *King v. John Hampden* the courts approved. Justice Berkeley, answering the contention of the defense that the king could have no revenue except with parliamentary consent, said succinctly:

> The law knows no such king-yoking policy . . . I never read nor heard that Lex was Rex; but it is a common and most true that Rex is Lex . . .[3]

Through the 1630's, "thorough" appeared to be a success. The revenue was adequate for the peacetime needs of the state. Then Laud overreached himself. His attempt to force the Book of Common Prayer on Scotland brought on the Bishops' Wars.

3. Carl Stephenson and Frederick G. Marcham (eds.), *Sources of English Constitutional History* (New York: Harper and Brothers, Publishers, 1937), p. 461.

With England invaded, Charles called Parliament, dismissed it, then summoned the Houses again. In the Long Parliament the fight between prerogative and privilege blazed forth. Because the issues could not be compromised politically, the parties appealed to arms, bringing on the Civil Wars, the execution of the king, and ultimately Cromwell's protectorate.

The political events described above affected American development by spurring emigration. The problem of Protestant nonconformity could only be resolved politically. The steady growth of royal power caused Puritan and Independent to despair and helped straighten their desire to come to America. Others, such as Thomas Hooker, the founder of Connecticut, would not live in a society where the law was variable and capricious.

The fight against the king's prerogative produced a body of thought and precedent that would at a later date be directly relevant to the American struggle for political liberty. The parliamentary struggle for privilege would be reproduced in microcosm in every colony, thus rooting deeply in the American tradition the principle of legislative supremacy. Coke's sturdy, eloquent defense of the common law, particularly his *Institutes*, furnished many an American brief against royal authority. His basic idea—the supremacy of law—grew vigorously in America.

Thus the factor having the most immediate effect on America was the poverty of the monarchy. Limited financial resources made it impossible for the Stuarts to undertake the work of colonization themselves. If Virginia or New England were to be more than geographic phrases, private capital had to be attracted to the ventures. The kings turned to private sources, to the corporation and individual proprietors, to undertake the western projects. America was settled as a result of independent enterprise rather than by royal fiat.

Chapter 2

The Early
Settlements

Elizabethan Efforts

*E*nglish attempts to colonize America during Elizabeth's reign were incidents of foreign policy. In diplomacy the queen necessarily trod a twisting path. The power factors directly affecting English security changed rapidly: the Low Countries blew up in revolt against the Hapsburgs; wars of religion rocked France; Philip II subjugated once-potent Portugal. As they shaped policy and committed resources, Elizabeth and her advisors gave first consideration to recurring European crises, especially to the growing strength of Spain. If colonizing ventures fit the pattern of national security, the queen approved.

One royal advisor, Sir Francis Walsingham, consistently supported colonization. A leader of the war party, he anticipated the Anglo-Spanish conflict and steadily urged an anti-Hapsburg policy. A precursor of the elder Pitt, he advocated overseas attack as the most efficient means of weakening a European foe. All who harbored malignant designs against Spanish America looked to Walsingham as advocate.

With security factors dominating policy, the first English attempts at settlement attracted a restless, belligerent crew. They showed little talent as colonizers. Going or coming to Virginia, they would detour into the West Indies to bag a Spanish prize. They were men of adventure, interested in plunder, gold mines, or a short northwesterly route to Asian spices.

The Florida ventures of the French Huguenot admiral, Gaspar Coligny, first attracted Elizabeth to the possibilities of trespassing on Spain's western domain. In 1563 she backed Thomas Stukely, who proposed a settlement in southern North America. Stukely promptly turned pirate, raiding the ships of all nations. For a decade, relations with Spain worsened steadily. The queen considered seriously a proposal of Richard Grenville to establish a privateering colony in America. Then Spain and England temporarily patched up their differences by the Convention of Bristol and the Privy Council shelved Grenville's scheme.

The man most active in Tudor colonizing schemes was Humphrey Gilbert, a Devonian gentleman-soldier. Gilbert's primary interest was the discovery of the northwest passage to the Orient. In 1565 he tried unsuccessfully to convince the Muscovy Company, then the queen, to license a northern voyage. During the next decade he attempted colonization in Ireland. In 1577, with Spanish diplomacy in a new crisis stage, Gilbert proposed an armed assault on the North Atlantic fisheries to be followed by raiding the Spanish Main. The next year a patent was issued authorizing him to hold any lands discovered in what amounted to free and common socage. For six years he could settle Englishmen in America where he would have rights of government and a monopoly of trade. The major Elizabethan efforts at colonization were made under this patent and what was essentially a later reassignment of it to Walter Raleigh.

Gilbert's voyage of 1578 failed completely. Though details are missing, it is clear that the government barred privateering because of fear of open war with Spain. In 1580 and again in 1582, Gilbert made assignment of his rights to individuals. One of the assignments of 1582 prematurely proposed the resettlement of English Catholics on a tract of one and a half million acres. In 1582, Gilbert made a great effort, his last. He obtained substantial support from Southampton merchants. Organized as an association, Gilbert promised subscribers land and trade advantages. Before sailing he willed his rights to Sir John Gilbert and two others. In the summer of 1583, four vessels made a northerly crossing to St. Johns, Newfoundland, where Gilbert formally took possession of the land for England. Then Gilbert went in search of the northern passage to Asia, but foul weather forced him to make a course for home. On the return voyage Gilbert's ship went down. By the testimony of the chaplain, we are told that he went to a watery grave exhorting those about him not to fear, "For heaven is as near, by sea as by land."

The next year (1584), a royal charter vested the Gilbert rights in Walter Raleigh. He immediately dispatched vessels to choose a site for a settlement. His captains used the Canaries-Indies route and chose Roanoke Island, off the coast of present North Carolina, as the site for the plantation. The first settlers, adventurers interested in gold and the passage to Asia, went out under Ralph Lane and Richard Grenville. Lane was governor, Grenville a general. From the beginning the expedition suffered from the divided command. Considering the nature of the enterprise, Lane made a good try. The party erected rude buildings, planted a crop, and contacted the Indians. In spite of their efforts, food was in short supply, and Grenville set out to replenish their store. In 1586, Drake stopped by on his way home from hammering the Spanish along the Main. After considerable parley, Lane and the remnants of his company shipped with Drake for England. Within weeks, Grenville arrived with supplies. He left fifteen men to hold the place and they subsequently disappeared.

Enlisting the support of prominent London merchants, Raleigh made his last Virginia effort in 1586. The corporation sent out 150 persons, including some women. John White, the governor, was instructed to settle Chesapeake Bay, but the marine leaders dumped him at Roanoke. Little is known of the colony. White returned to England to hasten the shipping of supplies. He arrived in the year of the defeat of the Spanish Armada, and we must imagine that his problems appeared to be of little consequence. In 1590, White went out with the supplies, but the colonists had vanished. The fate of the "lost colony" remains a mystery, and the best guess is that they were assimilated by friendly Croatan Indians.

Though no English settlement in America existed in 1603,

the work of the Elizabethans had not been futile. They had established the *de facto* English right to colonize. The hard lessons of Roanoke formed the beginning of a body of experience that in a relatively short time taught the sponsors of colonization much. Quick wealth would probably not be forthcoming. The need for substantial capital to see a colony through the early years recommended the joint stock corporation as the best agency to undertake the work. No crew of adventurers would succeed. The wealth of Virginia could be exploited only if the agricultural and commercial community of England could be transplanted to America.

The Virginia Companies

By the early years of the seventeenth century, Englishmen, mostly fishermen, sailed regularly to America. Interest in settlement gradually revived. The Earl of Arundel, desiring to relocate a group of Catholics, had a project afoot in 1605. This apparently stimulated Sir John Popham and Ferdinando Gorges to appeal to the crown for a settlement patent. The roster of petitioners included experienced mariners and others, such as Hakluyt, who had long been interested in colonization.

In issuing the Charter of 1606 to the Virginia Companies of London and Plymouth, James I exercised the royal authority directly. The grants defied Spain. They openly repudiated the Spanish interpretation of the Treaty of London and served notice to foreign powers that Virginia was a public undertaking. The grant established an area 100 miles square for each company. The Plymouth Company would work within the forty-first and forty-fifth parallels of latitude; the London group between thirty-fourth and thirty-eighth parallels. The area between was open to either group.

The provisions for the organization, financing, and government of the companies were unsatisfactory. James had before him the model of the East India Company, a fully incorporated joint stock, possessed of full jurisdiction within its sphere. Desirous of maintaining royal control in Virginia, the king ignored the example. No title to land passed to the companies. The

charter outlined an elaborate, unworkable system of government by council. A royally appointed council, located in England, would shape policy for all English America. In turn this
group appointed a council for each company. The companies
lacked adequate fiscal powers. Organized as associations or semi-
joint stocks, they could not offer stock to the general public.
They had, rather, to try to attract investors to single, specific
ventures. Though many of the patentees protested the large reservation of royal power and organizational defects, no amendment was made until the weaknesses had been demonstrated in
practice.

The first efforts of both companies make a chronicle of
catastrophe. The Plymouth Company quickly made its single,
unsuccessful bid. A first exploratory mission ended abruptly
when the party fell into Spanish hands. A second returned with
a good account of Maine. In the spring of 1607, two vessels
bearing about 120 men put out under George Popham and
Raleigh Gilbert. They located on the Kennebec (Sagadahoc)
River and failed to prosper. Food was short and the natives unfriendly. No commodity came to hand that could be sold profitably in England. Four dozen men hung on through a bleak,
bitter winter. George Popham died. When Gilbert decided to
return to England, the colony broke up.

The Virginia Company made its first effort in December
1606. The hope of gold and a northwest passage to Asia persisted and this fact dominated the enterprise. The first vessels
took out 144 passengers, all male, many of the gentleman-adven-
turer type. The company aimed to establish a commercial outpost rather than a real colony. The narrative of the first three
years is a tale of trouble. The miasmic climate of Jamestown
made the death rate truly horrendous: two out of three perished.
The limited acreage planted brought forth no harvest. The
surviving settlers lived on subsistence rations, measuring time
by the interval between the life-giving supply ships from home.
The council system worked badly at first, then not at all. The
products sent home were samples rather than cargoes. By 1609
it appeared that the London Company had sponsored another
Roanoke.

The London proprietors persisted. They reasoned that the

plantation had not prospered because of the basic defects of the charter, particularly in relation to government and finance. On their appeal, a new charter passed the seals in 1609, another in 1612. They may be considered together. The new charters reorganized the company as an incorporated joint stock, with the authority to govern vested in semi-annual meetings of the stockholders. In practice the treasurer and council had the power. In addition, the charter effected a vast expansion of the territory assigned to the company.

The great London merchant, Thomas Smith, undertook the job of reorganization. The company offered shares of stock to the general public and it sold well at £12·10/. To encourage emigration, all who went out in person were assigned a single share. The treasurer and council, assuming direct responsibility for government, decided to centralize authority in a single governor. In 1609, the company sent out a fleet of nine ships bearing five hundred persons and the new governor, Sir Thomas Gates. One of the vessels, with Gates and George Somers aboard, ran aground in the West Indies. The first ships to arrive at Jamestown discovered a handful of settlers wrangling bitterly among themselves. Gates arrived nine months later to find the colony all but wiped out by hunger, disease, dissension, and Indians. Week by week the crisis deepened until Gates decided to abandon Jamestown. The few remaining settlers boarded vessels for the return voyage. As they put to sea, they met incoming ships bearing reinforcements, supplies, and a new governor, Lord Delaware. Riding over any opposition, he introduced a stern military discipline, so that gradually the settlers rebuilt the village and planted crops. Virginia had been established.

The delay caused by the shipwreck of Gates and Somers led eventually to the establishment of a second colony under the auspices of the Virginia Company. The charter of 1612 added Bermuda, or the Somers Islands, to the domain of the company. With Jamestown in such a tenuous state, the company officials found it impossible to undertake directly the settlement of the islands. A voluntary association, formed out of the membership of the company, sent out the first party in 1612 under Richard Moore. Unlike the early mainland colonies, Bermuda had no "starving time." An excellent climate and the fortunate discov-

ery of a quantity of ambergris (a substance produced by sper-
maceti whales and much valued as an ingredient of drugs and
perfumes) encouraged the associates and settlers. In 1615 the
crown made the new colony independent of Virginia by incorporating the Bermuda Company.

The Pilgrims of Plymouth

Commercial and religious forces working in the second decade of the seventeenth century combined to establish the second
English colony in North America. By that time, the leaders of
the Virginia Company saw that the wealth of their domain could
be developed only if labor were applied consistently to New
World resources. To broaden their American beachhead, the
company granted some forty patents to groups who then acted
as private associations. Though few of the patents survive, they
probably were all similar in character. They made no land grant
but merely conveyed a right to settle. The associations directed
the local affairs of the plantation, subject to the general rules
of the company and the law of England.

The Independent, Separatist, and Brownist congregations
formed a potential source of plantation labor. Such congregations were compact, self-created communities of like-minded
believers. As early Stuart policy offered them no hope of toleration, these communities naturally considered emigration as a
means of effecting their religious purposes. Such a community
had gathered around the East Anglian squire, William Brewster,
and a nonconforming pastor, John Robinson. Though not themselves the object of persecution, they and their parishioners lived
in anxiety. In 1609, they made the decision to remove to the
Netherlands, the only European state then practicing toleration.
The Separatists sojourned briefly in Amsterdam, then located
in Leyden.

A decade of Dutch residence proved that toleration alone
was no panacea. These simple folk of rural England saw their
society corroding and dissolving in an alien, urban atmosphere.
The younger generation drifted from the church; they went to
sea; they began to speak Dutch. What testimony it is to how

well the Tudors had founded a nation that these unwanted, uprooted persons feared most their loss of identity as Englishmen!

Knowing both the perils and promise of American settlement, they opened in 1619 what proved to be complex negotiations. They turned naturally to the London Company of Virginia. Through family connections, Brewster had some influence with powerful Sir Edward Sandys. The precise timing of their application was inauspicious as Sandys and Smith were then fighting for control of the company. The matter did proceed as far as James I himself. As a condition, the Pilgrims had asked for official toleration. Though James rejected this, he promised not to molest them; and considering the Stuart record, such a pledge was as good as a sealed document. At this point the project failed, apparently because Sandys could not obtain the support of the council of the company.

The Pilgrims' progress became more involved. The attempt to come out under a patent granted to John Wyncop proved abortive. The Dutch West India Company offered New Netherlands, but Brewster rejected this on the advice of Thomas Weston, a London merchant. Then Weston became their agent. At first he proved effective, but ultimately his interests collided with the religious aspirations of the Separatists. A speculative entrepreneur, Weston obtained a patent from the Virginia Company in the name of a third party, John Peirce. After considerable delay, the Leyden Separatists decided to act under the Peirce patent.

Though the possibility exists that Weston acted in bad faith as an advance agent of the Council for New England, he organized an association under the Virginia Company grant. The associates formed a heterogeneous group. A few of the Leyden group, investing money and themselves, held multiple shares. Others of the Separatists held shares in proportion to the size of their families. For the London investor, it was a straight business proposition. Some who had no religious connection with the Pilgrims—John Alden and Priscilla Mullins, for example —invested their labor to come out as single shareholders.

It was a bootstrap operation, dependent on credit as well as capital in hand. After anxious delays, the *Mayflower* finally made a westerly course into the Atlantic in July 1620. The northern crossing was tempestuous but not as lethal as many on record. Making land at Cape Cod, the captain had made an apparent, but futile, effort to sail south to Virginia latitudes. The main party remained aboard the *Mayflower* while the others scouted the coast in the small boats. They chose Plymouth because of the harbor, good water, and unoccupied, cleared land from which smallpox had swept the natives. The *Mayflower* came up; the group signed the compact and gradually disembarked. Although a survey of Plymouth harbor shows clearly that the one place they would not be likely to attempt a landing in a small boat is on or near that huge rock, it remains the valid symbol of factual, heroic accomplishment. With Longfellow we may revere Plymouth Rock as "the cornerstone of a nation."

From the beginning, the interests of the Separatist settlers ran contrary to those of the London associates. Though there was little prospect of profit, each party suspected the other, and accusations and counteraccusations flew back and forth across the Atlantic. Weston abandoned the association. Peirce moved to strengthen his hand and obtained a deed poll from the Council for New England, which caused the Pilgrims to fear that he intended to reduce them to mere tenants. After years of wrangling, in 1627 the Pilgrim agent in England bought out the London interests for £1,800. To this amount, the colony debt of £600 was added. Bradford then formed a trading corporation, with all colonists as members, to sink the debt. From the 1630's until annexed by Massachusetts in 1691, Plymouth pursued its independent career.

The Council for New England

The Pilgrims had established themselves by chance on the land of the nearly defunct Virginia Company of Plymouth. The same year that the *Mayflower* sailed, a group of west country gentlemen had a proposal before Privy Council and Parliament to create a new company to develop northern Virginia. The moving spirit behind the petition was Sir Ferdinando Gorges, a man long interested in colonial ventures. Gorges had large, but impractical, vision. His status and sympathies identified him clearly as an aristocratic landholder.

Gorges proposed to transplant the English tenurial community to the New World. He hoped that a feudally based agricultural society would gain new strength in America. The patent creating the Council for New England made a magnificent grant of land between the fortieth and forty-eighth parallels. In most particulars the charter resembled the earlier grants to the Virginia Companies, but in one essential the council differed: it was a closed corporation, limited to forty members. The council was the corporation, a board of proprietors possessed of the right to dispose of and govern a huge domain. In essence, the Council for New England was a real estate company.

Gorges really never had a chance to realize his grandiose schemes. The inadequate capital resources of the landed classes predetermined failure. The merchants, invited belatedly and reluctantly, would not invest. From the beginning, mutual hostility marked the relations of the council and commercial interests. Gorges had attempted to obtain a monopoly of the northern fishery and this aroused the London Company. Their fight against the council, carried to the House of Commons, underlined the conservatism of the council's schemes. At all times the council emitted a strong odor of monopoly and prerogative; it repelled the merchants.

The Council for New England held its domain in free and common socage, as of the Manor of East Greenwich. Though land so held was normally not subject to subinfeudation, the council intended to distribute land by such a process. The recipients of the fiefs would be of two classes: members of the council and their families and friends, and private parties. Nonmembers would pay a large fee for their patent and the expectation was that this would be a major source of income. Except for the original fees, the council as a corporation could not expect to profit as landlord. Patent holders were not tenants of the Council for New England because the Statute of *Quia Emptores* intervened at the moment of subinfeudation to make the grantee a tenant of the crown. Most of the council grants specified that the tenant held the patent directly of the crown by knight service. This onerous restriction the Council tried unsuccessfully to have waived.

How, then, did the Council for New England hope to realize a profit? The members expected to profit as individual proprietors. Within grants they received they hoped to establish manors. As pristine seigneurs they would cash in on quitrents or other manorial dues. As a corporation the council retained the right to govern all New England. Probably they looked forward to a time when their principality would produce taxable wealth.

The Council for New England began operations in 1620. What its relations may have been to three early private planters remains unknown. Thomas Weston, the commercial agent of the Pilgrims, tried to establish a settlement at Wessagusset. A Captain Wollaston lived briefly at Mount Wollaston with a small party of gentlemen and servants. A third, Thomas Morton, established a short-lived but spectacular settlement named Merrie Mount. A thoroughgoing sensualist, Morton and his company drank deep, danced around a Maypole, wrote verse tending toward pornography, and cohabited with Indian squaws. The grimly moral Pilgrims and Puritans invaded this realm of pleasure on more than one occasion. Ultimately they drove Morton out.

The first provable patents were issued in 1622 and 1623, with John Mason and the Gorgeses, father and son, as the chief beneficiaries. To stimulate interest, Gorges subsequently made two divisions of land among the members. In spite of the presence of the monarch himself at the drawings, the majority were so little interested that they did not attend. Only Robert Gorges acted. He went out in 1623, carrying with him the seed of old England. The community had all the paraphernalia, including Governor General Gorges, Admiral West, and would-be bishop Morrell. One winter finished the feudal fantasy of Gorges.

Massachusetts Bay

While the Council for New England pursued its unrealistic course, mercantile and religious forces again combined to generate another successful plantation in English North America. The commercial impulse came from the ports of western England. The revived religious interest reflected the growing discontent of large numbers of Protestants.

The western ports had long been interested in America. Plymouth had held a potentially valuable patent; Bristol had tried a settlement in Newfoundland. All of the ports engaged more or less regularly in working the American fisheries. In 1622 the Council for New England granted a fishing license to a Dorchester merchant and the next year the council issued a plantation patent to Dorchester factors. In 1624, interested parties met and formed the Dorchester Company. Organized as an association, they raised a substantial fund. Through 1625 and 1626 the company attempted to found a fishing plantation at Cape Ann. As governor they chose a man already in New England, Roger Conant. Misfortune dogged the company. Saddled with high costs, it had the bad luck to arrive at the markets when prices were depressed. The type and location of the settlement guaranteed early bankruptcy. Cape Ann, too remote from good fishing, proved again that the occupations of farmer and fisherman were not readily interchangeable. The company wound up its affairs in 1626.

Two men, Roger Conant and Reverend John White, persisted. With a small group, Conant hung on briefly at Cape Ann, then resettled at Salem. Here, as the "Old Planters" they held a beachhead for Puritanism. White had been a moving force behind the Dorchester Company. An Anglican minister tending toward Puritanism, White saw in New England the chance to establish a purer church and the opportunity to convert the heathen in the bargain. The correspondence of Conant and White through the winter of 1627 revealed the common denominator of their thought, the desire to establish a reformed Anglican Church in America.

White set himself the task of implementing the idea. Mustering a roll of impressive names, he appealed to the Council for New England for a new grant. The nature of the negotiations remains a puzzle, for it seems unlikely that the nearly extinct council could have assembled the necessary quorum. Probably the Earl of Warwick, president of the council, merely reassigned a previous grant. However that may be, the extant copy of the patent created a voluntary association, vesting in the New England Company the right to settle between the Merrimac and Charles Rivers. Through the spring and summer of 1628, the new company buttressed the Old Planters at Salem with supplies and a new governor, John Endecott.

The lavish land grants of the Council for New England now rose to threaten the New England Company. Their patent cut deeply into a previous grant to Robert Gorges. Before committing more capital to the venture, the New England Company moved to put its title on a basis of undoubted legality. They turned to the crown, and Charles I bestowed valuable rights on a group tending toward Nonconformity. Why he did so at the expense of men like Gorges and Mason, strong royalists, is in part inexplicable. The times were troubled, Parliament belligerent, the nation at war. The best explanation seems to be that a hard-pressed, indigent king accepted a large sum of money and let the charter of Massachusetts Bay pass the seals.

The charter created a fully incorporated joint stock with authority to govern. Imperceptibly the New England Company disappeared as the Massachusetts Bay Company began to exercise its authority. For a time, the corporation acted as a straight trading company, strengthening Endecott's settlement with men and supplies. Soon it became apparent that the religious and economic aims of the interested parties were incompatible. At Salem, Endecott rode hard on orthodox Anglicans, thus threatening to embarrass the merchant factors. Soon it was clear that a determined minority of Puritans intended to use the settlement for their own purposes without regard for profit.

As the conflict between Puritan and merchant within the company became visible, Charles I launched his experiment in personal government. He began negotiations to end his wars, ultimately making peace with France and Spain at Susa and Madrid. Spurning the Petition of Right, he dissolved Parliament. Laud and Strafford pushed their high prerogative policy. This brought the English Puritan to a new point of despair; many began to consider emigration.

The experience of the prosperous East Anglican squire, John Winthrop, must have been typical of Puritan soul-searching.

Through a long period of doubt he weighed the factors for and against migration. Ultimately he reached the decision that it was indeed God's will that he come out, provided that the conditions were satisfactory. Winthrop made his decision sometime in early summer of 1629. In July he and others attended a general court of the company where the governor proposed that the residents in New England be given full power to govern themselves. For a month the Puritans debated among themselves whether such an abrogation of the charter would be legal. Finally, twelve of them signed a private contract, the Cambridge Agreement. They agreed to go to America with their families, if "the whole government together with the Patent" could be transferred legally to America.

Whether the transfer was legally effected remains a moot point. About one-fifth of the total membership of the company attended the special meeting that approved the Cambridge Agreement. So armed, the Puritans quickly reorganized the company, electing Winthrop governor. Through the winter they wound up their affairs. In March 1630, charter in hand, Winthrop departed with a fleet of eleven vessels. They represented the vanguard of the greatest emigration overseas in all English history.

Maryland

George Calvert earned and enjoyed the favor of the first two Stuarts. An Oxford graduate, he began a long public career as Sir Robert Cecil's secretary. For fifteen years he sat in the Commons. In 1619, James made him one of the principal secretaries of state. A man of peace, he opposed those who desired to reopen the Anglo-Spanish conflict. Approving of the proposal to marry Charles to the Spanish infanta, he conducted the diplomatic exchanges that looked to a Spanish match. This involved him with the papacy as well as Madrid. During the negotiations he became a Roman Catholic. The collapse of the marriage project, coupled with the Duke of Buckingham's violent denunciation of Spain, fired the war party. The surge of anti-Catholic sentiment forced Calvert to resign his office. Charles rewarded him for service rendered by raising him to the Irish peerage as the first Baron Baltimore.

Calvert had been interested in colonization from the beginning. He held stock in the Virginia Company of London and at one time was a member of the Council for New England. In 1620, he purchased territory in Newfoundland from a private party. During the next three years he came under the influence of Jesuit priests, probably William Blount and Andrew White. Perhaps Calvert, a tolerant man, had previously considered the possibility of a colony for religious minorities. Certainly the Jesuits expressed interest in a mission in English America.

In April 1623, the king caused letters to be patented granting Calvert a proprietary domain in Newfoundland. Five years later Calvert himself went out to found Avalon, and the next year he brought out his wife and children. The land was cold, bleak, and inhospitable. Only the dark, tempestuous sea promised a harvest. Leaving Newfoundland to the fishermen, he removed his family to Virginia where orthodox officials demanded that he take the oath of supremacy, a thing he could not do.

Back in England, he petitioned the king in council for a new grant south of Jamestown. The government looked with favor on any proposal to establish new colonies in the Virginia area. The Dutch had established themselves in the Hudson Valley, and the Spanish still claimed southern North America. New English colonies would preempt the land, thus keeping both rivals at bay. The charter proceeded as far as the seals, but then Virginia Company men blocked its passage. Baltimore next asked for a grant north of Virginia. Red tape, anti-Catholicism, and Virginia opposition twice blocked the second patent. On the third try it passed the seals, but George Calvert was dead.

Without interruption, Cecilius Calvert continued the work. The charter, clear evidence of the king's regard for Lord Baltimore, granted magnificent rights. The Baltimores held Maryland in free and common socage for two Indian arrows a year. No previous proprietor had enjoyed such unencumbered tenure. The charter created a palatinate and gave Baltimore all the power that any Bishop of Durham had ever enjoyed. This amounted virtually to vice-regal authority. The patent waived

Quia Emptores, thus permitting Baltimore to "assigne, alience, grant demise, or enfeoffe" the land. A further economic privilege forever exempted the colony from taxation. The proprietor had full right of advowson and the oath of supremacy was not required. The patent closed with the declaration that, should there be any dispute as to the meaning of the charter, the interpretation should always be that most advantageous to Baltimore.

In recruiting settlers, Baltimore faced a basic dilemma. The Jesuits had made no secret of the fact that the colony would be a haven for Catholics and a base for missionary activity among the Indians. In spite of Jesuit enthusiasm, few Catholics came out. With the injured Virginia factors playing up the antipapal theme, Baltimore had constantly to reassure the Protestants that they would in no way be molested. In 1633, a tolerant man walked the razor's edge.

After anxious delays, the *Ark* and the *Dove* slipped out into the Thames in November 1633. Baltimore's brother, Leonard, commanded as deputy governor. The party of over two hundred included two Jesuits and an unknown number of Catholics. That Baltimore expected discretion from the Jesuits there can be no doubt. A voyage of three months by the Canaries-Indies route brought them into Chesapeake Bay in March. Father White thought the bay "the most delightful water I ever saw, between two sweet landes." On the bank of the Potomac, White erected the cross and offered Mass publicly. With White and Leonard Calvert rode Baltimore's hope that Maryland would become a profitable, peaceful property.

Chapter 3

The Expansion
of New England

Through the five years after 1630, the Nonconformists poured into Massachusetts, driven there by the surge of Archbishop Laud's High-Church policy. To many English observers it seemed as if old England was breaking up and moving west. In New England, Winthrop and his associates labored to construct a Bible Commonwealth. The added burden of assimilating thousands of arriving immigrants posed a variety of problems, some of which seemed to threaten the very purposes of the colony. Most important was the question of religion. Though most of those coming out shared the Puritans' Calvinism, an age of religious contention inevitably produced dissent. Intimately connected to the religious issues were questions of government. In principle opposed to popular government, the Massachusetts leaders constructed an oligarchy which strove to impose a standard discipline on the community. In part, the incoming thousands had left England because Charles I and his ministers had repudiated constitutional government. Naturally some would resent the authoritarian rule of the governor and magistrates. To the crucial questions of religion and politics was added an economic problem, that of westward expansion. The Puritan leaders favored compact, contiguous settlements because they were easier to control. By 1635 the immigrants had created a pressure on the none-too-fertile lands of eastern Massachusetts. The rich valley of the Connecticut called them west.

During the first formative years, the issues of religious uniformity and the control of government agitated the community. The turbulent disputes, plus the desire for better land, engendered a series of new plantations, which ultimately developed into three new colonies.

Rhode Island

No colonial career illustrates better the interaction of advanced English ideas and primitive frontier conditions than that of Roger Williams. The son of a London merchant, his early career was shaped by the great jurist, Sir Edward Coke, whom Williams served as secretary. A graduate of Cambridge, he entered the ministry, inclined from the beginning toward Puritanism and dissent. In 1629, Williams became involved with Winthrop and a group of ministers who were interested in the overseas project. Though not of the original party, he came out aboard the first supply ship, the *Lyon*. Winthrop regarded him as a young man of great potential, "a godly minister."

Soon after his arrival, he refused the position as teacher in the Boston church because that congregation still maintained that it was the Anglican communion. In so doing, he revealed the spirit that would dominate his life. Born to dissent, Williams' ideas, always articulated, never stood still. He moved from Puritanism, to Separatism, to the Baptist faith, to end up the ultimate Protestant, a Seeker. Having attacked the Bostonians for failure to separate, Williams added another allegation to his indictment. In their judicial capacity, the magistrates had punished as civil crimes all violations of the first table of the Mosaic law. Williams denied that they had this right. Little wonder, then, that when the Salem church called him as teacher the authorities blocked his appointment. The young cleric moved to Plymouth where he conceived yet another objection, one that when announced would strike at the very foundations of the Massachusetts Bay Colony. On the ground that the king of England had no right to grant title to land possessed by the Indians, he declared the charter itself to be bad.

In 1633, Williams went to Salem as teacher and from that position he publicly blasted the charter. To a growing list of charges he added another, that the oath of fidelity that had been administered to nonfreemen was blasphemous. He argued that an oath by its very nature was spiritual and could not be tendered to the unregenerate. At this point Winthrop summoned him to come before the magistrates, but Williams' promise to mend his ways postponed the event. He did not mend his ways.

In the spring of 1635, the assistants examined Williams concerning the nonfreeman's oath. He remained unconvinced and the radical Salem church backed him by calling him as minister. That summer he appeared before the general court, charged with holding heretical opinions. Condemning his views, the court attempted to force Salem to deal with the rebel. They did so by withholding approval of a Salem petition for additional land. Williams fought back by calling upon all the churches to discipline the general court. After supporting their pastor for a time, his own parishioners abandoned him and Williams stood virtually alone. At the next general court, powerful Thomas Hooker debated with him but could not get the least recantation. The court ordered him banished from the colony, and in January 1636, Williams led a tiny party south toward Narragansett Bay.

Roger Williams had been more of an inconvenience than a menace. Scarcely had he been ejected when a controversy erupted that split the Bay Colony into two bitterly contending factions. Winthrop and John Wilson, the pastor of the Boston church, led the group defending the *status quo.* Conspicuous among the opposition were Harry Vane, Reverend John Wheelwright, and his sister-in-law, Mrs. Anne Hutchinson.

In 1636, the general court elected Vane governor. The election of the twenty-four year old youth probably was an expression of deference to his powerful father. On its political side, the conflict became a dispute between Vane and Winthrop for the control of the colony government. Mrs. Hutchinson, a vigorous, outspoken woman, precipitated the struggle. Though she shocked the sensibilities of the majority, she won over most of those with whom she had personal contact. The complex narrative can be reduced to the following scenes. Soon after her arrival, Mrs. Hutchinson began holding midweekly meetings in her home. At first she repeated the substance of the Sunday sermons to those women who had not been able to attend the regular service. Soon she began to expound her own ideas, and they were radical. She drew a sharp distinction between the covenant of grace and works. Those who accepted the covenant of works—and she put Reverend Wilson and most of the colony ministers on the list— were mere legalists, bound by the literal meaning of Scriptures. Those working under the covenant of grace were especially elect, for the Holy Spirit dwelled within them. Theirs was a religion revealed by direct divine inspiration. Naturally, Mrs. Hutchinson claimed to be under this covenant. Equally blessed, she said, were Wheelwright and John Cotton, the teacher of the Boston church.

After a preliminary round in the Boston church, whose members, including Vane, supported Mrs. Hutchinson, an *ad hoc* meeting of the magistrates and ministers considered the problem. Called upon for an explanation, Mrs. Hutchinson flatly accused the clergy of being under the covenant of works. A month later, at fast-day services, Wheelwright aggravated the differences by advocating the covenant of grace in a strong speech. At its next session the general court found Wheelwright guilty of sedition but postponed sentence. In the spring of 1637, the issue was resolved politically. In a bitter, violent session the court reinstalled Winthrop as governor. He moved quickly to nail down the victory. A general church convocation upheld the covenant of works and condemned a long list of the Wheelwright-Hutchinson opinions as heretical.

With church and state again in conservative hands, Winthrop proceeded against the leading dissenters. He summoned Wheelwright before the court and sentenced him to banishment. After the court had disposed of several others of the opposition party, the "trial" of Anne Hutchinson began. The charge against her amounted to libeling the ministers. She made a skillful defense, and when John Cotton intervened in her behalf it looked as if the prosecution might fail. In the end she condemned herself by stating that her criticisms of the clergy had been inspired by direct divine revelation. Found guilty, she inquired as to what specifically had been her crime. Winthrop peremptorily ordered her to be silent, saying the court knew of what she was guilty. In the spring Reverend Wilson cut her loose from the Boston church, declaring, with obvious relish, that she was irrevocably separated from the company of that congregation.

Between 1636 and 1641, the Massachusetts exiles established four towns in the Narragansett Bay region. Except for a dislike of Puritan policy, the founders of Rhode Island had little in common. Strong-minded individualists, they had no desire to form a colony. Ultimately they united, but they did so reluctantly, under strong external pressure that threatened their independence.

When Roger Williams left Salem in the winter of 1636, his future plans could not have been very definite. Perhaps he considered a life as missionary to the Indians. That winter he lived with Miantonomo, sachem of the Narragansetts. In the spring Williams began a settlement on the Seekonk River, but Winslow of Plymouth warned him off. Probably at Winthrop's suggestion, he crossed the river and purchased an indefinite tract along the Great Salt River. The party began constructing a simple village, which they named Providence. From the beginning, Williams' policies were simple and liberal. As a landed proprietor he resisted pressure to profit from his investment and sold land cheaply to all comers. The familiar covenant was the basis of government. From it and Williams' writings two principles emerge clearly. The government, rooted in consent, was operated by the people. Its sphere of activity was limited strictly to civil matters, thus effecting a complete separation of church and state.

In 1638, the defeated Massachusetts faction, led by the Hutchinsons and William Coddington, began arriving in the Narragansett area. Purchasing Aquidneck Island (Rhode Island) from the Indians, they began a settlement at the northern end calling it Pocasset, or Portsmouth. Coddington, a man of means and ability, dominated the enterprise. The original plantation covenant revealed Coddington's desire to create another Bible commonwealth, this time one that he could control. The subscribers agreed to live by the law of Christ and Moses. Coddington ruled as Judge, assisted by three Elders. This arrangement lasted about one year. Then the Hutchinsons ousted Coddington and he relocated at the southern end of the island. Under his direction the town of Newport began to take shape.

The founding of a fourth Rhode Island town, Warwick, was an incident in the stormy, eccentric career of Samuel Gorton. In a turbulent age, Gorton must be awarded the prize for contentiousness. His involved theology, heterodox at many points, was the product of a unique mind. His political theory was based on two apparently antithetical ideas. On the one hand, he regarded himself as perfectly capable of running his own affairs and would submit to no self-constituted American authority. Yet he always recognized royal power and insisted that government must be based directly on a specific royal grant. His ideas kept him on a merry-go-round of trouble.

Gorton first established a household in Boston, but soon removed to Plymouth. The Pilgrims ejected him for what they styled seditious behavior. From there he moved to Portsmouth and during a brief residence helped the Hutchinsons crowd out Coddington. His next stop was Providence, where he tried the patience of Williams. From Providence he moved to Pawtuxet, staying there until the leaders of that community decided to submit to the Massachusetts Bay Colony. He then bought an Indian tract called Shawomet and founded the town of Warwick. Claiming jurisdiction, Massachusetts intervened and brought him by main force to Boston for trial. Condemned as heretics, the Gorton party was distributed among the Bay towns. A year later the general court changed his sentence to banishment and, his travels over, Gorton returned to Warwick.

Deeply suspicious of any central authority, the ruggedly independent Rhode Islanders were forced toward union. Their orthodox neighbors—Connecticut, Plymouth, Massachusetts—resented and mistrusted these vigorous, unorthodox communities. Legally, the Narragansett towns were in a weak position because their territorial right was based on a series of Indian cessions. The Puritan neighbors, pressing their land claims hard, consistently made it clear that they would obliterate the towns if they could.

Coddington made the first move toward union by combining

Newport and Portsmouth into a loose federation. By 1643, the Puritan neighbors so threatened the autonomy of the towns that Williams decided to go to England to obtain a patent. He found the homeland ripped by civil war and religious dispute. He made his appeal to the parliamentary commission of the Earl of Warwick and in due course that body issued a patent authorizing the establishment of a government. The similarity of issues agitating the English communities on either side of the Atlantic became apparent during Williams' brief stay. The great debate between the advocates of a Presbyterian establishment and the Independent sectarians raged. Williams unhesitatingly threw his weight to the side of the Independents. He had interviews with Oliver Cromwell and John Milton. Before returning to America, he wrote a potent polemic, *The Bloudy Tenent of Persecution for the Cause of Conscience*. This strong argument for toleration had considerable influence among those who ranged themselves behind Cromwell.

Even after the Warwick patent was issued, the Rhode Islanders showed themselves to be somewhat less than eager to accept federation. Not until 1647 did they organize a government. In that year a primary assembly specifically contracted to establish a government, but it functioned poorly. Coddington, striving to maintain the independence of Portsmouth and Newport, opposed it. In England he obtained a document recognizing his proprietary right to Aquidneck. A weary Williams returned to England to frustrate Coddington's schemes.

Gradually, through the 1650's a general government began to emerge. At the time of the Stuart restoration, Rhode Island submitted immediately to Charles II. Through the agency of John Clarke the colony obtained a liberal royal charter in 1663.

The outstanding features of early Rhode Island government were the degree to which it was democratically oriented plus the complete separation of church and state. In all its aspects the little state was extremely reluctant to compel individuals and showed real deference to the popular will. Unique evidence of its liberal character is to be found in the efforts to use arbitration to settle civil disputes and in the use of a rude form of legislative initiative and referendum.

Connecticut

A variety of groups, located on either side of the Atlantic and variously motivated, effected the settlement of Connecticut. The Connecticut river, with trading potential and a rich arable valley, drew them in. The Dutch of New Netherlands, interested in the Indian trade, claimed the area. Of the New England colonies, Plymouth especially showed interest in the trade. Many within Massachusetts Bay were attracted by the rich, plentiful lands. In old England, Puritan leaders who feared the drift of politics in the early 1630's saw the area as a future refuge.

For a number of years the Plymouth Pilgrims had sought profitable trading opportunities in order to sink the debt owed to London factors. Edward Winslow often acted as their agent in such ventures, and in 1632 he investigated the possibilities of the valley. The Dutch, alarmed by the Plymouth activity, moved a small party into the area the next spring. They built a tiny fort and trading post, the House of Hope, at the future site of Hartford. The same year Plymouth followed up Winslow's exploration and established a trading post up river at Windsor. A third trading post, Wethersfield, was started by John Oldham, a far-ranging trader out of Massachusetts. In two years, Dutch, Pilgrim, and Puritan traders had located at the sites of the River Towns, the nucleus of Connecticut. The traders were soon disturbed by the advance guard of Massachusetts migrants. They began arriving in small numbers in 1635, locating first at Windsor. In short order their numbers overwhelmed the Plymouth traders, and in 1637 Massachusetts bought them out.

The year 1635 brought great interests to bear on the Connecticut settlement. One group emerges from a background made murky by the complex relations of the Earl of Warwick with the Council for New England. For several years Warwick had been president of the council. In the early 1630's, a group of powerful Puritans, the Lords and Gentlemen, led by Lord Say and Sele, appealed to Warwick for a patent. The Earl tried to get a patent by the seals of the council but failed, owing to Gorges's opposition. Nevertheless, Warwick deeded his apparently nonexistent right to the Lords and Gentlemen. That they were willing to proceed on such a flimsy legal basis is, perhaps, evidence of the measure of their fear of the future at the hands of Laud and Strafford in England. In 1635, one of the Lords and Gentlemen, Sir Richard Saltonstall, sent a party to Connecticut. The Massachusetts Puritans at Windsor made it clear that they were not welcome. Later that year the English Puritans decided to act on the Warwick grant. They sent out John Winthrop, Jr., with instructions to establish a settlement at the mouth of the Connecticut. Winthrop arrived at Boston just as Thomas Hooker was maturing his plans to move the Massachusetts congregation of Newtown to the Connecticut valley.

Though historians have had difficulty fitting Thomas Hooker into any neat category, it is abundantly clear and all agree that he was a tremendously able man, perhaps the greatest of the seventeenth century Puritan preachers. He was educated at Cambridge, the factory of nonconformity. His vivid, eloquent, and learned sermons attracted large congregations; they also attracted the attention of the authorities. Like Roger Williams, he had early been in contact with Winthrop and the emigrating Puritans. Hooker's travels took him first to the Netherlands. While he was there, a party of his supporters removed to Massachusetts to await his coming. Hooker returned to England in 1633 and, after a brush with the law, came out to the Bay Colony together with John Cotton.

In New England, Hooker immediately assumed a prominent position as the elected pastor of Newtown. Two things became clear in short order, that the leaders of the Bay Colony wanted him to stay and that he wanted to leave. The leader of a prosperous town, Hooker was a pillar of orthodoxy. The magistrates and elders turned without hesitation to Hooker when doctrine needed to be debated; witness the case of Roger Williams. Hooker was, indeed, one of the "wonders of New England." Though he and his parishioners had no quarrel with the saints in matters spiritual, they protested the policy that kept the population concentrated in the environs of Boston. The Newtown farmers, interested in raising cattle, found the available land inadequate for their purposes. In the spring of 1634 they petitioned the general court for permission to search out a better location.

Whether or not Hooker's motivation was more complex than land hunger remains a moot point. The records of the period prior to the removal speak only of this desire. Yet Hooker's subsequent course of action suggests strongly that he was not happy with the government of the Bay Colony. Though it would be a great error to picture Hooker as a democrat, he did think that Winthrop's oligarchy rested on too narrow a basis of consent. The indefinite state of Massachusetts law and the wide area of choice permitted to the magistrates were also distasteful to him. It seems reasonable to conclude that Hooker and the Newtown congregation had political as well as economic reasons for desiring to leave Winthrop's jurisdiction.

The arrival of John Winthrop, Jr., as the agent of the Warwick patentees posed additional problems. Through the winter of 1635–36, Hooker and Winthrop negotiated an agreement that permitted Hooker to settle on the patent. In return, Hooker recognized Winthrop as governor and admitted the right of the Lords and Gentlemen to settle the form of government. Provision was made for temporary government by asking Massachusetts to appoint an eight-man commission. Once this arrangement had been made, advance parties began to move into the valley. That winter a new congregation arrived from England and bought the Newtown properties. In the late spring Hooker and his company removed to the Connecticut valley; they settled at Hartford.

The younger Winthrop had already acted under his commission. In 1635 he began the construction of a fortified place at the mouth of the Connecticut which gradually grew into the town of Saybrook. Only one of the Lords and Gentlemen, John Fenwick, lived there. As the situation in England moved to the crisis of the Bishops' Wars, it became clear that the leaders of the Puritan party would not come out. Connecticut first assumed responsibility for maintaining the Saybrook fortifications. Though the dubious status of the Warwick patent confused the issue, Connecticut purchased some of the territory and then assumed full jurisdiction in the late 1640's.

As the River Towns expanded into a colony, another settlement was established within the ultimate boundaries of Connecticut.

New Haven

The history of the Puritan colony of New Haven begins again with an English parish and minister, this time London and John Davenport. A graduate of Oxford, he began his career as an orthodox Anglican but drifted gradually into Nonconformity. When Laud was elevated to the archepiscopal see, Davenport moved to Holland. There, during a residence of about three years, he decided to come out to Massachusetts Bay. Back in London, he gathered together a group of his former parishioners. Most prominent was the prosperous merchant, Theophilus Eaton. In one important respect this new party of saints differed from those who had gone before—they were urban rather than rural people, interested in commerce rather than agriculture.

The Bay Colony leaders welcomed the orthodox, prosperous Davenport-Eaton party and offered them their choice of land. For a variety of reasons they decided to move on. A mercantile people, they wanted a coastal location, which was not available in Massachusetts. Davenport, like many of the emigrant ministers, wanted his own religious community, one free of external control. After a short stay in Boston, they went around by sea to Long Island Sound and located at the mouth of the Quinnipiac River, early in 1638. The founders of New Haven purchased their land from the Indians and turned to the task of creating a government. The most rigid of the Bible commonwealths resulted. In the broad outlines, as Hooker had, they built on the Massachusetts model. Unlike Hooker, where Davenport and Eaton deviated from the type they moved toward an even more conservative settlement. They built on the Massachusetts rule that established church membership as the prerequisite to the exercise of every franchise. The basic instrument of government created what amounted to a self-perpetuating board of trustees that acted as a general court. This group made law and chose the executive and judicial officers of the colony. A more restricted, less popular government would be difficult to conceive.

From the beginning, New Haven was a commercially ambitious community, with large plans for expansion. In their planning they looked as far south as the Delaware, only to be frustrated there by the Dutch. Of the dozen Puritan towns that developed on the shores of Long Island Sound west of the Connecticut River, seven came to be closely associated with New Haven. The formation of the New England Confederation in 1643 forced the towns to join with some larger jurisdiction. Some chose Connecticut; the others federated, thus creating the colony of New Haven.

From 1645 to 1660, two self-created colonies, Connecticut and New Haven, existed between the Pequot River and the western boundary of New Netherlands. Connecticut, developing much better land, prospered; New Haven, unfortunate in its commercial venture and occupying poor land, did not. The crisis created by the Stuart restoration gave Connecticut the opportunity to absorb her weaker neighbor. New Haven remained true to the Puritan tradition, going so far as to offer asylum to several of the regicides. Connecticut proclaimed Charles II and then moved immediately to obtain a royal charter. John Winthrop, Jr., with adequate money and credit at his disposal, got a liberal charter for Connecticut past the seals in 1662. One by one the towns went over to Connecticut, until only New Haven and Branford remained. Through two years, Connecticut pursued an aggressive policy, finally absorbing New Haven as a result of an order of the royal commissioners who visited New England in 1664.

The Origins of Maine and New Hampshire

The histories of Maine and New Hampshire begin with the pretentious plans of the leaders of the Council for New England —specifically, with a series of grants made between 1622 and 1635. In making the grants, the Council, exhibiting a colossal ignorance of American geography, created a series of overlapping and competing jurisdictions and proprietorships. The confusion that inevitably accompanied actual settlement caused conflicts that clogged the calendars of English and American courts for generations. The grants were of two types. The first patents conveyed title to large areas and assigned rights of government to the holders. The second type granted smaller tracts for the purpose of getting the process of settlement started. The chief holders of the large grants were Sir Ferdinando Gorges and Captain John Mason.

The Council made the basic grants from which the Province of Maine would emerge to Mason and Gorges in 1622. It established the Merrimac and Kennebec Rivers as boundaries. At a later date Mason disassociated himself from the northern enterprise, and the southern boundary was moved south to the Piscataqua. Within and, in part, beyond this area a series of smaller proprietary grants were made on the Agameticus and Saco Rivers, at Cape Porpoise, on Casco Bay, and in the Muscongus-Penobscot region. On a few of these patents small settlements, sufficient unto themselves and without general government, developed.

In 1635, the Council for New England made a redivision that definitely assigned Maine to Gorges. Four years later the crown confirmed the grant with a royal charter. Gorges had just turned to the work of creating a government for Maine when the Civil Wars erupted. The Maine story of the 1640's and 1650's is an incredibly complex narrative of the conflict of minor interests. As the course of English events brought Charles I to the scaffold and produced the Commonwealth and Protectorate, Massachusetts revived her claim to Maine. The Charter of 1629 had assigned the Bay Colony a northern boundary three miles north of the Merrimac. When the northern source of that meandering stream was located, it made it possible for Massachusetts to claim most of Maine. In the early 1650's, the leaders of some of the northern settlements attempted to get a new charter from Parliament. Massachusetts then put the pressure on and by 1658 the last of the towns had submitted to her jurisdiction. Twenty years later Massachusetts extinguished the claims of the Gorges' heirs by purchase. Maine was to remain a part of Massachusetts for one hundred and sixty-two years.

However involved the early history of Maine may have been, it was a simple process when compared to parallel developments in New Hampshire. In 1629, the Council for New England made the basic grant to Mason. What he hoped would become New Hampshire was bounded on the south by the Merrimac and on the north by the Piscataqua. Settlers first moved into the region of the Piscataqua and quickly disturbed the tranquility of that peaceful stream. In the first instance they squabbled over boundaries, for the council had made numerous grants in the area. David Thomson, the representative of a small joint stock company, had settled at Odiorne's Point as early as 1623. Edward Hilton came soon after, establishing a tiny village at Hilton's Point (Dover). Thomson moved to Boston after a brief stay, and the Laconia Company took over the buildings left behind. The Laconia Company was a voluntary association controlled by Mason and Gorges. Under its auspices the old Thomson settlements were expanded to include Strawberry Bank (Portsmouth). In addition to never-ending boundary disputes, these little communities, particularly Dover, became the scene of acrimonious religious combat involving Anglicans, Puritans, and Baptists. In 1638, Reverend John Wheelwright, one of the exiles from Massachusetts, founded Exeter.

In the late 1630's, the status of the New Hampshire towns was much in doubt. The Council for New England had assigned the land between the Merrimac and the Piscataqua to Mason in the general division of 1635, but Mason died that year and the crown never confirmed the patent. By 1639, Massachusetts claimed jurisdiction on the basis of her extreme northern boundary. Through the next four years she annexed the towns one by one. After the Stuart Restoration, Mason's heirs contested the fact of Massachusetts control in English courts. In the late 1670's a court decision and an opinion of the attorney-general ruled that the Masons had proprietary, but not governmental, rights. At the same time the court rejected the claims of Massachusetts. The English government then cut the knot by buying out the Mason interest and making New Hampshire a royal colony.

The United Colonies of New England

The problem of federalism is as old as man's attempt to live together in a political society. The crux may be stated as follows: given any area that has ethnic, economic, religious, or historic reasons to exist as a political unit, two sets of interests, which may be in conflict, appear immediately—the special interests of specific locations and the general interest of the whole unit. The need to reconcile conflict between these interests poses a major problem for statesmen. The central problems of early American history were those of federalism—the imperial question of metropolis versus colony; the provincial problem of local versus whole-colony interest; the problem of intercolonial, ultimately of interstate, union.

The first experiment in federalism came in New England before 1660. By 1640, many factors had made an attempt at New England union logical. The New Englanders were of the same race—virtually unmixed English. They spoke the same language and shared the same heritage. With the exception of Rhode Island and Maine, they professed the same religion. Even more important than these several common denominators was the urgent pressure of problems that transcended the capacities of any one colony: Indian policy, boundary disputes, barriers to intercolonial trade, foreign relations.

The question of a Puritan confederation was raised as early as 1637 in a church synod. Through the next five years individual colonies proposed union on several occasions. Finally an eight-man commission representing Massachusetts, Connecticut, Plymouth, and New Hampshire met at Boston in the spring of 1643. The four Puritan colonies never seriously considered including Rhode Island and the Maine settlements because of their religious beliefs.

The articles of confederation, creating a "perpetual confederation," announced the purpose of union to be the protection of the purified American church-states from Indian and European neighbors. The government created was simple in the extreme. Each general court selected two commissioners who met annually in September. The place of meeting rotated. A majority of six was required for all decisions, and failing a majority, questions could be referred to the general courts. The commissioners had no executive authority. Though the sixth article seemed to create an absolute obligation on the part of individual colonies to carry out the decisions of the commissioners, in practice their authority was advisory. In fact, effective implementation of commission decisions needed unanimous consent. The articles are largely concerned with war and defense. In the event of threatened invasion, the commissioners were to meet, examine the case, and make preparation for defense. In a sudden emergency, all member colonies would come to the defense of the one threatened. At a later date the commissioners determined whether or not the call to arms had been justified. Offensive war could be undertaken only with the approval of the commissioners. The articles distributed the burden of the cost of war among the colonies in proportion to population. The nonwar powers are contained in the eighth article, which provides for settlement of intercolonial disputes, the formulation of a common Indian policy, a guarantee of unimpeded transit from one colony to another, and a general extradition clause.

Though the commissioners continued to meet well into the reign of Charles II, they were most active during the interregnum. A few selected examples illustrate the nature of their work. The Pequot War came before the union, King Philip's War after its demise. In the interval, the Indian diplomacy of the commissioners aggravated intertribal frictions and continuously threatened to produce a general war. The United Colonies backed the Mohegans in their running conflict with the Narragansetts. When the dispute produced a war, the Puritans gave their blessing to the execution of a Narragansett chieftain, thus further embittering the tribe. In the end the commissioners extorted a treaty from the Narragansetts which provided for tribute and established England as the mediator of tribal disputes. In these events one can detect the beginnings of what would become firm English-American policy: divide and conquer, then subject the tribes to the sovereignty of the whites.

While the commissioners developed their policy, they cooperated with the first of many altruistic and abortive attempts to civilize the Indian. The English-based Society for the Propagation of the Gospel in New England worked through the agency of the United Colonies. The zealous efforts of the missionaries to thrust education on unenthusiastic natives bore little result.

The animus of the Anglo-Dutch conflict in Europe spread naturally to America. Minor atrocities against traders and ill-defined boundaries produced the causes of local dispute. The Dutch of New Netherlands were the first to feel the power of the English thrust westward. Ignoring claims of discovery and overlooking in some instances actual prior settlement, the Puritans pushed into the Connecticut Valley and along both shores of Long Island Sound. By 1650 they had come within a few miles of Manhattan. A series of small altercations brought Governor Peter Stuyvesant to New England to meet the commissioners. The Treaty of Hartford (1650) drew a boundary most favorable to New England. It assigned to the English the greater part of Long Island and provided for a boundary close to the Hudson. Because the larger plan called for the annihilation of the Netherlands' American interest, no English government ever ratified the agreement.

Three years later England and the Dutch Republic went to war. This fact, plus rumors of Dutch intrigue with the Indians, produced a panic in southwestern New England. New Haven and Connecticut called the commissioners into a special session where they proposed an offensive war. The need for unanimity at once became apparent when Massachusetts opposed the desire of six commissioners. Putting a strained interpretation on the sixth article, Massachusetts argued that only the general courts could declare an offensive war. By defying the majority, Massachusetts prevented a needless war.

The power of Massachusetts was also made clear in the intercolonial disputes that came before the commissioners. For example, facts of geography seemed to dictate that Springfield belonged to Connecticut because the river bore her trade. Massachusetts never admitted this logic and, before the union, had established her jurisdiction. Connecticut countered by insisting that Springfield bear a share of the cost of maintaining the fort at the mouth of the river. She accomplished this by levying tolls on Springfield's trade. The town protested and brought the matter before the commissioners. Though not yielding on the principle, Massachusetts agreed to the toll system for a year. Gaining no satisfactory settlement, Massachusetts acted unilaterally by imposing duties on the trade of other colonies that moved through Boston. Under this pressure, Connecticut yielded.

Though the first experiment in American federalism produced no great result, it stood as an early warning that the development of effective Indian and foreign policies and of intercolonial comity lay beyond the competence of individual colonies.

Chapter 4

The English

on the First Frontier,

1606-1660

"*A*t the Atlantic frontier one can study the germs of processes repeated at each successive frontier. We have the complex European life sharply precipitated by the wilderness into the simplicity of the primitive conditions."[1]

The English emigrant of the early seventeenth century was part of an ancient society that had been reinvigorated by economic and intellectual change. Undoubtedly the varied stimuli of a new environment would cause him to modify his way of life. Equally obvious, however, is the fact that Old World ways would persist. The frontier process molded the American character, but it did so by modifying, rather than obliterating, traditional attitudes and institutions. The story of the English on the Atlantic frontier is the first phase of a peerless social experiment that ultimately produced a unique nation.

1. Frederick Jackson Turner, "The Significance of the Frontier in American History," *American Historical Association Annual Report for 1893* (Washington, 1894), pp. 199–227.

The Impact of Environment

"The stubborn American environment is there with its imperious summons to accept its conditions."[2] The first effects of that new environment were nearly disastrous. Excepting courage and ingenuity, the English came to the task poorly prepared. Though subject to variation, the initial assault on the new world can be generalized. Captains had the choice of two routes, each fraught with its own hazards. The favored route took the emigrant ships south to the Canaries then west to the Indies. Along the southern route, the threat of Spanish interception created a major danger, and the long sea voyage increased the chance of disease. The other route lay directly across the Atlantic. Though the time of transit might be as little as forty days, contrary winds and foul weather increased the hazards of a northern crossing. On either route, the voyage was a debilitating process. The vessels, small and crowded, were often pestilence ridden. If a majority might die on the voyage out, surely most arrived in a weakened physical condition.

A variety of criteria affected the choice of site for the plantation: a harbor of sufficient depth, yet defensible; proximity of potentially arable land; fresh water. Once located in these first settlements, the English learned in the hard school. Accustomed to a temperate climate, the settlers suffered from the extremes of the North American weather. The twin specters of disease and starvation quickly moved in. Smallpox, pneumonia, typhoid, dysentery were the killers. Though few actually starved, the diet through the first years was at a mere subsistence level. There is even evidence of cannibalism. The vital statistics of Virginia underline the grim nature of the business; during the first nineteen years only 20 per cent of the immigrants survived.

The forest and its human inhabitants were mixed blessings. Given the crude tools of the day, the task of clearing the forest was a huge one. Where possible, they chose land previously cleared by the Indians. In the process of reducing the obstacle of the forest, the settlers produced their first crop—lumber for

2. *Ibid.*

buildings, barrel staves, shingles, and naval stores and potash for export.

Mutual curiosity best describes the original relationship between the English and the Indian. On the positive side, from the English point of view, was the introduction of Indian maize. As the English cereals originally grew poorly in many locations, corn became the staple, literally the staff of life. To supplement their diet, the settlers quickly appropriated Indian knowledge of fish and game. The Indian trade, mostly for furs, contributed to a slowly growing volume of colonial exports. Expediency ruled Indian relations. The ultimate bases of English policy—that the Indians were separate, dependent nations with title to the land which had to be extinguished—evolved slowly. In some instances, notably Rhode Island, the settlers proceeded on such assumptions. More often, the English regarded the Indians as an inconvenient, inferior people, and from the beginning the history of interracial frontier relations was written in blood. For years the Indians kept the Virginians pinned down in the valley of the James. In the massacre of 1622, over three hundred settlers lost their lives. In Maryland the Susquehanna sporadically raided isolated plantations until frontier incidents came to climax in the Indian war of 1644. Maryland counted nearly five hundred casualties.

The early comers suffered much but learned quickly. The first generation developed the techniques of survival that made the task of founding the later settlements much less hazardous. Maryland and Massachusetts Bay had no starving time. By the 1640's that essentially new man, the self-reliant American pioneer, was on the way west.

Emerging Economic Patterns

As the hope of gold and silver strikes evaporated, it became clear that American prosperity would be based on land and labor. The major economic problems were to recruit and organize labor and to develop workable systems of land disposal. Through the first cycle of settlement, the managers tried various systems of labor organization and land disposal.

Some colonies, Virginia and Plymouth, for example, began

with land title vested in the company. This was the chief capital resource. The companies planned, at least during an initial seven-year period, to hold the land. The first comers were either stock-holders in, or employees of, the company. Labor would find its reward at the septennial division of accumulated profits. The corporate or communal system worked poorly. In a famous passage, William Bradford explained why. The prospect of an equal division dulled the initiative of the able and ambitious. Men hesitated to put improvements on the land, not knowing to whom it would belong at the division. As early as 1623, Bradford recognized the motive power of private ownership and assigned garden plots to individuals: "This had very good success. . . . The women now went willingly into the field, and took their little-ones with them to set corne." Virginia experienced a similar lack of success with communal tenure and, under the charter of 1612, the company began to grant land to individuals.

In proprietary Maryland feudalism and manorialism furnished the model of organization and distribution. The proprietor parcelled out estates, large and small, in free and common socage. The obligations of the contract would be discharged by an annual quitrent, perpetually due the proprietor. This system worked little better than communal tenure. With cheap land available, the settlers wanted an unencumbered title. For decades, the Calverts fought a losing battle to collect their quitrents.

In the South, the problem of an adequate labor supply was persistent. The chief inducements to labor were the promise of land ownership or high wages. Several colonies attracted immigrants with the headright. Virginia first used the system and there, any person coming out at his own expense or paying the passage of another obtained title to fifty acres. Maryland used a similar system, originally conveying one hundred acres per person. Though designed to attract labor, the headright was also an effective method of land distribution.

The system of indentures proved to be the most effective means of relocating English labor in the southern colonies. By such an agreement, an individual sold his labor for a term of years. In return the master paid his way out and furnished subsistence. Though a normal term of service was five years, a skilled artisan could redeem himself in less time. It was a mutually profitable venture. In spite of the rapid turnover, the master profited. In his promotional literature, Calvert estimated that a 100 per cent profit could be realized on a servant during his term. In a short time the skilled redemptioner paid his costs and was a free man. Once free, a career for his talent opened to him.

In 1619, an enterprising Dutch trader landed a cargo of African Negroes in the James River valley. Though introduced early, Negro slavery grew very slowly for a half century. A few of the greater planters bought slaves and prospered as a result. That Negro labor was not exploited more rapidly was largely because England had been excluded from the slave trade. Until the last decades of the century the proportion of Negroes in the total population remained insignificant.

The early southern colonist diversified his economic effort. Though far from self-sufficient, the planter, large or small, avoided the intense specialization that later made him economically dependent. Well-balanced farms produced a variety of fruits and root crops as well as grain. Livestock, particularly cattle and swine, multiplied rapidly. The planters made every effort to furnish themselves with whatever consumer's goods could be manufactured on the place. They did not shun trade but bartered briskly with Indians, Dutch, and English. As a result, the seventeenth century plantation South bore little resemblance to what came after. Though a handful of large planters emerged, factors during the first seventy-five years favored the small, yeoman planter. As early as 1612, John Rolfe planted a crop of tobacco, and it rapidly became the staple. Down to the Stuart restoration, the planter sold legally or illegally in a free market. Since expensive labor kept the crop small, prices held firm and profits were substantial. Until he had to compete with the masses of slave labor, the southern yeoman prospered.

The land distribution system of New England illustrates how the form of Old World institutions could be applied with radically different results in America. The New England town appeared to be a transplanted manor, stripped of its seigneurial features. Actually it most resembled the ancient English free village. Both the original Plymouth and Massachusetts Bay settlements fragmented rapidly, expanding in the process. The new communities were compact units, organized as towns. The general court gave the new towns land outright without any charge or fee. The town then constructed a village with each householder owning a plot of land adjacent to his house for garden and outbuildings. The remaining land was divided into large fields in which a man owned acreage in proportion to his wealth or to some degree to his need. Sometimes the villagers cultivated the fields in common, but this was the exception. The town used the rest of the land as commons for grazing and wood.

Both the town and the individual farmer aimed to establish a self-subsisting unit. The village had its blacksmith, its miller, cooper, and whatever other artisans a simple life required. The farmer diversified his effort, seeking first to grow what his family consumed. Stubborn effort gradually wrung from an infertile soil a small surplus that could be bartered for those goods that the family could not make.

From the earliest days, the coastal towns turned to the sea. They reaped their first harvest in the fishery, and the industry soon produced a surplus which the merchants sold in southern Europe or the West Indies. The needs of the fishery stimulated shipbuilding. In 1631, John Winthrop launched *The Blessing of the Bay* and a great New England industry. By the 1650's the yards produced vessels for export. The industry was so important that Massachusetts instituted a system of rigid inspection to maintain quality.

Merchant shipping formed the third branch of New England maritime enterprise. Its channels were not obvious because Dutch and English traders monopolized the major export—tobacco. Since other agricultural surplus did not find a ready market in England, the triangular trades began to emerge. They pivoted in the West Indies where the produce of the northern colonies—fish, grain, meat, lumber—could be sold for cash or exchanged for goods that were saleable in England and Europe. By the mid-seventeenth century an economic pattern had been fixed in New England. It would endure until modified by the industrial revolution and development of the trans-Appalachian West.

First Foundations of the Republic

The most significant aspect of our colonial heritage is political. Through almost two centuries the colonist transferred English political institutions to America and gradually reshaped them to the needs of republican government. Though it would be non-historical to assume that the colonists anticipated the result, we can state categorically that American government is what it is because of the colonial experience.

At the base of all American government is the concept of constitution. In America the concept has come to mean a fundamental, superior law, by nature a contract, which establishes a form and process of government and guarantees individual rights. The precedents for the concept run back through the colonial experience to ancient English practices.

The first American governments were formed in the context of a vigorous debate about the nature of the English constitution. The great opponents of the Stuart prerogative, men like Coke and Sandys, illuminated the old documents. Protagonists of the supremacy of law, they made Magna Carta practically a household word. The various proposals of the period—the Great Contract, Petition of Right, Nineteen Propositions, Heads of Proposals, the Instrument of Government—are all evidence of a desire to specify the rights of the subject and powers of government. Though the actual course of events in the early seventeenth century seemed to negate these theories, the founders of the early American colonies were influenced by such arguments.

The original sources of American constitutions were covenant and charter. Their use in America illustrates how older institutional forms could be adapted to the needs of a frontier community. At English law a corporate charter was no constitution. Any such grant could be revoked for cause by process of law under the writs *scire facias* or *quo warranto*. Yet the charters met several of the criteria of a constitution. The intent was to grant power in perpetuity. The word *forever* conditions almost every clause. They created a public authority, a body politic. They granted full power to make and execute law. They suggested, sometimes mandated, the form government should take. They guaranteed the rights of the subject. When three thousand miles of ocean separated the holders of such a franchise from king and courts, the charters became constitutions in fact.

The transformation of a corporate charter into a *de facto* constitution is best illustrated in the case of Massachusetts Bay. The charter of 1629 created a standard joint stock with power to govern. Through the first year the governor and assistants conducted the business from London, with the quarterly general courts meeting regularly. This normal pattern of operation changed abruptly as the result of a Puritan meeting held at Cambridge. There John Winthrop and eleven others agreed to come out to Massachusetts with their families. To this pledge they attached the novel provision that they would do so only if "the whole Government together with the Patent" could be taken with them. When Winthrop went aboard the *Arabella*, patent in hand, the charter became a constitution. As such it was jealously guarded by the Puritans as the basis of their authority and right.

The concept of covenant or contract as the foundation of government was rooted deeply in the theory of Puritan and Independent. Calvin and Beza, the great Protestant apostles, stressed the fact that authority finds its justification in an original agreement. From Geneva the idea of voluntary association as the basis of social order spread. It permeated Huguenot thought, justified Dutch resistance and independence, was the watchword of Knox and the Scots covenanting lords. In England it stimulated and undergirded the resistance to the Stuarts.

Since the English Independent congregations lived under the ban of the law without status as organizations, they formed their local churches by voluntary association. The covenants of the Separatist churches were declarations of common purpose and rules by which the community could be organized and ruled. In the fall of 1620 the Plymouth Pilgrims found themselves, without title or grant of authority, located on the lands of the Council for New England. They turned naturally to the familiar covenant and used it to create political authority. The Mayflower Compact is a short, simple document:

> [The signers] covenant and combine [themselves] together into a civill body politick, for [their] better ordering and preservation . . . and by vertue hear of do enacte, constitute, and frame such just and equall lawes, ordinances, acts, constitutions, and offices, from time to time, as shall be thought most meete and convenient for the generall good of the Colonies, unto which we promise all due submission and obedience.

Aside from a pious preamble, that was all there was to it.

The argument that the Compact was of little significance because the Council for New England made a proper grant of authority the following year must be dismissed. In fact, the Compact was a constitution. It created a government, a direct democracy of the signers, and it contained a pledge of obedience or allegiance, the very sinews of public authority. Most significant is the self-reliant attitude it reveals. Finding themselves beyond the line of law, the Pilgrims regarded themselves as capable of creating a government.

In the process of expansion, Massachusetts used the covenant regularly. As new towns formed under the authority of the general court, they created by covenant the nucleus of their community, a Congregational Church. As settlers went, or were driven, further afield, they established new governments by compact. The plantation agreements establishing Providence, Portsmouth, and Newport were essentially church covenants used for political purposes. The Rhode Island towns federated in 1647 by voluntary association.

Connecticut furnishes an excellent example of the explicit, conscious use of compact to form a government. Hooker's removal from Massachusetts is in part explained by his dislike of the politics of the Bay Colony. In Connecticut he became the firm, articulate spokesman of voluntary association. In 1638, he preached a powerful political sermon. Taking Deuteronomy 1: 13 as his text, he defended the proposition that "the foundations of authority is laid, firstly, in the free consent of the people." Within the year, such thinking produced the Fundamental Orders of Connecticut. By the Orders, the people "associate and conjoin [themselves] to be as one public state or commonwealth." They did this to "preserve the liberty and purity of the gospel" and the "discipline of the churches" and to establish the rules of law. The document proceeds to frame a government consisting of governor, magistrates, and general court. It regulates the processes of election in detail and assigns authority to the various branches. This clear-cut case of voluntary association may be regarded as the first American constitution.

These processes would be repeated on every frontier until the last vigilance committee laid down its arms. Voluntary association for public or quasi-public purposes, introduced thus at the very beginning, has been a powerful force in shaping American institutions.

Though legislatures were established in every colony at an early date, many began with power concentrated in the executive. In some cases, the struggle for survival in the early days dictated such a course. In others, the leaders feared that the religious or economic purposes of the venture would be threatened if authority was shared.

The original plan of government for Virginia vested power in a three-man council. In the face of the desperate problems of the early days, the councilors quarreled bitterly among themselves. From these squabbles John Smith emerged as strongest, and his vigorous, arbitrary, unauthorized rule saved the colony from extinction in 1608–1609. While events in America produced a one-man government, the company officers in England decided that a single executive would be sound policy. In 1609, they made the Lord Delaware lord governor and captain general with full authority to make law, judge offenses, and if necessary, rule by martial law. In the colony Delaware began to tighten discipline, a process continued until ill health forced him to return to England. From 1611 to 1617, Sir Thomas Gates and Sir Thomas Dale ruled the colony under a set of regulations formulated by the three governors. The Lawes Divine, Morall and Martiall, since known as Dale's Laws, are remembered for their severity. The code consisted of three major heads. It made church attendance mandatory and enforced the obligation with minute regulations. It established as capital crimes a series of offenses, some of which were relatively minor. Finally it embodied the military experience of Gates and Dale in what amounted to articles of war. The governors, enforcing the code rigorously, conducted the whole enterprise along the line of a military establishment. By sometimes arbitrary action, they guaranteed the survival of Virginia.

As early as 1617, the faction within the Virginia Company which ousted Thomas Smith in 1619 became visible. Its leading spirit was Sir Edwin Sandys who hoped to revivify the company with liberal economic policies and political concessions. A series of acts of the general court passed in 1618 became the basis for instructions to a new governor, Sir George Yeardley. These instructions, styled by the colonists as "the great Charter," authorized the first American representative assembly. Though this concession probably reflected Sandys' advanced political notions, it had immediate practical purposes. The company was attempting to attract new investors with liberal land policies. The establishment of a legislature guaranteed that those associating themselves with the company would share in making policy.

In July 1619, twenty-two burgesses, together with the governor and council, assembled in the Jamestown church. The burgesses had been elected by the free inhabitants. Though every act needed to be approved by the general court of the company, the assembly acted from the beginning as a micro-parliament. Claiming the privilege so recently won by the House of Commons, they judged their own returns, refusing to seat the representative from Martin's Brandon. Proceeding to business, the assembly reviewed Yeardley's instructions and framed several petitions to the company requesting changes. The legislation of the session dealt, among other things, with trade, religion, and Indian affairs. In its judicial capacity the assembly heard one civil and one criminal case. Then this first American offspring of the mother of parliaments adjourned.

The evolution of representative government in Massachusetts is the story of the transformation of the machinery of a commercial corporation into a self-governing commonwealth. It is also a narrative of the desire of the Puritan leaders to maintain control of the colony in the face of a persistent demand for less authoritarian government. From the beginning Winthrop personally held the charter and ruled with little regard for its exact provisions. Through the first months the governor and assistants made law, enforced it, and sat as judges. Since the charter required four general courts each year, it became necessary to create a membership. In October 1630, 108 men accepted an invitation to become free of the company. Since the charter empowered the general court to select the governor and make law, it was essential that the freemen be properly orthodox. To guarantee this Winthrop barred all who were not members of a Puritan church from the next meeting of the court. The subsequent evolution of representative government was always conditioned by the absolute requirement that the franchise be restricted to church members.

Even with such controls built in, Winthrop did not trust the general court and the assistants continued to govern. A tax levied by them in 1632 drew a protest from the residents of Watertown. Arguing that a tax so levied threatened to subvert basic English liberties, the protest raised the underlying question of the proper authority of the assistants and general court. Though Winthrop prevailed in the matter of the tax, the protest may well have forced the decision to give to the general court the authority to elect the governor and assistants. Two years later, the freemen asserted themselves vigorously and won full legislative power for the general court.

The inconvenience of having all freemen attend each general court caused the adoption of the representative system. After 1635, each town elected two deputies who, together with the governor and assistants, sat as a single house legislature. Within this framework, Winthrop and the assistants continued to assert a special authority. They claimed and exercised the right of the negative voice. Had the general court made its decisions by a simple majority vote, the assistants would have been outvoted easily. Since the charter had stated that a quorum of the assistants had to be present before business could be done, these magistrates claimed what amounted to a veto power in the general court.

The hotly debated question of the veto power, or negative vote, came to a decision as a result of the famous case of *Sherman v. Keayne*. The point at issue was the ownership of a sow. Mrs. Sherman brought suit for the recovery of the pig against Keayne, a prosperous merchant and moneylender. The assistants, sitting as a court, found for Keayne and then Mrs. Sherman carried the case to the general court. On the division, a majority of the assistants voted for the merchant, a majority of the deputies for Mrs. Sherman. The debate on the negative voice erupted again. Two years later the question of the special power claimed by the assistants found its resolution. The general court divided into two houses, the assistants sitting as the upper house, the deputies as the lower. Concurrence of both houses was necessary before laws could be enacted. The formation of a bicameral legislature under such circumstances created a significant example of an upper house as a custodian and guarantor of property rights.

The New England Way, 1630–1660

Religion shaped the culture of early New England, and in time that culture influenced powerfully the development of America. A historian of the first generation of saints states categorically, "Without some understanding of Puritanism . . . there is no understanding of America."[3] Here agreement about the Puritans ends. From then until now they have been the center of an acrimonious dispute concerning the nature of their influence. Was it positive or negative?

The Puritans constructed their society on the base of a coherent and articulated religious philosophy. In the main, the emigrating groups were not innovators. They brought well-formed and tenaciously held ideas of church dogma and polity with them. When John Norton wrote, "we only changed our Climate, not our mindes," he spoke truth. With the important exception of the covenant or federal theology, the New World Puritans worked out their destinies with Old World ideas.

Puritan theology began where Calvin's did, with man's original sin. From this premise, logic carried them irresistibly to a complete theory of religion and life. Adam's fall from grace, both absolute and permanent, was endlessly heritable. The power of salvation lay outside the capacity of men, all of whom were fundamentally corrupt and explicitly damned. Only all-powerful God could restore a man to grace and guarantee salvation. Since God was an omniscient being, He knew at once and for all time who would and who would not receive the divine favor. Thus each individual's ultimate fate had been predetermined.

Such a view of salvation resulted from a literal reading of the Bible. As an act of faith, the Puritan accepted the text as absolute, literal fact. But the New England Puritan, as much a product of the Renaissance as of the Reformation, had to buttress faith with understanding. To this end, the learned ministers evolved the covenant or federal theology, which made the scriptures not only a logical argument, but also a rational record. This

3. Perry Miller (ed.), *The American Puritans: Their Prose and Poetry* (Garden City: Doubleday, 1956), p. ix.

doctrine held that after the fall from grace, God of his own volition set out, in the form of a covenant or contract, the conditions necessary for salvation. This covenant was "nothing else but His purposes revealed." Though one might meet the terms of the covenant and still be damned, it did increase the odds of being assured of salvation. A God who would enter into such a contract would not be capricious. He would respect reasonable human rules in the majority of cases. He would make the fact of election known to those touched by his grace.

> The blessed God hath evermore delighted to reveal and communicate Himself by way of Covenant. He might have done good to man before his fall, as also since his fall, without binding Himself in the bond of Covenant; Noah, Abraham, and David, Jews, Gentiles, might have had the blessings intended, without any promise or Covenant. But the Lord's heart is so full of love (especially to His own) that it cannot be contained so long within the bounds of secrecy—*viz.* from God's eternal purpose to the actual accomplishment of good things intended—but it must aforehand overflow and break out into the many streams of a blessed Covenant. The Lord can never get near enough to His people, and thinks He can never get them near enough unto Himself, and therefore unites and binds and fastens them close to Himself, and Himself unto them, by the bonds of a Covenant.[4]

For himself, the Puritan had not only reconciled but united faith and reason. "His principal argument for the satisfaction of reason would be that once the Bible is believed by faith, it appears wholly and beautifully rational; it contains a consistent doctrine, that of the covenant, which makes it at once the source of belief and the fountain of reason."[5]

There has been much misunderstanding of the sources of Puritan polity and church organization. They evolved a form of Congregationalism, and because of surface similarities, many

---

4. Thomas Shepard, *The Gospel-Covenant; or the Covenant of Grace Opened* as quoted in Miller, *The American Puritans: Their Prose and Poetry*, p. 145.
5. Perry Miller and Thomas H. Johnson (eds.), *The Puritans* (2 vols.; New York: Harper & Row, Publishers, Inc., 1963), I, p. 58.

have concluded that they appropriated the Independent mode of church organization from their Plymouth neighbors. This is not true. The Puritans brought with them a highly sophisticated and complex theory of polity, that of non-separatist Congregationalism. From the beginning the English Puritans accepted the twin principles of religious uniformity and royal or civil supremacy. There was to be one church imposed on all by the crown. Though they accepted these general principles, the Puritans tended to emphasize the divine responsibility of kings rather than their divine right. They were also convinced that the Bible dictated the form of polity in its smallest detail and that they and they alone had read the Bible aright. Nonetheless, their view on religious uniformity and civil supremacy were orthodox.

When the Puritans came to the task of squaring compulsory uniformity with Calvin's doctrine of the divine election of a minority, they faced a major dilemma. The Brownists or Independents took the logical course to Separatist Congregationalism with its twin tenets of voluntary association and separation of church and state. The great majority of Puritans refused even to consider this solution. The other apparent alternative was Presbyterianism with its highly centralized control. Many Puritans found themselves in agreement with the aphorism of James I, "Your new presbyter is but old priest writ large." Committed to uniformity and civil supremacy, rejecting Separatism and Presbyterianism, attracted to the Congregational idea of a church as a union of the elect, they evolved the theory of non-separatist Congregationalism.

The apostle of this theory was William Ames. He held that the Anglican Church was a true church, but that it erred in certain particulars. These errors he was prepared to identify and eliminate. Miller says of Ames and company: "It takes, to say the least, a large audacity to pretend when you are amputating limbs that you are only removing warts and moles . . ."[6] The Ames argument ran as follows: At its heart the Anglican Church was implicitly but unconsciously Congregational; the elect joined the Church by associating with it and that the nonelect were there also made no difference; though the bishop or patron might

6. Perry Miller, *Orthodoxy in Massachusetts 1630–1650* (Boston: Beacon Press, 1959), p. 86.

nominate the minister, he was in fact called by the congregation; the episcopal hierarchy was not wrong as such, for the bishops and archbishops each had his parish, evidence of a proper "calling"; the prelates had merely overstepped the bounds by appropriating the royal authority to enforce uniformity.

Through the first decades of the seventeenth century, the Puritan Congregationalists remained convinced that they could convert king and Parliament to their views. When Charles I and Laud finally made it clear that this would not be the case, they emigrated. They left England in the name of uniformity, committed to Congregationalism and professing allegiance to the king. In New England the logic of their dogma and polity immediately created problems. The adjustment of their theories to the real job of creating a commonwealth created the New England Way and that force that we have labeled Puritanism.

An analysis of the main features of the New England Way and its impact on America must be by way of essay. There can be no absolute, certainly no monistic, interpretation of anything so complex as the development of national characteristics. Yet the following features of early seventeenth century American Puritanism seem to have had long-range influence: compulsion, intolerance, materialism, austerity, and a "zeal for education."

From the beginning, the elect saints amounted only to a minority of the total population of New England. Committed to uniformity they used the civil law to force the unregenerate to attend church. Such persons, in the church but not of it, at all times amounted to about 75 per cent of the total population. The Puritan oligarchs not only compelled individuals to attend church, but also forced a uniform doctrine and practice on the churches. Because the Puritan was convinced that the Bible was explicit and clear on all points of dogma and polity, it followed that each new church would be an exact replica of the older churches. It did not work out this way. Heresy reared its head. To make the Word clear to all, the leaders assembled two general synods before 1660. The first, coming in the wake of the Williams-Hutchinson troubles, labeled a specific set of ideas as erroneous and hence heretical. The second, held at Cambridge in 1647–1648, crystallized doctrine by adopting the Westminster Confession of Faith and set the form of Congregational polity.

The magistrates gave the decisions of both synods the force of law. Stated generally, then, the Puritan minority, absolutely convinced of its rectitude, stood ever ready to force the majority to accept its views.

The next question is whether one can find substantial traces of this compulsory moralism in later American history. The American people have always been secular-minded, but churchgoing. This is nothing else but a different expression of the Puritan idea that, though the majority be reprobate, the church is an agency of social control. Another example may be found in the desire of moralist minorities to compel acceptance of their views; witness the prohibitionist and abolitionist. John Brown, Carrie Nation, and William Lloyd Garrison were all "Puritans." Or again, modern sociology has identified a social structure in which a small dominant group controls a society for its own advantage with the acquiescence, even perhaps the approbation, of the majority. This describes precisely what the New England saints did in the seventeenth century. The large southern planter and the business tycoon played the same role in the nineteenth and twentieth centuries. The covenanted saints achieved their identity by voluntary association. Though there is an obvious inconsistency between voluntarism and compulsion, the moral purposes of the minority override logic. Every vigilance committee on each frontier was essentially Puritan, as are, in differing degrees, the host of voluntary associations that would improve our lot whether or not we want to "progress" in their direction.

Intolerance and persecution inevitably followed compulsion. Those who could not be forced into the church, even on a nominal basis, the Puritan forced out of the community. The first dissenters—Hutchinson, Williams, Coddington—came from within the ranks. Without hesitation the magistrates had ejected the erring brethren.

The Baptists of the Old World and the New arose simultaneously and from many sources. The common denominator of their thought was rejection of infant baptism. Such a view was logically consistent with Calvinism, for not until an individual had reached a mature age could evidence of his election be seen clearly. The so-called Particular Baptists held this view. More dangerous, from a Puritan standpoint, were the General Baptists who rejected the idea of election and held that Christ had died for all. Both kinds of Baptists appeared early in New England, especially in Rhode Island. The Puritan colonies tended to lump all Baptists together and to tar them with the same brush. Perhaps this followed from the fact that the Baptists, regardless of doctrinal differences, all held to Separatism. In condemning the Baptists, the Puritans went beyond the issue of their Separatism and labeled them, indiscriminately and inaccurately, as Anabaptists. By so doing they accused the Baptists of adhering to the radical social and ethical notions of the extreme left wing of German Protestantism. Unpopular minorities are rarely described with precision.

The tendency of Rhode Island toward Baptism alerted Massachusetts officials to the danger. During the early 1640's, the magistrates reprimanded several persons for expressing Baptist opinions. In 1644, the general court condemned the Baptists and prescribed banishment for all who advocated adult baptism. Several years later three Baptists—John Clarke, Obadiah Holmes, and John Crandall—visited Salem. All three were substantial businessmen, certainly not dangerous sectaries. Arrested in a private home, they were hauled off to church where they affirmed their belief. Salem shipped them to Boston for trial. Clarke and Crandall paid their fines and left. Holmes, either unable to pay his fine or desirous of suffering for his faith, felt the lash. Regardless of such persecution, the Baptists continued to filter into the Bay Colony. After 1660, the magistrates grudgingly tolerated them, and several Baptist churches were founded.

On the heels of the Baptists came the Quakers. All of New England, including Rhode Island, regarded the Quaker as an active subversive, a menace to both church and state. The followers of George Fox rejected the concepts of organized churches, professional ministries, and definite dogma. Their faith consisted of the belief in a one-to-one relationship between man and God expressed as the mystical and inspirational Inner Light. This light they refused to hide in any conventicle. They became active, articulate missionaries. Drawn largely from the lower classes, they expressed radical social, economic, and religious ideas. They invited persecution, and officials on both sides of the Atlantic obliged.

Every New England colony legislated against the Quakers. Punishment ran the gamut from fine to death. The first Quakers arrived in Massachusetts Bay in 1656. The magistrates quickly clapped them in jail, held them incommunicado, and then deported them. The general court responded with a statute, which the New England Confederation made general by resolution. Driven by their missionary zeal, the Quakers kept coming back, only to be imprisoned, whipped, and banished. In or out of jail, the Quakers were treated as less than human by the Puritans. For several years the animus and fear deepened. Three Quakers, previously banished, returned to Boston. Deported for a last time, they returned, obviously seeking martyrdom. Massachusetts Bay took their lives in the spring of 1660, thus setting the stage for the tragedy that had its climax in the witchcraft trials.

In the context of the seventeenth century, the New England Puritan certainly had no monopoly on intolerance. Yet he was the main vehicle for letting persecution loose into the stream of American history. Though Puritan intolerance was consistent with their theology, and thus understandable, there remains on the record the inconsistency of a persecuted people walking through "a wide door of liberty" and then slamming it shut. We remain to this day heirs of seventeenth century dualism. Tolerance and intolerance, persecution and magnanimity, have existed cheek by jowl with us from the beginning. Taking a long view, it becomes apparent that though the objects of intolerance may change, the principle does not.

The critics of the Puritans have charged that their piety was merely a thin veneer covering a hard core of crass materialism. Certainly they did not shun the work of this world. Rather, they gloried in it and made it a positive virtue. The injunction that the devil made work for idle hands (and minds) must have been reiterated constantly. But the Puritan philosophy of labor was not a resignation to toil that the bare necessities of life might be obtained. The spirit of the entrepreneur moved them. They searched out opportunities for profit in land, commerce, and the fisheries. Profit and material increase they regarded as evidence that they were following their "calling," and this as a consequence of divine favor. In unprecedented fashion, America offered the career for talent. The Puritan seized that opportunity and made of himself the typically American, divinely sanctioned, self-made man.

To what degree the spirit of capitalistic enterprise that motivated the New England Puritan can be ascribed to his religion remains a moot point. In a famous essay the German sociologist and economist, Max Weber, advanced the thesis that the Protestant ethic, particularly that of Calvinism, generated the spirit of modern capitalism. The Weber thesis, at once sophisticated and challenging, may be stated as follows: Catholicism, emphasizing the other world rather than this, regarded the work of this world as "morally neutral." The Church prohibited practices essential to capitalistic enterprise with its rules concerning usury and the just price. With the emergence of a more complex society the Church made grudging concessions to capitalistic methods. Though the Protestant leaders condemned usury they created "psychological sanctions" and applied them to the entrepreneur. Calvinism exhorted the elected saints "to make fast one's own call" and to attain certainty of one's own election and justification in the daily struggle of life. It recommended "intense worldly activity" as the best means of assuring the saint of the fact of election. "The God of Calvinism demanded of his believers not single good works, but a life of good works combined into a unified system."[7] God called the elect to labor and profit.

> "If God show you a way in which you may lawfully get more than in another way (without wrong to yourself or to any other), if you refuse this, and choose the less gainful way, you cross one of the ends of your calling, and you refuse to be God's steward, and to accept His gifts and use them for Him when He requireth it: you may labour to be rich for God, though not for the flesh and sin."[8]

To a large extent it is true that Americans have measured the good man by his worldly competence and the good life by material success. The New England Puritans must share with

7. Max Weber, *The Protestant Ethic and the Spirit of Capitalism* (New York: Charles Scribner's Sons, 1958), p. 116.
8. Richard Baxter as quoted in Weber, *op. cit.*, p. 162.

other groups and factors the early and steady commitment of Americans to material progress. Yet the saints surely are responsible for sanctifying work and glorifying gain. Their influence runs like an unbroken thread to Benjamin Franklin's pervasive aphorisms and on ultimately to find apotheosis on the Social Darwinism of the Gilded Age.

It is axiomatic that New England life was austere. Yet the symbolic representation of the Puritan as grim, somber, and rigid is misleading. It is true that they pushed their austerity to extremes by abolishing the drama, abandoning traditional holidays, and by maintaining the strictest Sabbath. Though later American generations have highly regarded the Elizabethan and early Jacobean dramas, contemporaries held the theater in low repute. The early New Englanders, in common with other colonists, brought their aversion with them. With players banned from Zion, the saints created a more somber calendar by abolishing Christmas and May Day as holidays contaminated by pagan practices. But New England gave us Thanksgiving. Weekly the Puritan kept a rigorous and ascetic Sabbath. The injunctions against all forms of nonspiritual labor on Sunday went to ridiculous extremes.

In regard to music, dress, and drink, the Puritans counseled moderation rather than silence, drabness, and prohibition. Seeking the utmost simplicity in their religious service, they stripped the churches of instrumental music. They did, however, publish a famous metrical version of Psalms. Since the *Bay Psalm Book* contained no music, the rendition depended on the ability of some member to set the music. The result, undoubtedly, was somewhat less than melodious. Yet they had no particular aversion to either instrumental or vocal secular music so long as it was "decent." The image of the Puritan garbed always in black persists but is erroneous. Clothing inventories and orders for dry goods indicate that they loved colors and bright ones. There are, however, many admonitions against overdressing, and definite distinctions were made as to the mode of dress appropriate to various classes. The statutes and sermons over and over again warned against tavern dwelling and drunkenness, but the Puritans could never have conceived an eighteenth amendment. One of their seers put it succinctly:

Drink is in itself a good creature of God and to be received with thankfulness, but the abuse of drink is from Satan. The wine is from God, but the Drunkard is from the Devil.

In several areas—literature, architecture, and household artifacts—Puritan austerity created works of simple beauty. Writing prolifically in a wide range from history to poetry, they evolved the plain style. Thomas Hooker and John Cotton were early masters of this style, which aimed first to make meaning and logical organization crystal clear. The result was not a dull prose, for they freely used the standard literary devices to give color and drama to their work so long as such devices did not obscure meaning. Such a style was adaptable to various *genre*. Hear the plain style of the Puritan poet, Anne Bradstreet:[9]

> If ever two were one, then surely we.
> If ever man were loved by wife, then thee;
> If ever wife was happy in a man,
> Compare with me ye women if you can.
> I prize thy love more than whole Mines of gold,
> Or all the riches that the East doth hold.
> My love is such that Rivers cannot quench,
> Nor ought but love from thee, give recompense.
> Thy love is such I can no way repay,
> The heaven reward thee manifold I pray.
> Then, while we live, in love lets so persever,
> That when we live no more, we may live ever.

The first generation of New England Puritans exhibited an amazing, lively "zeal for education." Within thirty years of their coming they created a comprehensive system of schools ranging from the elementary school to a degree-granting college. They built their college first. In the stormy year 1636, the general court voted £400 for the establishment of a college. The following year the colony bought land at Cambridge and enrolled a freshman class. In 1638, John Harvard perpetuated his name by leaving the college a substantial part of his library and a bequest of about £800. Under a pettifogging, corrupt first president the college failed to prosper. Its real educational be-

9. Miller and Johnson, *The Puritans*, II, 573.

ginnings coincided with the presidency of Henry Dunster; in a decade he established a liberal arts curriculum, trained additional teachers, and built a college building.

The founders of Harvard College built after the model they knew best, Cambridge University. Harvard was a true college in the English sense, with the scholars in residence and immediately responsible to a tutor. The college executed its curriculum by lecture, a great amount of independent reading, and regular oral quizzing by the tutor. The curriculum was classical and consisted of the three philosophies and the seven liberal arts. In addition the students, already masters of Latin, studied Hebrew and Greek.

The college was supported by public grants, private gifts, and tuition. Not only Massachusetts Bay, but also Connecticut and New Haven as well as individual towns, made contributions. Both the public grants and tuition (£2 per year) were often paid in the produce of the country. The bursar needed to be an imaginative man to use or dispose profitably of shoes, grain, lumber, wine, and livestock, to list some of the commodities delivered to his door.

During the 1640's, Massachusetts Bay laid the base for American public education with a series of statutes making compulsory the maintenance of elementary and, under certain conditions, secondary schools. The central concern was to teach the children to read. An act of 1642 required parents to see that this was accomplished. The act of 1647, the "old deluder, Satan" law, has attracted much more attention. It required each town of fifty families to maintain a teacher to instruct the children to read and write. Towns of a hundred families were ordered to establish secondary or grammar schools. These statutes were not merely pious declarations. The seventeenth century record is studded with examples of individuals and towns presented and fined for failing to meet the minimum standards. Most of the public schools charged a nominal tuition. As those who could not afford to pay were admitted free, it is fair to state that by 1650, Massachusetts Bay had established the principle of the universal availability of basic education.

The elementary school teacher concentrated on the first "R," paid some attention to the second, and probably ignored the third completely. He taught an ungraded class with children ranging in age from late infancy to adolescence. The length of time spent in school varied with family circumstances and the speed with which the child learned to read. The facile student, at least, did not linger long in the primary school. Typically he matriculated in the grammar school at the age of seven or eight. The first text in the village school was the time-tried hornbook. From this the student graduated to primers or spelling books. The first native primer was *Spiritual Milk for Babes in either England Drawn out of the Breasts of both Testaments for their souls' nourishment.* Before the end of the century, the standard *The New England Primer or Milk for Babes* was published. Before it had run its course some six million copies came off the press.

The majority left school when they had learned to read. Those who continued went to one of the grammar schools. There the curriculum had a single major aim—to teach mastery of Latin. In addition, the scholars began Greek. The boys hammered away at Latin grammar and literature for seven years before moving on to Harvard.

What explains this early and extensive commitment to education of a people on a raw frontier? Most commentators have assumed that the purpose was exclusively religious—to train a ministry and to rivet orthodox Congregationalism on the communities. The preamble of the statute of 1647 is cited to support the thesis that the sole reason for the establishment of the public schools was to foil "that old deluder, Satan." Also cited is *New England's First Fruits*, where the reason given for the founding of Harvard College was the fear of leaving "an illiterate ministry to the churches when our present ministers shall lie in the dust." That religious training was an important aim of New England education cannot be doubted. Yet equally important were the aims of "training for citizenship and service in a civilized state"[10] and of thoroughly grounding the leaders in the best tradition of humanistic learning as that tradition was then understood. That the schools were neither secular nor democratic can scarcely be

10. Samuel E. Morison, *The Intellectual Life of Colonial New England* (New York: New York University Press, 1956; originally published in 1935 as *The Puritan Pronaos*), p. 67.

laid against the Puritans as a criticism. The Puritans established a basic, durable principle of American education: that the public school exists to secure and advance the public welfare.

The Idea of Religious Toleration

The Protestant and Catholic Reformations of the seventeenth century left a Europe deeply divided on matters of religion. With few exceptions, princes applied policies of uniformity and compulsion. Southern Europe had been held for Catholicism. In the Germanies the rule *cuius regio, eius religio,* established by the Peace of Augsburg, permitted the ruler of each principality to choose between Lutheranism and Catholicism. Within each jurisdiction uniformity prevailed. Scandinavia was Lutheran. The reformed religions, based in Calvinism, prevailed in Switzerland, Scotland, and the Netherlands and claimed substantial minorities in France and England. Examples of even limited toleration were rare. The Dutch Republic tolerated all Protestants who professed a belief in the Trinity, but the Reformed Church was regarded as official. Henry IV had granted toleration to French Huguenots in the celebrated Edict of Nantes. Louis XIV reversed this policy and, after a long campaign of attrition, revoked the edict. All over Europe intolerance prevailed and the great colonizing states extended their policies of uniformity to their empires overseas.

The majority of Englishmen coming to America during the first half of the seventeenth century brought the concept of religious uniformity with them. In four New England colonies, Congregationalism was not only established but was so closely identified with government that near theocracies resulted. To the south, Virginians protected the Anglican Church rigorously. Only two colonies—Maryland and Rhode Island—practiced toleration and they did so for quite different reasons.

Without any public announcement, Lord Baltimore practiced toleration in Maryland from the beginning. There were compelling reasons that he should have done so. Realizing the deep prejudice against Roman Catholics, he knew that any anti-Protestant act or opinion would endanger his interests as proprietor and frustrate his effort to establish a refuge for persons of his faith. Baltimore also knew that there were too few English Catholics to populate his province. He was the first proprietor to use a policy of toleration to lure labor to his domain. Baltimore specifically instructed the Jesuit priests, who went out on the first ships, to practice their religion as covertly as possible and to do nothing to annoy the Protestants. The Jesuits had different ideas. Through the first years they tried to make Maryland a Catholic enclave in Protestant, English America. They said Mass publicly, proselytized openly, and engrossed land. Baltimore challenged them and applied the rule of the ancient Statute of Mortmain (1279), which forbade societies or corporations to acquire land. While the proprietor quarreled with the Jesuits, the colony filled up with Protestants who vastly outnumbered the Catholics by the mid-1640's.

The rise of the English Puritan party during and after the Civil Wars created a threat to Baltimore. In this context he moved to put the implicit toleration he had practiced on an unequivocal basis. In 1649, the Maryland assembly passed the famous "Act Concerning Religion." The law, negatively stated throughout, established toleration by applying harsh criminal sanctions to certain acts. It punished with death blasphemy and the denial of the divinity of Christ or disbelief in the Trinity. Reviling the Virgin Mary, the Apostles, or the Evangelists was punished by the confiscation of the reviler's estate. The calling of a person a "heretick, Scismatick, Idolator, puritan, Independant, Prespyterian, popish prest, Jesuite, Jesuited papist, Lutheran, Calvenest, Anabaptist, Brownist, Antimonian, Barrowist, Roundhead or Sapatist," brought a fine of 10/. Anyone who disturbed or molested a person "professing to believe in Jesus Christ" was to be fined or publicly whipped.

As a result of the visit of parliamentary commissioners in 1655, Baltimore temporarily lost control of his province. In the interval, a Protestant-dominated legislature denied toleration to those believing in "popery or prelacy." In 1658, Cromwell's council of state restored Baltimore's rights on the condition that he reinstate the policy of toleration. This he promptly did.

Led by Roger Williams, Rhode Island went far beyond the limited concept of mere toleration or forbearance of diverse religions to put the principles of liberty of conscience and separation of church and state on a positive basis. Several factors make an historical analysis of Williams' ideas difficult. His ideas evolved sometimes gradually, sometimes by spurts, and they were expressed in polemics and practice rather than in official acts. Also, we are so far conditioned to religious liberty that it is almost impossible for us to comprehend the explosively radical nature of his ideas in their seventeenth century context.

At the root of his thought concerning church and state are two basic ideas. The choice of a religion was an individual intellectual or emotional act. Compulsion might bring an outward conformity but it was absolutely powerless in the face of individual choice and conviction. The individual had to be left free to make his own religious decision. "The Church of Christ doth not use the Arme of secular power to compell men to the true profession of the truth, for this is to be done with spirituall weapons, whereby Christians are to be exhorted, not compelled." If one side of the coin dictated the spiritual integrity of the individual, the other side denied a divine right or mandate to any particular government. The boundaries of government were prescribed rigidly by the distinction between things civil and things spiritual. Government was to proclaim reasonable rules and work out compromises between conflicting interests; but it was never to touch the churches, which stood in relation to government as any other corporation or society. Williams severed absolutely the connection between church and state.

Williams first openly denied the divine basis of government and affirmed the spiritual freedom of the individual by defying the magistrates of Massachusetts Bay. At that point, no thorough statement elaborated his theories. At Providence, the original instrument of government was a stark, frugal agreement to abide by, or at least not to resist, the decisions of the majority. Williams' whole concept of separation is contained in the statement that the assembly could make decisions "Only in civill things." Through their first, erratic thirty years, the Rhode Island towns, alone or in combination, reconfirmed this simple declaration.

Williams made the first full statement of his ideas in three pamphlets published during his London visit of 1644. The most influential was the powerful, difficult *The Bloudy Tenent of Persecution for the Cause of Conscience*, a work described by a contemporary as "unforgivably ragged for the talent that produced it, and also magnificent." The introduction outlines the argument: Jesus Christ, as the Prince of Peace, required no blood sacrifice; there is no Biblical authorization for persecution; all governments are civil, without authority in matters spiritual; the only weapon in religious combat is the Word of God; the Old Testament Israelite state was not a pattern for subsequent governments; God does not require uniformity of religion; without toleration there can be no peace.

Eight years later Williams published *The Bloody Tenent Yet More Bloody* in answer to John Cotton's rebuttal of the earlier pamphlet. His later works included *The Hireling Ministry None of Christ's* and *George Fox Digg'd out of his Burrowes.* The latter pamphlet resulted from a debate between Fox and Williams during the Quaker founder's tour of America. In it Williams stated that religious liberty was not unlimited. He denied such liberty to the Quakers because their provocative behavior threatened the civil order.

Williams' final victory came in the third year of the reign of Charles II. The Stuart restoration forced all of the American colonies to establish or re-establish their right to exist. Rhode Island had never had a charter. Through agents, Williams appealed for one, asking that it contain a guarantee of religious freedom. The charter that passed the seals in 1663 contained the provision "that noe person within the colonie, at any time hereafter shall be in any wise molested, punished, disquieted or called in question for any differences in opinions in matters of religion. . . ."

Surely Roger Williams "comes as close as any American to being the embodiment of a fundamental principle of democracy."[11]

11. Clinton Rossiter, *Seedtime of the Republic* (New York: Harcourt, Brace & World, Inc., 1953), p. 199.

Chapter 5

The Origins
of the Empire

*B*etween 1606 and 1660, early Stuart statesmen turned to the task of incorporating the American colonies into an imperial system. They were not novices, for by the early seventeenth century the English had had a long experience with empire. Two main bodies of precedent—one legal, the other economic—constituted the raw materials for a theory of empire. Lawyers and judges drew on the practices of the old feudal empire to construct what amounted to an imperial constitution. In the area of economic policy, the planners had available as guidelines the already articulated major principles of mercantilism.

The Legal Theory of Empire

Simultaneously with the settlement of America, the English faced another essentially imperial problem. Because James I of England remained James VI of Scotland, the question of the relationship of the two realms necessarily came. James pressed for union. Balked in the House of Commons, the king turned to the law courts. In the name of Robert Calvin, a Scottish infant born after the accession of James to the English throne (hence postnatus), two actions involving real property were brought. The cases started in King's Bench and Chancery but were removed to the chambers of the Exchequer where the matter was argued before the Lord Chancellor and the fourteen judges of the common law courts. The issue, on its face, was simple: Could English courts entertain the case? The question could be answered affirmatively only if Robert Calvin was not an alien.

Sir Edward Coke, who reported the case, made a detailed analysis of the essentials of sovereignty under the heads of ligeance, laws, kingdoms or realms, and alienage. Throughout the opinion Coke relied on the fundamental medieval distinction between the realm and the dominions. The realm was England and Wales. This unit was defined in terms of jurisdiction, specifically as that area within the regular jurisdiction of the common law courts. The dominions and realms achieved their status as a consequence of the means by which they were acquired, either by inheritance or conquest. For example, Scotland was an inherited realm and within it the king governed with the consent of the Scots Parliament. Ireland was a dominion conquered from a Christian king. There the English kings had used the local law until John introduced the law of England. Subsequent kings could not change Irish law without the consent of the English Parliament, and the Parliament could legislate for Ireland if that area was named specifically in the statute. Coke further distinguishes a dominion created by the conquest of infidel territory. In such a dominion "the king by himself, and such judges as he shall appoint, shall judge them and their causes according to natural equity." Having restated the status of the realm and the dominions, Coke then provided the nexus that bound all together into an empire. That nexus was a common allegiance owed to the king. He then ruled that Robert Calvin was competent to sue in English courts.

This celebrated case was to have great significance at the beginning and at the end of American colonial history. At the beginning it served as a "conduit" through which the precedents and practices of the medieval empire could flow to be adapted by the lawyers to the purposes of the seventeenth century overseas empire. The core of Calvin's Case, so far as America was concerned, was that part that assigned to America the status of a dominion conquered from the infidel. The concept of dominion permitted imperial planners to apply a continuous stream of medieval precedent to America. As a result of this application the basic rules concerning jurisdiction, administration, and the authority of Parliament emerged.

Both American and English historians, assuming an inevitable progress toward democracy, have tended to establish institutional origins in ancient democratic practices. The facts rarely support such assumptions. The history of the administration of the seventeenth and eighteenth century empire is a story of the application of the royal prerogative.

The medieval judges of the common law courts, faced with the fact of a diverse and expanding empire, had resorted to a convenient but inflexible concept of jurisdiction. The courts had always regarded the lands actually held by the crown to be in a special category. Within the realm these lands were known as the ancient desmesne, lands owned by the crown as of 1066, the year of the death of Edward the Confessor. The regular processes of the common law stopped at the boundary of these lands. Occasionally cases came to the central courts on appeal from the ancient desmesne. The courts were reluctant to intervene and the rule emerged that "the King is so prerogative in his lands that he will have no one over him." Gradually the courts transferred the special immunity of the ancient desmesne to the dominions. The king remained "a pristine feudal suzerain as to his outlying possessions. It is in this guise that he is clothed when America is discovered, and from the moment that the first colonizing charters are sealed, the struggle commences to maintain in the New World establishments the capacities and powers conceded by the common law to inhere in the King as to his possessions outside the kingdom."[1]

From this assumption the basic rules of the new empire emerged. In the first instance the American dominions were the king's lands in both a proprietary and a political sense. He granted and governed them as he saw fit. So far as administration

1. Julius Goebel, Jr., "Matrix of Empire" which is the introduction to Joseph H. Smith, *Appeals to the Privy Council from the American Plantations* (New York: Columbia University Press, 1950), p. xxiv.

was concerned, the king normally acted through the Privy Council, which acted in colonial affairs as the old medieval *curia regis*. The similarities between the administration of the medieval and modern empires are many and striking. For example, the key administrative position in America was to be the royal governor. His commission and instructions were almost exact replicas of the commissions and instructions to his feudal counterparts, the lord deputy and the seneschal. The brief commission made the appointment. The instructions, originally a contract, filled in the details of rights and responsibilities.

The problem of the review of unjust judgments of dominion courts furnishes another example of the transfer of medieval practice to America. The dominion courts were, of course, outside the jurisdiction of the common law courts. Appeal, or more properly transfer, from the dominions came as a consequence of the application of the prerogative, either in response to a petition or because the king expressed special interest in the case. Such a dominion case was transferred *coram rege*, to the court of the king. It could be determined by King's Bench, but in its ancient capacity as a specialized agency of the *curia regis*, rather than as a common law court. The ultimate control of colonial justice, then, rested with the king in council.

The question of the authority of Parliament in relation to the dominions ultimately became the crucial point in the debate that preceded the American Revolution. This fact has tended to confuse analysis of the exercise of that authority through the colonial period. The matter is made even more opaque by lack of understanding of the actual origins of Parliament. The fact is that whenever Parliament acted in relation to the dominions it did so because the king chose to use that alternative to respond to a petition. This calls for further explanation. The origins of parliamentary statute-making are to be found in the prerogative rather than in representation. The king, as the mouthpiece of the law, spoke through his Council or *curia regis*. Any subject, either of the realm or dominions, could petition the king in council. The king might respond as he saw fit. He could ignore the petition, answer it as a particular case, or answer in terms of general principles of law. If he chose the last alternative, he had two methods from which to choose. He could answer through the Council, stating the law as an ordinance, or he could answer through Parliament, stating the law as a statute. So far as the dominions were concerned, Parliamentary authority remained on this footing in the seventeenth century. Where matters of general concern were involved the king tended to respond by statute. The response "could be thrust upon all by the formula of grant out of special grace and affection." As late as the Stamp Act of 1765, this formula was applied.

At the opening of the colonial period, the king was in a strong position. The American dominions were literally his property. Through the Privy Council he could control colonial administration and act as the ultimate judicial authority. He could enact new law through Council or Parliament. Yet all this power stood on a precarious footing; in fact, the king faced something of a dilemma. Medieval precedent concerning the dominions also presumed that the provincial subject was entitled to "the law of the place." Certainly it was in the royal interest that the law of the place, that is, American law, be reasonably consistent with English law. Yet if the crown formally introduced the common law, the rule of Calvin's Case intervened to minimize royal authority. For once the common law was introduced, only Parliament could change the law. The kings sought to establish reasonably uniform colonial polities while at the same time evading Parliamentary interference. They did so by inserting into each colonial charter a phrase conditioning every grant of power. The exercise of charter-given authority was never to be inconsistent with the colonists' rights as Englishmen. These various expediencies created the formula of royal control of America. In the end, they produced a still greater dilemma. Though the common law was not a part of the English American's birthright, he acted as if it had been. Through a century and a half the colonist unofficially imported the common law. By the eighteenth century the "law of the place" resembled the law of England. Unrepresented in both fact and theory, the thirteen colonies ultimately advanced a theory of revolution that was consistent with the medieval concept of empire. They declared themselves to be independent of a king who was "so sovereign in his lands that he would have none over him."

The Economic Theory of Empire

Though a great many historians and economists have written about mercantilism, they have not agreed what the system was. Indeed, some have argued that there was no system of mercantilism as such. Most of these scholars would disagree with the use of the word "theory" as descriptive of mercantilism. One historian has described mercantilism as a state of mind. Others have described it variously as a unifying system, a system of power, a system of protection, a monetary system, a conception of society. Mercantilism was all of these things.

It is true that by the early seventeenth century there was no system of English mercantilism in the sense of precise policy or an authoritative statement of theory. Yet a reasonably consistent body of precedent for policy existed by the time of James I. These precedents revealed assumptions about methods and aims that would guide policy makers through the seventeenth and eighteenth centuries. In the first instance, the economy was not free. Rather, the basic economic decisions were matters of state to be settled in the arena of politics. Though the precedents revealed considerable difference of opinion as to how the aims of policy might best be realized, there was agreement as to the aims themselves. In an era of intense international competition, the planners strove to use economic policy to guarantee English prosperity and security. Mercantilism was one of those major changes that marked the shift from medieval to modern society. The roots of the concept were in the Middle Ages. English medieval precedent revealed a series of general principles that became the foundation of mercantilism—the protection of agriculture, the protection of industry, the protection of navigation.

An Elizabethan Parliament succinctly stated the role of agriculture in a mercantilist economy: "The strength and flourishing estate of this kingdom hath been always, and is, greatly upheld by the maintenance of the plough and tillage. . . . The said husbandry and tillage is a cause that the realm doth more stand upon itself." To serve the end of national self-sufficiency, the government had regulated the import and export trade in grains since the later Middle Ages. The choice of controls revealed a conflict of interest. The control of exports reflected a social policy designed to protect the interests of the lower classes by maintaining an adequate supply of cereals at reasonable prices. The statutes emphasized the regulation of exports down through Tudor times.

The seventeenth century brought a gradual change to an import control policy. This shift reflected basic changes in the agricultural community. During the Tudor century, agriculture had become commercialized and specialized. A new land-owning class, economically alert and politically powerful, came into being. This group demanded and got a protected internal market. During the early seventeenth century, Parliament experimented with new Corn Laws, essentially a series of protective tariffs. By 1670, the demand for protection had hardened into policy. Though successive laws varied in detail, they all provided a sliding scale of duties which increased as the domestic price of grain decreased. The Corn Laws were a basic part of the foundation of the mercantile system.

The fostering and protection of domestic manufacturing had been a concern of government long before the accession of James I. Woolen manufacture, the premier industry, furnished the precedents of policy. Underlying the maze of medieval statutes and ordinances were some common assumptions concerning English manufacturing: it created a ready, sure market for native raw wool; it provided large scale employment for the poor and the materials for a lucrative trade; the crown profited from taxes on the trade.

The government moved in a variety of ways to regulate and encourage the industry. Henry I's Assize of Cloth set standards of quality that were reaffirmed by Magna Carta. Another line of policy encouraged foreign weavers and clothiers to relocate in England. The core of mercantilist industrial policy would be direct protection from foreign competition. The modern policy of prohibition and tariff had ancient origins. The town-centered medieval guilds had always striven to protect their local market. As the special immunities of the towns began to yield to a national free-trade area, interested parties naturally demanded protection of the larger market. Though the policy was never uniform and was as often dictated by diplomatic as by economic considerations, the principle of protection was well established before the seventeenth century. Intermittently, the government gave advantage to the English manufacturer by prohibiting the export of raw wool. On the other side of the coin of protection it restricted or forbade the importation of foreign cloth. Edward II's Ordinance of the Staple permitted only the upper classes to purchase the finer foreign fabrics. During the reign of Edward III a series of statutes and ordinances restricted imports, and this policy his successors pursued with reasonable consistency. By 1600 the principle of protection of native industry had taken firm root.

The aim of the mercantilist system of navigation was to make shipping a national monopoly. England pursued such a policy primarily for reasons of security and secondarily for economic gain. Medieval government finance prevented the creation of a permanent navy, but a large well-founded merchant fleet and a multitude of seafaring men were easily converted into a navy in time of national emergency. Though the Dutch wars of the seventeenth century were to give the greatest stimulus to the English navigation system, early precedents were there, though perhaps dimly seen.

The first navigation act came in the late fourteenth century in the reign of Richard II. The statute forbade English merchants to use foreign vessels in the import-export trade. Like many later statutes, it soon had to be modified because of the inadequacy of the native merchant marine. The early Tudors restricted certain specific trades to English vessels. Though the events of Elizabeth's reign underlined the relationship of sea-power to English security, the queen realized that a blanket ban on foreign shipping was unrealistic. She did, however, restrict the coastwise trade to English ships, make import-export duties preferential in favor of English vessels, and bar foreign vessels from specified trades. Since the fishery provided an invaluable "nursery for seamen," the queen moved to strengthen the industry by proclaiming "political Lent." At one time the eating of meat was forbidden on Wednesday, Friday, and Saturday for the purpose of the "maintenance and increase of the navy."

The Colonial Policy of the Early Stuarts

Though financial distress and political instability forced the first two Stuarts to rely on private capital to begin the work of colonization, at all times they maintained the royal prerogative. The executive agencies shaped policy, and Parliament was effectively excluded from the colonial area. On more than one occasion, the colonists, particularly the Virginia Company of London, petitioned Parliament to redress grievances or confirm grants. Though colonial matters were several times debated in the Commons, the legislature never acted in an American matter until the 1640's.

The basic weaknesses of the royal administration became apparent in the first period of colonization: the multiplicity of English agencies concerned with colonial affairs; the original lack of resident royal officials in America, and later the fiscal inability to pay such officials; above all, the remoteness of the transatlantic dominions.

Both James I and Charles I exercised their authority through the Privy Council. The Council approved the grants and charters, received petitions, heard appeals, and through its orders shaped policy and controlled administration. The stormy politics of the period dictated that the Council could give its full attention only intermittently to American affairs. The logical answer to the colonial problem was a special committee or commission to be concerned only with dominion matters. The Virginia charter of 1606 provided for a royal council resident in England, but the experiment proved abortive, coming to an end with the charter of 1609. In 1623, James I appointed a special commission to investigate the activities of the Virginia Company. After the dissolution of the company, the commission cooperated with a committee of the Privy Council, ultimately making recommendations to Charles I concerning the reorganization of Virginia government. By a proclamation issued in 1625, Charles I re-emphasized the fact that all American colonies were responsible to the crown. The Virginia commission continued to exist, but the main colonial business was done in Privy Council. During the 1630's, while Strafford and Laud strove to push the policy of "thorough," Charles appointed a special commission for foreign plantations with the archbishop as chairman. The membership of the Laud commission was also appointed as a standing committee of the Privy Council. The commission, in turn, appointed a subcommittee of persons presumably expert in colonial matters to conduct the routine business of administration and to recommend policy. Through this agency Laud pushed a policy of centralization, particularly in relation to New England, until the Bishops' Wars stalled the policy of "thorough" on both sides of the Atlantic. In addition to the Privy Council and its committees, the Treasury, the Admiralty, the law officers, and the King's Bench as *coram rege*, sporadically concerned themselves with colonial affairs.

On two occasions, once successfully and once unsuccessfully, the early Stuarts moved dramatically to demonstrate that the American companies were dependent corporations subject in their very existence to the ultimate sovereignty of the crown. In October 1624, the attorney general began *quo warranto* proceedings against the Virginia Company at King's Bench. The theory that James moved against the company to punish its treasurer, Sir Edward Sandys, for opposing the crown in Parliament, is now discredited. The causes of the dissolution were multiple: a dispute between the Smith and Sandys factions about the management of the company; wrangling between the government and the company over the control of the tobacco trade and modification of the charter; the debility of the colony after the Indian massacre of 1623. When the Sandys-dominated company refused to compromise, the king appointed a royal commission to visit Virginia. The tangled knot was then cut decisively by the *quo warranto*. The actual hearing was, as always in such cases, strictly a formality. The court ruled that the company had exceeded its franchise and quashed the charter.

James I died before the government of Virginia could be reorganized. Charles had several options and for a time it appeared that a charter similar to that of 1606 would be issued. The royal commission for Virginia continued to exist but was inactive. The standard pattern of the royal province soon emerged. A crown-appointed governor and council assumed the responsibility of representing England in Virginia. Receiving their instructions from England, they exercised broad executive, judicial, and legislative power. As it extended its direct authority to America, the crown refused to assume fiscal responsibility for the maintenance of its agents or for the defense of the colony. Repeated requests that a specific portion of the American revenue be assigned to cover these costs were rejected. In due course the popularly elected assembly was revived. Soon the classic conflict between governor and legislature emerged, with the advantage inevitably accruing to the assembly because it controlled the purse.

The nearly autonomous community of Puritans in Massachusetts Bay ran afoul of two men, Sir Ferdinando Gorges and Archbishop Laud. The grant to the corporation had cut drastically into Gorges' territory at a time when the Earl of Warwick controlled the Council for New England and Gorges labored for the Stuart state. In 1632, Gorges regained control of the council and revived his ambitious American plans. So far as Laud was concerned, every aspect of Winthrop's church and state was antithetical to his concept of public policy. Reports of New England Congregationalism and rumors of a supposed desire for independence regularly came back to London. Puritan justice, purging the colony of undesirable elements, sent back to England a series of men burning for revenge. Thomas Morton, expelled for his merry doings, became an implacable foe. Philip Ratcliffe had his ears lopped off before being shipped home. Sir Christopher Gardiner, a prominent, immoral man, probably an agent of Gorges, was merely banished. Back in England, these men met frequently with Gorges, and their tales undoubtedly furnished the evidence to support a petition to Privy Council requesting an investigation of the colony. Shortly a committee of the council turned in a report, one favorable to the Massachusetts Bay enterprise.

As soon as it was formed, Gorges took his business to Laud's commission on plantations. The archbishop, alarmed by the exodus of Nonconformists, stopped outbound vessels until the emigrants swore the oath of allegiance and subscribed to the Act of Supremacy. Encouraged, Gorges proceeded to dissolve the nearly moribund Council for New England. His plan was to seek new grants in knight service for himself and his supporters and to become the governor general of New England. Gorges next convinced Laud to bring the charter of Massachusetts Bay before the King's Bench where its validity could be examined. The writ *quo warranto* ran in the spring of 1635, addressed to the individual members of the company, rather than to the corporation itself. The patentees who lived in England came into court where judgment was given for the king. Against those who had removed to America the court began the process of outlawry. Since the crown never pursued the outlawries to a conclusion, the corporation remained intact in law and in fact.

In any event, the enforcement of an English court order would have been difficult, if not impossible. The New England Puritans had watched the proceedings with intense interest. They evolved a plan that became permanent policy—procrastination and preparation for armed resistance. When asked to surrender the charter, the governor and assistants stalled. This, they wrote, needed to be authorized by the general court, which would not meet for several months. In the area of direct resistance, John Endecott of Salem performed a rash, symbolic act by cutting the cross of St. George from the national flag. By Winthrop's order, the officers brought the militia units up to strength. Significantly, they drilled under ensigns that bore no cross. There is absolutely no question but that Massachusetts Bay would have met any attempt to enforce the *quo warranto* by main force. As the saints drilled, old England moved to the crisis of the Civil Wars. The attempt to compel New England into the empire was now abandoned for half a century.

The emergence of economic colonial policy before 1640 is best illustrated by the attempts of the English government to regulate the tobacco industry. In the first instance, the mother country had hoped that the colonies would supply a variety of goods that had been purchased previously from foreign nations. From Virginia and Maryland they expected cargoes of naval stores, dyewoods, silk, cotton, and sugar. Instead they got tobacco. Spanish tobacco had been introduced in Elizabeth's time and grew rapidly in popularity. The government consistently opposed its use on the grounds that it endangered both health and morals. James I wrote a famous tract, *Counterblast against Tobacco* and Charles I shared his father's aversion. Since royal condemnation failed to check the demand, the kings moved to regulate the trade and in so doing established several basic tenets of colonial policy. For fiscal purposes, the government regarded the colonies as outside the realm; that is, their trade with England was subject to all normal and special import taxes and duties. Under Stuart policy, England became the staple for colonial produce. All American commodities designated by the government could be shipped only to England. This policy of funneling valuable American products through England, with its obvious advantage to merchant and monarch, would expand into the policy of enumeration. Having denied the colonies free access to their best markets, the crown gave the Americans a monopoly of the English market. The colonists were, of course, never allowed to compete with desirable English industries. Finally, the colonial trade was to be carried in English ships.

Inevitably, American tobacco became involved in the disputes that arose out of Stuart attempts to raise a revenue without Parliamentary consent. The Virginia charters of 1609 and 1612 had provided exemption for a term of years from all import duties except the traditional tonnage and poundage, which amounted to 5 per cent *ad valorem*. Manipulation of the book of rates made it possible for the crown to raise these duties. After the impost victory in Bate's Case, James, over the protest of the Virginians, imposed special duties on tobacco. As a result, tobacco taxes furnished a valuable revenue through the second decade of the century. In the 1620's the rapid expansion of production forced tobacco prices down. Since the commodity could no longer bear the high impost, James turned to the favorite device of monopolies designed to restrict importation and to augment the revenue. In 1619 and again in 1621, James negotiated monopoly contracts with individual merchants. Virginia protested loudly. In 1622 the company itself negotiated a contract that proved unsatisfactory to both parties and was subsequently annulled by Privy Council. From time to time both James and Charles revived the plan of monopoly, but a durable contract was never negotiated.

As production soared, the American planters demanded exclusive access to the English market. The Council responded with a series of proclamations prohibiting the cultivation of tobacco in England. Doubtless the councilors were in part motivated by a desire to strengthen the colonies. More important, the domestic crop failed to square with mercantilist principles. Locally raised tobacco was not easily taxable and thus represented a loss in public revenue. The diversion of English acreage to a luxury crop ran against the idea that agriculture should help the realm "stand upon itself." The injunctions against local tobacco culture were extremely unpopular in rural England and local officials met real resistance as they rooted out the crop. Having won this point, the colonies asked for the exclusion of Spanish tobacco. At times the crown prohibited such imports, at times permitted importation under license. At all times the superior Spanish tobacco was much more heavily taxed than the American.

From the beginning the government had insisted that all American tobacco be shipped to England. In ten years, the colonists supplied, then oversupplied, then glutted the English market. Virginia clamored without results for a free market. This policy made the English merchants middlemen in a valuable trade. The government encouraged this trade by allowing a substantial drawback on import duties at the time of re-exportation. Throughout the colonial period the southern planters paid a heavy toll to English factors.

The desired English monopoly of the colonial carrying trade was very imperfectly realized during the early period. The inadequacy of the merchant marine is reflected in the repeated rulings that colonial produce coming in foreign bottoms would be assessed an additional 25 per cent customs.

Interregnum

The early Stuarts had founded an empire and sketched out the main lines of a colonial policy based on prerogative and mercantilism. The seating of the Long Parliament (1640), the Civil Wars (1642–1648), and the execution of Charles I (1649) necessarily interrupted the progress of the Stuart empire.

In 1642 the Long Parliament appointed a committee for plantations under the chairmanship of the experienced Earl of

Warwick. The committee did whatever business came before it but let policy drift. The urgent pressures of English domestic affairs permitted the colonies to develop unhindered by external controls. The provincial attitude toward English political developments differed. New England naturally looked with favor on the triumphs of the English Puritans. Virginia and a majority of the Caribbean colonies expressed strong royalist sentiments. Maryland, with its Catholic proprietor, tried to maintain a neutral position. Whichever side they took, the American colonies acted in similar ways. All of them threw their ports open to foreign shipping and the Dutch moved in rapidly. None of them would admit that the overthrow of the king in any way modified their rights; none admitted the right of Parliament to legislate for them.

For the American colonists, the execution of the king proved to be decisive. The act had horrified Europe, united continental opinion against the revolutionary state, and forced England to reconsider her security. This concern for security led to a series of measures that directly affected the economic interests of the colonies. Politically, the theory of an empire founded and administered by prerogative was interred temporarily with the execution of Charles I. Parliament moved immediately into this vacuum and assumed sovereign power over the dominions. This was done in May 1649 in the act by which the Rump Parliament established the Commonwealth.

> Be it Declared and Enacted by this present Parliament and by the Authority of the same, That the People of England, and of all the Dominions and Territories thereunto belonging, are and shall be, and are hereby Constituted, Made, Established, and Confirmed to be a Commonwealth and Free-State: And shall from henceforth be Governed as a Commonwealth and Free-State, by the Supreme Authority of this Nation, The Representatives of the People in Parliament . . .

This declaration revolutionized the imperial constitution as it had been understood since at least the time of Henry II. It marks the beginning of the constitutional conflict between metropolis and province. "In a sense, then, it was the temporary abolition of kingship which created the constitutional issue from which in time the American Revolution resulted."[2]

No dominion accepted this declaration of Parliamentary power to bind them. The only thorough statement of constitutional right came from Ireland, which had been subjected to direct Parliamentary control as early as 1641. The Irish House of Commons flatly rejected the power of the English Parliament: "The Subjects of this his Majesties Kingdom of Ireland, are a free People, and to be Governed only, according [to] the Common Law of England, and Statutes made and established by Parliament in this Kingdom of Ireland." This point of view was ably defended before the Irish Commons by Patrick Darcy. A short time later the Irish argument was expanded into a pamphlet, which contended that the only tie that bound Ireland to England was allegiance owed "to the King's sacred Majesty." Here one has precisely the interpretation of the imperial constitution that John Adams and others would advance 134 years later in the crisis of the Revolution. In terms of the precedents of the Constitution, this interpretation was and remains fully as respectable as the counterview that Parliament had the power to bind the dominions "in all cases whatsoever."

Four American colonies—Virginia, Antigua, Barbados, and Bermuda—refused to accept Parliamentary authority and proclaimed Charles II. Parliament first retaliated with economic sanctions by barring all foreign vessels from trading with the rebellious colonies. The Council of State then sent two expeditions, one to the islands, another to Virginia, to obtain the submission of the recalcitrants. All submitted, but with conditions reserving the rights of the local legislatures and guarantees of at least a relative freedom of trade. The New England colonies, led by Massachusetts Bay, needed no coercion. Though they quickly gave their blessing to the English Puritan experiment in government, they were equally fast in making it clear that their old rights remained intact and that they would not tolerate Parliamentary interference in their affairs.

As soon as royalist opinion in America had been suppressed, the Commonwealth permitted the colonies a broad autonomy.

2. Charles H. McIlwain, *The American Revolution: A Constitutional Interpretation* (Ithaca: Cornell University Press, 1958), p. 26.

Cromwell pursued a similar policy during the period of the Protectorate. The Council of State assumed the role of the Privy Council and, together with a variety of committees, intermittently considered American matters. In their sporadic deliberations one can find no trace of the Laudian drive for greater centralization and control.

Foreign affairs dictated English commercial policy during the 1650's. With a single exception, the colonies were virtually free from restriction. For example, the policy of staple, which limited American exports to England, was implicitly abandoned with the result that the colonists enjoyed a much freer market. The exception to this trend away from emerging mercantilism was the tightening of the navigation system. The Navigation Act of 1651 aimed to guarantee English security by strengthening her marine power.

Through the reigns of James I and Charles I, England had been permitted the luxury of an ineffective foreign policy because of the preoccupation of the continental powers with the Thirty Years War. The Stuarts pursued a dynastic diplomacy which led them into two futile wars. While they did so, the continental balance of power was altered radically, and the Dutch rose to a position of unprecedented maritime superiority. Cromwell shaped the foreign policy of the 1650's. From the beginning he faced a dilemma. He hoped to create a powerful Protestant coalition. The natural ally for such purposes was the Dutch Republic, but that nation was the chief commercial rival. In the end the nationalist, sectarian spirit of the age prevailed and Cromwell's England went to war with the Dutch.

The Navigation Act of 1651 is evidence of English concern for the decline of her maritime power and a symptom of her resentment of the Dutch rather than a cause of the first Dutch War. In the area of colonial policy the chief significance of the law is that it drew together the scattered ordinances and statutes of the earlier period and became the precedent for the definitive act of 1660. The law required that all products from the colonial areas of America, Asia, and Africa be imported into England in ships manned by a majority of Englishmen; that European goods come into the empire only in English ships or the ships of the nation producing the import; and that foreign vessels be excluded from the coastwise trade and from the import-export trade in fish and fish products.

The Navigation Act contributed to steadily worsening Anglo-Dutch relations. The causes of the war were many and deep-seated. The demise of Portugal had drawn the English and the Dutch in as the main contenders for the rich prize of the oriental trade. In 1619, Dutch factors effectively cleared the English from the East Indies by slaughtering the English at an island outpost. Though but an incident, this massacre at Amboyna gave the English a prime propaganda piece that was real evidence of the rise of the Netherlands' oriental interests. Other causes of war concentrated in the North Atlantic. The two nations disputed with acrimony for control of the Greenland whale and North Sea herring fisheries. The body of seapower hung on a skeleton of naval stores. The main sources of such stores were the Scandinavian nations. In 1649 the Dutch negotiated a most favorable treaty with Denmark by which they virtually excluded England from the Baltic. Most galling was the question of English sovereignty in the Narrow Seas. James and Charles had made much of this, demanding that foreign vessels salute and lower their colors. The Dutch rode the Narrow Seas with impunity. On one occasion, the great Dutch admiral, Van Tromp, destroyed a Spanish fleet in the Downs while the king negotiated terms for its protection. As he sailed out, Van Tromp mocked English impotence by derisively dipping his colors.

Through 1651 the two nations negotiated without result. The next year Van Tromp refused to salute a squadron under Robert Blake, and the war came on. The Dutch undoubtedly expected easy victory. Instead they suffered defeat. This amazing reversal resulted from three factors. Through the 1640's Parliament had pushed an energetic program of ship construction, concentrating on heavily armed men-of-war. The Dutch, relying on converted merchantmen, were outgunned. Throughout the war Dutch naval effectiveness was limited by the need to protect her vast merchant marine. Finally, England found again in Robert Blake the spirit of Drake. By the treaty ending the war the Dutch recognized the salute, acknowledged the navigation system, and entered a defensive alliance. On the strength of the victory, England negotiated a treaty with Denmark which gave her access to Baltic naval stores.

Having revived English seapower, Cromwell turned to more ambitious schemes for its use. The conflict between France and Spain dragged on. Though England had grievances against both Catholic powers, both courted her. France harbored the Stuart exiles and this led to a bitter, undeclared naval war. As the French war proceeded, Cromwell formulated his "Western Design." This policy aimed to drive Spain out of the western hemisphere and marked a return to Elizabethan diplomacy. In 1654, an expedition under Robert Venables and William Penn was fitted out. The instructions to the commanders gave them discretion as to where they might strike in the Caribbean. The events of the campaign soon proved that Cromwell had underestimated Spanish power in America. The army that he had sent was by far the worst to take the field during his period of ascendancy. It was turned back at Hispaniola and San Domingo and had to be content with seizing weakly held Jamaica. Though the "Western Design" was abortive, it recommitted England to a policy of vigorous overseas expansion. It was also evidence of the growing conviction that the real wealth of America was to be found in the sugar islands of the Caribbean.

Chapter 6

Charles II:
Imperial Definition
and Expansion

The Restored Stuart

During the decade between the deaths of Charles I and Oliver Cromwell, England experimented radically with a variety of forms of government. Whatever the form, the clear fact was that behind each revision was the military power of the Protector. He died in 1659 and that power passed into the hands of his incompetent son, Richard Cromwell. Parliament and an army faction were soon at loggerheads, with ineffectual Richard uncomfortably between. Under army pressure, Parliament was dissolved summarily and reconvened without even the formality of election. No longer subject to iron Oliver's command, the army itself divided. A nation weary of strife and change stood on the verge of renewed conflict. A situation created by force was ended by force. General George Monck brought a major part of the army down from Scotland to end the business once and for all. With Monck pledged to both the army and Parliament, the nation returned the Convention Parliament, whose main business was conceived to be the working out of the conditions for a Stuart restoration. But Monck, moving ahead, had agreed to support a virtually unconditional restoration. The nation, faced with the alternatives of accepting the royal Declaration of Breda or plunging back into the era of violence, chose the former course. On a summer day in 1660, Charles II assumed his birthright.

The reign of Charles II began in necessarily unsatisfactory compromise and developed on the basis of unresolved tensions. The religious settlement, though it tacitly abandoned the principle of uniformity, was embodied in a series of laws that made possible sporadic but violent persecution of nonconforming Protestant sects as well as Catholics. In foreign affairs the traditional policies of maritime expansion and continental balance of power came into conflict as expediency dictated shifting patterns of alliance with or against the maritime Dutch or militant French. Politically the reign witnessed a revival of the contest between king and Parliament which found no real resolution. Acrimonious conflict created the beginnings of the two-party system and a series of violent episodes.

In contrast to the sharp differences concerning religion, foreign affairs, and politics, there was general agreement as to the main lines of commercial and colonial policy. Stuart leaders gave new life to the Cromwellian desire to expand the empire and to use commercial regulation as an instrument of national policy. A diverse group of statesmen, courtiers, dedicated bureaucrats, and merchants found common cause in commerce and the colonies. The nexus binding them together was economic gain. The king, courtiers, and statesmen, always hard pressed for funds, saw in an expanding commerce a lucrative source of taxation and in colonial ventures an opportunity for profit. The interest of the merchant coincided exactly.

Both the king and his first chief minister, Edward Hyde, Earl of Clarendon, were interested actively in the main business of the councils, commissions, and committees that shaped emerging imperialism. The heir apparent, James, Duke of York, concerned himself continuously with overseas affairs. Many of the great men who had supported the king in his exile or who had been foresighted enough to abandon the "Old Cause" in time were active in colonial affairs; among them were Shaftesbury, Albemarle, Culpeper, and Craven. A group of merchants represented by such men as Thomas Povey and Martin Noell pressed for policies of expansion and consolidation. Povey, especially, formed a link with the past when he urged successfully the adoption of precisely the same measures he had advocated in Cromwell's time. Among the working officeholders, William Blathwayt stands out as a man who through a generation strove to perfect the imperial system. These men worked openly in a most favorable climate of opinion. The last quarter of the seventeenth century brought on a flood of pamphlet literature about the merits of trade and plantations. Though the theorists might disagree about particulars, they accepted and popularized the major tenets of mercantilism. Over and again they played the theme that England's security and prosperity lay at sea.

The combination of public and private interest in imperial matters created the most productive policies of the reign of Charles II. Under Charles the English obtained Bombay and Tangiers, intruded further into the slave trade, drove the Dutch from North America, consolidated their Caribbean holdings, established six new colonies in the New World, gave statutory form to the navigation system, and identified, if they did not solve, the main problems of the administration of a transoceanic empire.

The Acts of Navigation and Trade

At the Restoration, crown lawyers held all of the acts and ordinances of the Interregnum to be null and void. This made it necessary for the first Parliaments after 1660 to re-enact many laws in addition to dealing legislatively with new problems created by the return of the Stuarts. In the rush of legislation, mercantilism was given its basic statutory form. Though the Old Subsidy of 1660 and the Navigation Act of the same year, the Statute of Frauds of 1662, the Staple Act of 1663, and the supplementary Navigation Act of 1672 were by no means limited to colonial matters, the laws did define the commercial system of the old empire. One of the statutes stated succinctly the general purpose of the legislation to be making the colonies "yet more beneficial and advantageous" to England. Specifically, the laws aimed to increase the royal revenue; either exclude foreign shipping from the empire or at least discriminate against it; protect existing English economic interests; guarantee England an adequate, cheap supply of valued colonial products; make of the whole empire a protected market; establish England as the staple for a large part of the colonial import-export trade.

Charles II returned to an economically distressed England. The public debt stood at an all time high and to this indebtedness was added the cost of Charles' expenses during the long exile. The hopelessly inadequate system of public finance was not reformed. In apparent good faith, Parliament provided a revenue that it regarded as sufficient for the normal operation of the government. But it was not enough and the royal income continuously fell short of expense. As it had before the Civil Wars, Parliament took advantage of the king's perpetual poverty to gain concessions before voting new taxes. Ultimately Parliamentary penury drove Charles to the dangerous policy of seeking the financial support of Louis XIV.

Parliament passed the most important customs duty in the form of the Old Subsidy of 1660. By this subsidy it granted the king the ancient duties of tonnage and poundage for life. The tonnage, a fixed tax levied on imported wine by volume, was of little imperial consequence. The poundage fees were the heart of the imperial tax system. By the law of 1660, these duties amounted to 5 per cent of the value (hence *ad valorem*) of all goods imported or exported. The value of commodities was not determined by what they could command in the market; rather, Parliament established artificial official values in the Book of Rates. The rates bore little relationship to real prices. For example, English exports were always rated low in order to put such commodities in a strong competitive position in world markets. At the other extreme was a commodity like tobacco, which was given a book value five times as great as its price in the English market. In some instances, import duties were prohibitive. English cereals, for example, were given complete protection. Wherever the duties were low enough to make importation feasible, the colonists enjoyed a preferential rate over foreign producers.

Through the last quarter of the seventeenth century the tendency was to push the rates of the basic subsidy steadily upward. By the end of the Stuart period the import rates averaged between 20 and 25 per cent of the true value of commodities coming into England. The Old Subsidy made it possible for England to toll the import-export trade of the American colonies. It only remained to force the main streams of colonial trade to flow through England. The Navigation Acts accomplished that.

A substantial common interest in England assured the easy and early passage of the Navigation Act of 1660. It was an omnibus bill for English maritime interests. Its preamble announced its purpose to be "the increase of shipping and encouragement of . . . navigation." In regard to the merchant marine the law renewed the attempts to make shipping a national monopoly. Under this head the law was pointedly anti-Dutch. With certain exceptions, the statute barred from the empire trade all vessels not built in the empire and owned by English subjects. On the question of build and ownership the wording of the law was sufficiently ambiguous so as to require clarification. An act of 1662 required that a ship needed to be English built and owned to qualify. Since all colonial vessels were regarded as English, this amounted to a substantial privilege. In addition, the master and three-quarters of the crew needed to be English.

A second group of provisions regulated trade between England and Europe by setting out a long list of goods that could be imported only in English ships or in foreign ships carrying goods produced by that foreign nation—for example, French goods in French ships. The list was so drawn as to give full protection to the vested monopolies such as the Levant and Muscovy Companies. Because of vague wording, the statute failed to accomplish the major intent of its authors, the destruction of the re-export trade of the Dutch and Hanse merchants. This was accomplished two years later in the Statute of Frauds. The law flatly prohibited importation from the Netherlands and Germany.

As the Navigation Act came out of committee, its sponsors tacked on a provision of immense importance. Section eighteen announced the policy of enumeration or control of colonial exports. Six valuable commodities of tropical or subtropical origin —sugar, tobacco, cotton, indigo, ginger, and dyewoods—were enumerated. This meant that these products could be shipped only to England. In the years following, commodity after commodity was added to the enumerated list. By the 1760's, virtually all colonial commodities were on the list. The trade in enumerated commodities was bonded and importation could not be nominal. Colonial goods, though bound ultimately for a foreign market had actually to be unladen, sold and reladen. Enumeration denied the colonists access to foreign markets and guaranteed that certain valuable goods would come into England where the subsidy could take its toll and the merchants profit from domestic sale or re-export. Englishmen recognized the fundamental importance of the Navigation Act of 1660. They styled it the Magna Carta of the Sea.

Having funneled selected American exports into England, Parliament turned to the regulation of colonial imports. The Navigation or Staple Act of 1663 resulted from the clamor of a great variety of English interests for protection from foreign competition. The relevant provisions of the law provided that all goods of foreign manufacture destined for the colonies be brought first to England. As in the case of the enumerated commodities, the landing had to be bona fide. The law gave the crown the opportunity to tax foreign goods and regulate re-export. It gave the merchants the chance to realize a profit on goods that were permitted to go to the colonies. It gave the manufacturer complete protection and was, in effect, a protective tariff thrown around the already vast and rapidly growing market of the English empire.

Though the policy of staple was not new, the Act of 1663 marked an important turning point. By 1660 the hope that the colonies would produce large quantities of precious spices and metals had largely evaporated. Though the English continued to try to develop colonies that could return valuable commodities such as dyewoods, silk, and naval stores, they had little success. The value of the North American colonies as markets became increasingly clear.

The policy of staple created the economic dilemma of the colonies. They measured their standard of living largely by the use of manufactured goods and the law forced them to buy in England. The southern colonies soon fell into the classic pattern of economic dependence which awaits any area that buys its goods and services with an agricultural staple that can be produced in surplus quantities. Since the products of the northern colonies were not wanted in England, they developed the intricate triangular trades in order to convert the produce of field, forest, and fishery into things acceptable in return for English manufactured goods. By 1700, the pattern of colonial commerce had been set.

In one important branch of trade, colonial ship captains evaded the intent of Parliament and yet stayed within the letter of the Navigation Act of 1660. Before leaving an English port, an English captain bound for the colonies had to give a substantial bond that he would return to an English port with any enumerated commodity he might load. A colonial captain loading an enumerated commodity had to post the same bond to guarantee that he would carry his cargo to England *or* to one of the plantations. Often colonial captains would enter such a bond, proceed to another colonial port, and, having technically complied with the law, clear directly for a European port. A substantial trade in tobacco developed along such devious routes. Parliament interrupted this practice with the Navigation Act of 1673. Any captain loading enumerated commodities who could not produce a certificate that he had deposited a bond in England either had to bond himself in the colonial port to carry his cargo to England or pay a tax on it. These plantation duties of 1673 (1*d* per pound of tobacco) effectively blocked indirect exportation to Europe. They did so because they were roughly comparable to the duties of the Old Subsidy levied at the water's edge in England. When a merchant re-exported an enumerated commodity from England a substantial drawback on the Old Subsidy was permitted. Since there would be no rebate of the plantation duties, the colonial merchant trading indirectly with Europe could not compete in those markets with the English re-exporter.

It was an easy matter for Parliament to place these laws on the books, quite another for administration to see that they were obeyed. The lawmakers, mindful of the problem, had ordered the Admiralty to assist. By executive order the crown had enjoined governors and customs officials to enforce the law strictly. The Act of 1673, by requiring that duties be paid in America, necessitated the creation of customs officials across the Atlantic. In this it achieved its significance by heralding a sustained conflict to come. The colonists resented the acts of navigation and, with three thousand miles of ocean as a shield, translated resentment into effective evasion.

Before the death of Charles II the attempt to force the colonies into the pattern of mercantilism had begun. The attempt revealed the central problem of the old empire, that of law enforcement. On that rock the empire would finally split.

The Central Administration

Several factors blur the picture of English government in the latter half of the seventeenth century. The tension between Crown and Parliament continued through two reigns before producing any further definition. The Privy Council, though nominally a potent agency, underwent decline as the Cabinet developed. A great expansion of the volume of public business expedited the growth of specialized executive offices and caused the creation of many special committees and councils. Old and new agencies gradually adjusted themselves to the task of governing an expanding empire, and they did so with little concern for a logical assignment of authority to appropriate public bodies.

Before the Civil Wars, the kings had effectively excluded Parliament from acting in the colonial area. During the Interregnum, Parliament had necessarily assumed full authority for the empire. After 1660, Parliament frequently passed basic legislation affecting the colonies. Yet in the absence of specific, positive evidence, it cannot be assumed that this amounted to a surrender of royal prerogative in imperial matters. The positing of any hypothesis of Parliamentary supremacy in the empire on the evidence of the Navigation Acts would produce a tenuous, inaccurate thesis. In fact, the evidence runs the other way. The "realm and dominions" ordinance that had followed the execution of Charles I in 1649 perished absolutely with the restoration of his son. Expedient Charles II never raised constitutional questions unless events thrust the issues upon him, as, for example, in the exclusion crisis. Since the community of interest concerning colonial affairs produced no real conflict, he proceeded along the efficient lines of least resistance. The weight of precedent was always on the side of stating general economic law through parliamentary statute. The petitions upon which the Navigation Acts were based came from Englishmen within the realm. The statutes concerned them as much, perhaps more, than the subjects across the Atlantic. It would have been unthinkable to respond to these petitions in any other way than by statute. The statute in no way modified the constitutional concept of the dominions as jurisdictions primarily subject to the prerogative of the crown. Though Parliament legislated, the dominions remained His Majesty's.

So long as there had been an empire, feudal or modern, the business of the dominions had come before the king in council. Throughout the history of the first modern empire, either really or nominally, the business of the dominions pivoted in the Privy Council. During the last half of the seventeenth century, the real power of the full Council declined steadily, to be replaced by select groups drawn from the membership of the Council itself. These small, efficient, and regally dependent groups were variously called the Cabal, the Committee on Foreign Affairs, or most often the Cabinet. Around these small, often secret groups a continuous conflict ensued as Parliament tried to force the king to take his advice in the open great Council where opinions could be identified and advisers punished, if need be, by the threat or fact of impeachment or attainder. In most matters, Privy Council became a place where previously made decisions were entered formally on the record.

By 1660 it was apparent that the complex business of administering an empire called for continuous and expert attention. Prompted first by the merchant Thomas Povey, the Privy Council created a series of councils and committees to recommend policy and supervise administration. The delegation of authority was never complete, and the special agencies always needed to come back to the Privy Council where recommendations were translated into orders. Between 1660 and 1675, the committees and councils came and went with confusing frequency. Immediately after the Restoration, the Privy Council appointed a committee of its own members to hear all petitions concerning the colonies. The committee turned at once to important business concerned largely with proprietary rights in the Caribbean. Within a few months, the Earl of Clarendon himself assured the merchants that the king was interested by promising to create two select councils—one for trade, one for plantations—with personnel drawn from the mercantile world, from the Privy Council, and from "gentlemen of equality and experience." In November 1660, the king established a Council of Trade. The letters patent, a pure mercantilist document, pledged the power of the state to the regulation and expansion of commerce. Within the month new letters issued, creating the Council for Foreign Plantations. The document reassured interested parties that the crown recognized the growth and value of the colonies. It announced one of the main themes of later Stuart policy, that of consolidation, with the statement that the plantations "should now no longer remain in a loose and scattered State but should be collected and brought under . . . an uniform inspeccon and conduct." The council sat in the Star Chamber.

The councils of trade and foreign plantations were active for about four years. To a considerable degree their functions overlapped. The work of the Council for Foreign Plantations ranged from the humdrum, petty routine of administration to such important policy recommendations as the extinction of proprietary rights in America. A variety of factors explain the early collapse of both councils. Though the letters patent had indicated a different intent, they acted only in an advisory capacity and this tended to vitiate their effort. The year of their demise, 1665, was one of unparalleled catastrophe—the plague, the fire of London, the Dutch War. Such events pushed provincial affairs into the background and the councils quietly expired.

Through three years the committee of the Privy Council concerned itself with colonial affairs, until in 1668, as a part of the reorganization of the Council that followed the fall of Clarendon and the rise of the Cabal, the king created a new standing committee for trade and plantations. But before 1668 was out, the pressure of business on the great councilors in committee led to the recreation of the special councils on trade and plantations. In 1672 the two councils were combined and shortly they came under the presidency of Anthony Ashley Cooper, the Earl of Shaftesbury. For three years the ebb and flow of colonial busi-

ness ran through the chambers of the committee, and its recommendations were translated into Privy Council orders. The
activities of the Council ended formally in 1675. Its principal
officer, Shaftesbury, had moved into opposition to Charles and
the new first minister, Danby, objected to the annual expenses of
£7,000 that the council had incurred. In 1675, the king assigned
colonial affairs to the Committee for Trade and Plantation of the
Privy Council. As the Lords of Trade, this committee directed
colonial policy and administration through twenty important
years.

The Lords of Trade spoke with greater authority than any
of the preceding agencies. Since its membership included the
leading councilors, its decisions carried the weight of the Privy
Council and its actions were approved automatically. Though
the membership of the committee changed with the rise and fall
of statesmen, professional administrators gave continuity to policy. The most influential of these well informed professionals was
William Blathwayt, who served the committee in one capacity
or another throughout its career. The deliberations of the lords
ranged over the whole of colonial administration. They gave the
colonial governors their instructions and demanded periodic reports. They reviewed colonial legislation and heard cases on appeal. If colonial problems appeared to be too complex to be
solved by remote control, the lords appointed special commissioners to go out and survey the problem on the spot. At all
times they gave priority to the effective enforcement of the acts
of navigation. Their efforts moved always in the direction of
uniform rules, effective enforcement, and consolidation of overseas units.

Though the development of imperial administration located
the center of power in Privy Council, the Treasury also had a
large stake in colonial affairs. The Treasury lords had the prime
responsibility for collecting the trade duties. From 1660 to 1671,
they entrusted collection to private collectors, the customs farmers. After 1671, the Commissioners of Customs, public agents of
the Treasury, supervised the enforcement of the laws of trade.
Under their direction a large staff of officials developed. In addition to actually collecting the duties, the commissioners stood
responsible for the complicated bonding and registry provision

of the laws and for the suppression of smuggling and other forms of illicit trading. Their influence was not limited to enforcement, for their many reports often shaped policy as stated by the Treasury, Privy Council, or Parliament. Seated at London, the commissioners faced the huge task of enforcing the laws of trade throughout the empire. After the passage of the Navigation Act of 1673, they became directly concerned with law enforcement in the colonies and their agents appeared in all major American ports.

The traditional hostility to the tax agent is rooted so deeply that the observer is apt to fasten on examples of malfeasance or bureaucratic intransigence when characterizing any customs service. But the Lords of the Treasury and Commissioners of Customs wrote an outstanding record of professional competence. In the seventeenth century the first lord was always a statesman, never a spoilsman. The key post of secretary went to able men; for example, the energetic and efficient Sir George Downing. The commissioners themselves were able public servants. Nonetheless, the commissioners in action generated a good deal of friction. Beyond the fact of natural human reluctance to pay taxes, the commissioners were plagued by factors that they had not created. The ambiguity and inconsistency of the statutes created substantial problems. The commissioners faced the major barrier to efficient enforcement when they attempted to apply the law outside the realm. Ultimately the collision of the commissioners with the subjects in the dominions produced fundamental constitutional conflicts. In the seventeenth century and through the greater part of the eighteenth, the barriers to enforcement were proprietary privilege rather than political rights. Substantial interests in the dominions resisted the intrusion of the commissioners' authority into their jurisdictions by citing the provisions of the charters granted in earlier days. This resistance was not limited to New England. West Indian proprietors stood firmly on their rights. Nor was it simply a matter of the inevitable delays imposed by the remoteness of the transatlantic dominions. From the Isle of Man, forty miles off the English coast, the Earls of Derby defied the commissioners with an audacity that made the Puritans of New England appear timid by comparison.

By the 1680's the efficiency of the Treasury and commissioners had been frustrated sufficiently by statutory vagueness and proprietary obtuseness so as to have created an insistent demand for new policies. This demand produced the attack on the proprietaries of the 1680's and the comprehensive administrative statute of 1696.

Until the 1690's, the Admiralty played a relatively minor role in the administration of the empire. The Act of 1660 had specifically ordered the navy to help in the job of enforcement. Since some of the other statutes did not mention the navy, there were questions concerning the Lord High Admiral's responsibility. Generally, English officials expected and got cooperation, though naval officers themselves disliked the duty. It must have appeared degrading for the members of a proud combat service to assume the task of a revenue patrol.

The Navigation Acts stated that legal proceedings against offenders could be instituted in any court of record. Most of the violations in England were prosecuted before the Barons of Exchequer who presided over the common law court, which traditionally heard cases involving public finance. Though the bulk of the business went to the Exchequer, the commissioners occasionally prosecuted before the High Court of Admiralty. Not until the definitive statute of 1696 extended its jurisdiction to America did the Admiralty assume real significance in the area of imperial commerce.

In addition to Admiralty, Exchequer, Treasury, Commissioners of Customs, Lords of Trade, Privy Council, Parliament, and king, there were other English officials who concerned themselves with American matters. All of the agencies consulted the law officers, the attorney and solicitor general, and their advisory opinions often shaped policy. Two of the king's chief councilors, the principal secretaries of state, tended increasingly to be held responsible for colonial affairs. By the early eighteenth century, the Secretary of State for the Southern Department, whose main business was to conduct the diplomacy of England with France and Spain, was regarded as the chief executive officer in the colonial area.

The administrative experience of the Restoration period served as an object lesson to imperial planners. The substantial calendar of necessary reform included clarification of the statutes, centralization of responsibility for policy making and law enforcement, consolidation and standardization of the colonial units. Before 1700, the reforms were attempted. That they were only partially realized in the short run and failed in the long, was due to factors either unchangeable or at least not easily changed. The administrative system remained enmeshed in politics. Procedural changes were difficult in a system of government that clung tenaciously to traditional forms. The Atlantic remained a barrier to effective enforcement. Beyond it grew a self-generating population with a lively sense of self-interest. Finally, at precisely the moment that the English came to understand their imperial problem, they committed themselves to a titanic struggle with France, which pushed other problems into the background.

The Renewal of Colonization

After a lapse of thirty years, England vigorously renewed her colonizing efforts. In little over a decade, six new colonies were established in North America and the English position in the Caribbean was consolidated. All of the older motives and methods of colonization reappeared, but the accents had changed. Commercial considerations dominated the new enterprises on the mainland, in the Caribbean, and in West Africa.

The same merchant groups that had backed the Navigation Acts advocated foreign and imperial policies that would extend the English colonial area. Though they did not utter the exact words, they would have agreed with the aphorism of their nineteenth-century cousins that trade followed the flag. As orthodox mercantilists they favored the development of colonies that would produce valuable subtropical commodities. They looked with particular favor on the further development of the Caribbean and southern mainland areas. Their desires led them into an inconsistent pattern. These men advocated imperial centralization, and this meant that they opposed private or proprietary interests. Yet they supported the creation of new proprietary colonies. Their reasons for doing so were expedient. The earlier experience with the joint stock corporation as the agency for creating colonies had left a dismal record of financial failure. The initial costs were too great to justify the risk. The trend of the times was toward royal colonies, but indigent Charles II was in no position to sponsor such costly ventures. He could, though, reward those who supported him. The Poveys and Noells found in the great courtiers and statesmen like the Duke of York, Clarendon, Albemarle, and Shaftesbury men with the inclination and influence to undertake new colonial projects. This explains the apparent anomaly of an empire, at once mercantilist and modern, choosing the essentially medieval device of a proprietorship as the vehicle for expansion.

In an age of intense national competition, the new expansion took the form of a race for the control of islands, coastal regions, and river valleys. The posture and policy of three European nations located the critical areas for Charles and his advisers. The Dutch had reached the peak of their maritime power. They dominated world trade and stood in particularly strong positions in Northern Europe, West Africa, and the Far East. Spain, well along the road to decline, remained the major power in South America, Central America, and southern North America. During the reign of Louis XIV, France became the dominant force on the European continent. Louis' driving minister of finance, Jean Baptiste Colbert, launched a comprehensive campaign to make France a strong mercantilist nation. Under Colbert, the French built a powerful navy and pushed a policy of overseas expansion. From their tenuously held Canadian base, the French pushed west and south along the inland waterways until their American empire stretched in a great crescent from New Orleans to Quebec. The chartering of East and West India Companies gave evidence of French intent in the Caribbean and the Orient.

By the 1660's, the major commercial nations regarded the West Indies as the area having the greatest potential for profitable development. The long process by which what had once been a Spanish lake was transformed into the crossroads of international commerce culminated in the first decade of Charles' reign. In the 1620's, the English and Dutch began to breach the Spanish monopoly of the Lesser Antilles. A Dutch fleet under Piet Hein broke the back of Spanish naval power in 1625. After that the Northern Europeans poured into the Antilles. With typical inconsistency, Charles I granted and regranted islands in the Leeward and Windward groups to different individuals. By 1627, the Earl of Carlisle regarded himself as the proprietor of St. Christopher (Kitts), Nevis, and Barbados. St. Christopher filled up rapidly and the surplus population overflowed into Antigua and Montserrat. At the same time a Puritan-sponsored corporation, the Providence Company, took over a small English settlement at Tortuga in Hispaniola. The company also developed colonies directly off the Spanish Main on the islands of Providence and Henrietta. In time the Spanish destroyed the latter settlements and the French prevailed in Hispaniola. To these possessions gained under the early Stuarts, Cromwell added a valuable island in the Greater Antilles. At the conclusion of the First Dutch War, the Protector unveiled his "Western Design," an ambitious revival of Elizabeth's anti-Spanish policy overseas. The "Design" secured Jamaica for England.

The Dutch West India Company led the assault on the Spanish trading routes but showed little interest in colonization. The company established its main base on Curaçao which became a valuable producer of salt. The Dutch also occupied St. Eustatius and St. Martins in the Leeward group. Though French privateers had been active in the Caribbean since the sixteenth century, France began settlement late. In 1635, the French moved onto Guadelupe and Martinique. Later they settled Marie-Galante, Désirade, St. Lucia, and Grenada.

Through the 1660's Charles pursued a tortuous, twisting path in foreign policy. At one time or another he was at war with the Netherlands, France, and Spain. At all times naval warfare continued in the Caribbean with little regard for European truce or treaty. It was the great age of the buccaneer, of Henry Morgan and Edward Mansfield, and there was "no peace beyond the line." The tale was one of daring, destruction, and rapidly shifting fortune. When, toward the end of the decade, the fog of war lifted, the distribution of Caribbean territory took a form that was to last for a century. The Treaties of Breda (1667) between England on the one hand and France and the Netherlands on the other crystallized possession. France gained most by the provisions that recognized her rights to Tobago and St. Eustatius. England was left in possession of her islands in the Lesser Antilles and Jamaica. In the two Treaties of Madrid (1667, 1670), England and Spain settled their accounts. Both parties agreed to end privateering, thus bringing to a close the classic era of the buccaneer. More important, Spain for the first time recognized England's rights to her West Indian and North American possessions.

Peace in the Caribbean made possible the regular, orderly growth of English West Indian holdings. The legal and economic foundations of that growth had been laid while the international struggle for control moved to its climax. At the Restoration, considerable confusion existed about the status of the proprietary rights in the area. The Carlisle patent of 1627 had had an erratic history because of stormy English politics. Revoked during the Interregnum, the rights were restored when the Earl of Carlisle submitted to Parliament. The matter was further complicated because Carlisle had leased his rights to Lord Willoughby. Soon after his return, Charles endorsed the Carlisle patent. This caused discontent among merchants trading to the area and the actual owners of the Caribbean plantations. A year later the Privy Council conducted an intensive investigation and canceled the proprietor's right of government. When Willoughby's lease expired, the islands in the Lesser Antilles became royal colonies outright. Jamaica had never been a private colony and Bermuda was to be royalized in 1684.

Beginning in the 1640's, the economy of the islands developed rapidly. In the earlier period, the planters had devoted themselves almost exclusively to tobacco culture. So long as they concentrated on tobacco they failed to prosper because their product was much inferior to that of Virginia. In the 1640's Dutch merchants encouraged the planters of the Antilles to attempt to grow sugar. That crop quickly became the staple and the islands prospered. With the discovery of a profitable plantation crop, the planters sought a large supply of labor and found it in Negro slaves.

The Duke's Friends: The Carolinas

The friends and associates of the Duke of York seized the major commercial and colonial opportunities of the early Restoration period. All, or most, of their names—the Berkeleys, Sir William and Lord John; Sir Anthony Ashley Cooper, later Earl of Shaftesbury; Sir George Carteret; the Earls of Clarendon and Craven; George Monck, Duke of Albemarle; Sir John Colleton —appear again and again on the rosters of new overseas enterprises. Members of the group dominated the Privy Council and controlled the various special committees of trade and plantations. They had much in common. Most of them had previous experience with investments in the dominions, either in Ireland or America. As informed statesmen, they knew the drift of diplomacy and its relationship to expansion. They shared a common antipathy to the Dutch. Probably they all regarded extension of the empire as a national advantage. Certainly they had faith in the economic potential of the empire and expected to profit immediately from such activities as the slave trade and ultimately as proprietors of vast new world estates. In a crass age, they did not hesitate to use their considerable influence with the king to gain huge concessions for themselves.

Between Albemarle Sound and the Savannah River lay a long coastline and a vast, untouched hinterland. By 1660, Spain had surrendered no part of her right to the area, though James I had granted the land south to the thirty-fourth parallel to the London Company of Virginia. Whatever English claims to the area existed reverted to the crown with the royalization of Virginia. In 1629, Charles I regranted the tract between the thirty-first and thirty-sixth parallels to Sir Robert Heath. The patent fixed the name of the territory as "Carolana," or Carolina, in honor of the king. A few years later Heath conveyed the property to Lord Maltravers, and in course of time it came into possession of his son, the Duke of Norfolk. Though Maltravers made plans for a colony, it is not clear whether settlement was actually attempted. Another effort by Samuel Vassall and his Huguenot associates was also abortive. A group of New Englanders tried a colony in the Cape Fear region in 1660, but moved on after a brief stay. By the time of the issuance of the Carolina charter of 1663, the only English settlers known to exist in the area were a scattered few who had drifted south from Virginia and located on the Chowan River and around Albemarle Sound.

The initiative for a new charter came from men with American experience who presumably knew something of Carolina's potential. Probably Sir John Colleton, an ardent royalist who had weathered the storm of the Interregnum as a Barbados planter, first conceived the idea. Sir William Berkeley, back in London after a tour as governor of Virginia, early became interested. Colleton and Berkeley then involved a rising politician, Sir Anthony Ashley Cooper. The three realized that they would need to bring in some great names to guarantee success. They set out to enlist men of influence, beginning easily enough with Berkeley's powerful brother, Lord John. They then drew in Clarendon, Craven, Albemarle, and Sir George Carteret, a particular favorite of the king. Such a combination guaranteed Privy Council approval.

The notion that Charles II granted Carolina to this group of courtiers as lightheartedly as he showered gifts on the courtesans who surrounded him is fictitious. Modern scholars agree that he probably opposed the grant originally but yielded to the pressure brought to bear. The charter was issued in March 1663. Before it could be implemented, the Duke of Norfolk and Samuel Vassall polished up their rights under the Heath patent and asked the Council to cancel the new grants. The issue was never in doubt and in June the Council peremptorily voided the old patent on the grounds of no settlement.

In its major provisions the charter resembled the earlier proprietary grants. The eight men held a huge territory stretching from sea to sea between the thirty-first and thirty-sixth parallels (extended in 1665 about thirty-five miles north and one hundred miles south). They held in free and common socage for twenty marks a year. Their rights were those of the Bishop of Durham with the Statute of *Quia Emptores* specifically waived. The charter contained several liberal concessions. The proprietors were instructed to make law "with the advice, assent and approbation of the freemen." For a seven-year period they were exempted from import duties on silk, wine, currants, raisins, capers, wax, almonds, oil, and olives. The charter waived the duties of the Old Subsidy for goods exported to the colony. Finally, those persons who could not "conform to the public exercise of religion, according to the liturgy, form and ceremonies of the church of England" were to enjoy religious freedom. Such concessions are evidence of a realistic attitude toward Carolina's economic possibilities. The proprietors hoped to develop an agricultural community that would produce commodities such as silk, wine, and rice, which England had been forced to import from foreign sources. Carolina's wealth would be based on labor, some of it skilled, applied to the land. The liberal provisions of the charter were designed to attract labor from other American colonies, from England, and from Europe.

With the charter past the seals, the proprietors quickly attempted to stimulate settlement at widely separated areas along the coast—at Albemarle Sound, Cape Fear, and Port Royal. They concentrated first on Cape Fear, probably because they had a good account of the area from William Hilton, who had twice visited the area. Before 1663 was out, they tried to interest a group of New Englanders in the area without result. Their best hope for an immediate start was with the surplus population of Barbados. There the Colleton interest gathered a party, but the Barbadans made excessive demands for land with rights of government and the proprietors turned them down. In the same year, Sir William Berkeley returned to America as governor of Virginia. The proprietors commissioned him to look after and develop the Albemarle Sound region. In 1664, Berkeley appointed William Drummond as governor. The northern region gradually grew, as landless Virginians and others drifted in. Albemarle was always in fact a separate colony. By 1700 this was apparent to all, and in 1712 the autonomy of North Carolina was recognized formally.

In 1664–1665, the proprietors again attempted to develop the southern reaches of their domain. They advertised Carolina and offered substantial concessions to attract settlers. In 1664 they published William Hilton's *Relation*, which painted a most attractive picture of Carolina. The land, "covered with black Mold," was so good that even primitive Indian agriculture produced fine crops. Land, sea, and air teemed with wildlife. Cape Fear had "as good Land, and as well Timbred, as any we have seen in any other part of the world, sufficient to accommodate thousands of our *English* Nation." Appended to the *Relation* are six curious letters that Hilton had exchanged with a Spanish captain. The only inference that can be drawn from them is that the Spaniards would not be hostile to English settlement in southern latitudes. The document closes with a liberal, sliding scale of head rights. For a limited time the proprietors offered land in free and common socage at a half penny per acre, subject only to the obviously nominal quitrent of an ear of corn per hundred acres. The next year, the proprietors threw out another lure, the *Concessions and Agreements*. They promised full religious freedom so long as the colonists did not use "Liberty to Lycentiousness." They instructed the governor to permit the election of a general assembly that was to have broad legislative power. Finally, they promised to share the charter-granted commercial privileges with the Carolinians.

The proprietors hoped to begin settlement near Port Royal at the extreme southern limit of the patent. They employed two Barbadans, John and William Yeamans, to get the project under way. The Yeamans enlisted a group of Barbadans and launched the venture in the autumn of 1665. They avoided Port Royal, perhaps because they feared that Spain, though weakened, might sever such an extended English appanage. The Yeamans' party located at Cape Fear; from the beginning the colony faltered. Bad weather wrecked supply ships; leadership was feeble, the colonists restive; the terms of the land grants were unsatisfactory. In 1667, the colonists abandoned the Cape.

After 1667, the Earl of Shaftesbury directed the efforts of the English proprietors. Discouraged by the attempts to begin colonization cheaply with persons already in America, he raised a substantial fund and in 1669 sent out three ships from England. The vessels detoured to Barbados, stopped at, but bypassed, Port Royal, and went on to begin a town on the right bank of the Ashley River. The next year they relocated on the point of land between the Ashley and Cooper Rivers. Charles Town grew rapidly and by the end of the century was already the queen city of the south.

Simultaneously with the renewed and successful effort at settlement the proprietors issued a formal frame of government for Carolina. The Fundamental Constitutions were drafted by Shaftesbury's secretary, John Locke. This document, the most elaborate basic law of the colonial period, was a fantastic blend of medieval institutions and seventeenth centry liberal ideas with a strong dash of James Harrington's *Oceana* thrown in for good measure. The preamble to the Orders announced the purpose of creating a government "agreeable to the monarchy" which would "avoid erecting a numerous democracy." The eldest of the proprietors was named the palatine and seven other titles with a strong medieval flavor were bestowed on his associates. The document went immediately to the main business—land distribution—by dividing the province into counties, seignories, baronies, precincts, and colonies. With the grants to the nobility went extensive seigneurial privilege, including a right of jurisdiction in the form of the court leet. Sixty per cent of the land could be taken up by freemen, but the remainder was perpetually reserved for an hereditary nobility consisting of the proprietors, landgraves, and caciques.

The Orders provided for an extremely elaborate government. Each proprietor had a supreme court with a "college" of twelve assistants. The courts had different executive or judicial functions. The courts together made up the grand council, which, among many other things, proposed all legislation in "parliament." The legislature was heavily loaded with nobility and ownership of considerable property was prerequisite to exercise of the franchise and to office holding. The "parliament" normally sat at a unicameral legislature, but became quadricameral when constitutional questions arose. The negative vote of one chamber nullified any act judged to be contrary to the Orders, which were unamendable.

In its more liberal provisions, the constitution blended common law with late seventeenth-century opinion. It specifically provided for jury trial and protected the individual from double jeopardy. In an elaborate system of courts, the voice of a lawyer was not to be heard for "it shall be a base and vile thing to plead for money or reward." In a verbose section of almost a thousand words, the Orders promised religious toleration.

Perhaps John Locke thought of the Carolina frontier as a *tabula rasa* upon which he could write government as he wished. In this he was much mistaken. Though the proprietors strove for twenty-five years to get the settlers to accept the Fundamental Orders, the better sense of the colonists prevailed. They would have no such theorizing. Rather they built their government, as other emigrating Englishmen did, out of those time-tried institutions of the homeland that proved to be serviceable in the New World environment.

The Duke's Interest: Africa, New York, New Jersey

In 1660, Charles II appointed his brother James to be Lord High Admiral of England. From that vantage point the Duke of York vigorously directed national maritime affairs. Certainly he clearly understood the relationship of sea power to colonial and commercial expansion. The facts pointed directly to a revival of the conflict with the United Netherlands. At the court and in the counting houses, the duke found men eager to support an anti-Dutch policy. Foremost among them was Sir George Downing who occupied the key post of minister at the Hague. Downing never wearied of writing memorials and letters that set out the grievances against the Dutch. Samuel Pepys came to see the matter clearly a few years later: the seas of the world were not large enough for England and the Netherlands.

Though many of the old grievances, such as the North Sea fisheries, remained, the direct cause of the Second Dutch War arose out of the West African trade. By the early seventeenth century, the Dutch had largely replaced the Portuguese along the West African coast. English traders had visited the area as early as Elizabeth's time to try to establish a regular, incorporated trade. The premature English Guinea companies sought to profit by exchanging manufactured goods for gold and ivory without much success.

In the 1650's Dutch factors demonstrated the real wealth of Africa. Across the Atlantic, in the English Antilles, they encouraged Brazilian sugar as a crop and then introduced African slaves to work the plantations. With sugar as a staple, the economy of the English West Indies, particularly Barbados, boomed. The rapid growth of the sugar plantations first created and then accelerated the demand for Negro labor. To the mercantilist mind it was unthinkable that the lucrative business of supplying English colonies with slaves should be monopolized by foreigners, particularly the Dutch. Underlying the new interest in Africa of the 1660's was an old, persistent desire—the hope of Hawkins—that England might secure the *asiento,* the right to supply the never-ending Spanish-American demand for Negroes. The revived African interest brought on a new Dutch war.

In 1660, the East India Company held whatever English rights existed on the West African coast. At the Restoration, the crown gave the privileges to the Company of Royal Adventurers into Africa. The company was reorganized once in 1663 and again in 1672 as the Royal African Company. The Duke of York headed these companies and their rosters carried the familiar names of Noell and Povey, Cartaret, Colleton, and John Berkeley. The charters made magnificent grants of soil from twenty-first parallel to the Cape of Good Hope. Through a thousand years the corporation was to enjoy a monopoly of trade.

It was one thing to make sweeping grants at Whitehall, another to make them good along the African coast. The Dutch had won their position by force and showed their intent to maintain it by the same means. To expedite matters, the Admiralty ordered Captain Robert Holmes to seize some Dutch African factories. He did; the Dutch retaliated and for three years an undeclared naval war blazed out intermittently along the African coast.

As they cast the die in Africa, the duke and his supporters turned coolly to the task of dispossessing the Dutch in North America.

Beginning in the 1620's, the Dutch West India Company had begun to build upon the claim resulting from the earlier voyage of Henry Hudson. Though the claim stretched between the Connecticut and Delaware Rivers, the Dutch concentrated on the valley of the Hudson. They located first at Fort Orange (Albany) and then established New Amsterdam on Manhattan Island. Other small settlements were scattered along the Hudson, on western Long Island, in northern New Jersey, and on the Delaware. Throughout its career, New Netherlands was a private, rather than public, undertaking. The West India Company, interested in commerce, pushed the fur trade and this drew company officials deep into the tangle of Indian diplomacy. Often engaged in war with the Indians, the Dutch were able to form a durable alliance with the Iroquois which was to have long-range influence in the colonies. Aside from the Indian trade, New Amsterdam served as a base for ocean marauders and illicit traders. From the beginning a polyglot population seated itself on Manhattan Island. Visitors often compared it to Babel.

To stimulate agriculture with little cost or effort the company resorted to a policy of making lavish land grants. The Charter of Freedoms and Exemptions of 1629 authorized the creation of patroonships. These were to be huge seigneurial estates with the patroon possessed of full rights of jurisdiction. Though the company made many grants, only one person, Kiliaen van Rensselaer, took full advantage of the privileges. His vast estate, Rensselaerwyck, covered one million acres around Fort Orange.

The government of New Netherlands never worked well. The company chose to operate through a resident executive, the director general or governor, and an appointed council. It erred in its choice of men, sending over a series of five governors who were either incompetent or arrogant or both. The generation of Dutch rule was punctuated steadily by popular protest. At any time a substantial minority who felt very little loyalty to the Dutch Republic would welcome change, even work actively for it.

The English design on New Netherlands accorded well with the rising anti-Dutch sentiment. For years Maryland, New England, and Long Island had complained of Dutch encroachment. After 1660, the volume of these protests increased. The continued existence of New Netherlands was antithetical to the new English concept of empire. The port of New Amsterdam provided the merchants of Massachusetts with a convenient place to drive an export-import trade that evaded the navigation system. In addition, Restoration statesmen had a vision of empire which included a continuous stretch of English territory along the North American coast. The Dutch had to go.

Since the English government never had recognized the Dutch North American claim, the Duke of York did not have to engage in any legal sophistries before acting. Late in 1663, the Privy Council appointed an *ad hoc* committee to consider grievances against New Netherlands. By April a charter had been rushed past the seals and a special commission had been appointed to carry out the occupation.

In regard to government, the New York charter of 1664 resembled those establishing the earlier proprietaries. The question of restricting the proprietor must have appeared unnecessary since the duke's domain would become a royal province at the time of his elevation to the throne. The novel feature of the charter was the territory granted—a fantastic conglomeration of noncontiguous territory. The main tract intruded deeply into New England by establishing the Connecticut River as the eastern boundary. To New York was added what was to become New Jersey and Delaware with Maine between the St. Croix and the Kennebec thrown in for good measure. Charles M. Andrews, normally sympathetic to the exercise of imperial power, described the charter as "in territory granted and powers conferred...the worst example in the history of English colonization of a proprietary lordship..."[1]

To Richard Nicolls, duke and king assigned the dual responsibility of governing New York and heading the royal commission. In addition to Nicolls, the commission included Colonel George Cartwright, Sir Robert Carr, and Samuel Maverick. Their open and secret instructions, in addition to authorizing the seizure of New Netherlands, empowered them to make a general inquiry into the practices of the New England governments.

The commissioners arrived in Boston in the summer of 1664 and proceeded to the Hudson within the month. The four warships and regular English troops were complemented by colonial militia, which turned out in substantial strength. The Dutch governor, Peter Stuyvesant, was in no position to fight and he knew it. He blustered and stalled, seeking to negotiate. Nicolls refused to negotiate and after a few days' delay Stuyvesant surrendered New Netherlands without resistance. Cartwright and Carr finished the occupation by seizing Fort Orange and securing the Delaware country.

As governor of New York, Nicolls exercised a vice-regal authority. He and three successors governed without a popular

1. Charles M. Andrews, *The Colonial Period of American History* (New Haven: Yale University Press, 1934–1938), III, 58.

assembly. They stated the law and levied taxes through an appointed council; they gave judgment through a court of assize. The resident Dutch, having no provincial tradition of self-government, adjusted easily. So far as they were concerned the settlement had been liberal. Nicolls confirmed the property rights of individuals and the parent Dutch corporation. The governor's troubles within his jurisdiction came from the English, particularly the Puritan towns of Long Island. From the beginning, the English protested the lack of an assembly and effectively blocked the governor's attempts to raise revenue for the Duke of York from duties on trade.

Nicolls strove with no success to establish the boundaries granted by the charter. Connecticut stood on her own charter and refused to accept the Connecticut River as a western boundary. The duke's rights to Maine never really existed except on paper. To the south, Baltimore contested the duke's claim that the Delaware River was the boundary. The duke himself further frustrated Nicolls by giving away New Jersey.

The history of New Jersey in the seventeenth century is a confusing record of lease and release, transfer and retransfer. Soon after his charter passed the seals, the Duke of York conveyed the title to New Jersey to Sir John Berkeley and Sir George Carteret. To accomplish the transfer, the duke used an ordinary instrument of English land law. Though no powers of government could be granted by such a device, Berkeley and Carteret acted as if they were absolute proprietors. This insecure and indefinite base of government caused trouble from the beginning.

Both Berkeley and Carteret were proprietors of Carolina. New Jersey offered them an additional opportunity to extend their American speculation. Knowing that profit depended on locating labor upon the land, they issued the *Concessions and Agreements*, which were patterned after the Carolina document. They promised political rights in the form of an assembly, easy access to land, and religious toleration.

In 1665, the proprietors sent out young Philip Carteret as governor. Carteret found his territory already thinly settled. In northern New Jersey, Nicolls had made the Monmouth and Elizabeth town grants. Puritans from New England and Long

Island had located in that area and had immediately established town governments. They defied Carteret, refusing absolutely to accept his authority. Through a decade the governor found his sphere of influence limited to the southern part of New Jersey.

During the Third Dutch War (1672–1674), the Dutch reoccupied New York and New Jersey for about a year. The Tready of Breda restored the territory to the English. At this juncture, Berkeley sold his rights to two Quakers, John Fenwick and Edward Byllinge. The sale marked the beginning of the division of the territory into two distinct jurisdictions. The Fenwick-Byllinge area was known as West New Jersey. After Berkeley sold out his share, the Duke of York regranted the rest of the area to Carteret and this became East New Jersey. In the late 1670's, other groups of Quakers took advantage of the confused situation in the Jerseys to establish a haven for the sect. Fenwick sold West New Jersey to William Penn and two associates. After Carteret's death in 1680, Penn headed another group that bought East New Jersey. The second Quaker association was not identical with the first because Penn had to draw in others to obtain the necessary capital.

For ten years, East and West Jersey continued as separate jurisdictions. They were united temporarily when James II incorporated them into the Dominion of New England. At the dissolution of the Dominion, the two tiny provinces again went their separate ways. In 1692, a group of English merchants combined as the West Jersey Society and purchased that area. They then appointed the incumbent governor of East New Jersey, Andrew Hamilton, to be governor of West New Jersey. On the basis of this limited union, the Jerseys existed for the rest of the century. Disputes over government, commercial rights, and land titles were continuous. In 1699, the case of New Jersey came before the Board of Trade. Three years later the Privy Council cut the tangled knot by purchasing the whole area and making New Jersey a regular royal colony.

The Holy Experiment of William Penn

Many of the major forces that moved Englishmen in the seventeenth century blended in William Penn to produce an outstanding man, perhaps a unique one. Deeply involved in the most radical English religious experiment, he avoided its excesses. Often the object of the harsh criminal law of his day, he won a major victory for the rights of Englishmen and helped carry the basic concept of the supremacy of law to America. A philanthropist, he understood both the economic needs of the common Englishman and the great potential of the empire. A rich and varied experience as a youth prepared the man. William's father, Admiral William Penn, had been in and out of favor with Cromwell. At the Restoration, the Admiral won the confidence of both Charles and James and this trust his son inherited. His father, a man of means, provided the opportunity for an excellent education. Two years at an Oxford dominated by brittle Anglicanism awakened Penn's religious curiosity and brought his expulsion. Later he studied at a French Huguenot college and still later read law at one of the Inns of Court. Along the way he went to sea with his father during the Second Dutch War. Sent to Ireland at an early age to manage the family estates, he gained practical business experience. In Ireland he became a Quaker.

George Fox was one of those brooding, intense men who discover or invent religions. The religion called Quaker derived from Fox's inspiration that the divinity dwelled within the soul of every man. Once recognized, this indwelling spirit became the Inner Light that would guide the individual in all matters moral and spiritual. What was implicit in such a highly personal creed, Fox soon made explicit. A man so moved needed no organized religion, certainly no priest. The Inner Light created an individual independent of social forms. Such a person was beyond compulsion, and unreasonable law could not confine him. A fiery missionary, Fox defied church, state, and society. Under his leadership, the Quakers became the most feared, most persecuted persons in a seventeenth-century England that might have accommodated almost any variety of religious opinion but would tolerate neither the leveling tendencies of the Quakers nor their essential denial of external political sovereignty.

Penn became a Quaker after the movement's first zealous enthusiasm had somewhat abated. A thoroughly convinced Quaker and an intimate associate of Fox, he avoided extremities and became a leader of the organization of the Friends. Penn journeyed three times to the European continent seeking converts. At home, his activities exposed him to fine and imprisonment. On one occasion, his knowledge of English law won a notable victory for the rights of the subject, namely, that a jury may return a verdict contrary to the law as stated by the judge. Before Penn began his work in America, his ideas had taken definite form: he accepted the essential doctrine of the Inner Light; he was a pacifist; in matters of government he was a relativist who equated good government with a rule of law; he believed that the odds were all against effecting a reformation of society in England.

Penn's experience in East and West New Jersey convinced him that he should try a new experiment in a larger area to which he had unequivocal title. In 1680, he petitioned the king for a grant between New York and Maryland. Factors favoring the grant were the king's affection for Penn and the fact that the government owed him £16,000, which his father had expended in public service. Arguing against the grant was the growing conviction of English officials that the policy of establishing proprietary colonies should be arrested. For nine months his petition went the rounds of London offices. In March 1691, the last proprietary charter, a unique document, issued from the chancellor's office.

The charter granted the land in free and common socage for two beaver skins a year. In only one sense was Penn the true and absolute proprietor. With the Statute of *Quia Emptores* again waived, he had an unrestricted right to dispose of the land. In granting powers of government, the charter laid on all of the old restrictions as well as many new ones. Penn was to make law "with the advice, assent and approbation of the freemen." The law was to be consistent with the law of England. The new restrictions reflected the growing conviction at London that the provinces should be subject to central control. The right was reserved to appeal any judgment of a Pennsylvania court to the Privy Council. All acts of the colonial assembly had to be sent to London where the king could exercise a veto power. The charter contained an injunction that the Navigation Acts be obeyed strictly and provided specifically for the entry of English officials to enforce the law. The document required Penn to maintain an attorney or agent at London "to answer for any misdemeanours." Though religious toleration was guaranteed, the charter made a further reservation by requiring that, upon the request of twenty persons, Anglican ministers were to be admitted to the colony.

In a series of documents and pamphlets, Penn began immediately to prepare for settlement. A detailed code of laws revealed Penn's assumption that in a clean, new environment men would be rational and good. His "Frame of Government" made himself or his deputy the governor. The council, a very large body, was elected. As the upper house of the legislature, it had the sole right to initiate legislation. In common with other provincial councils, it had a general executive and judicial authority. A modest property qualification controlled the franchise for members of the assembly.

Having provided for government, Penn began the work of attracting the people to his land. His advertising campaign, by far the most thorough and extensive conducted by any proprietor, was not limited to England. His pamphlets circulated in all the British Isles and were translated into Dutch and German. In the "Concessions" he set out the terms of a liberal policy of land disposal. His pamphlet, *Some Account of the Province of Pennsylvania*, was a shrewdly argued economic document. He stated the basic mercantilist argument for colonies succinctly and then described those classes of persons who would benefit both the realm and themselves by emigration. From the beginning, the publicity given the province produced results. Pennsylvania, drawing its people from all over Northern Europe, filled up rapidly. In April 1681, Penn sent out William Markham as his deputy to establish the proprietary.

Before Penn himself went out to America, he succeeded in adding to his holdings. The Delaware River provided the sole access of his province to the sea. The eastern shore of Delaware Bay was within the jurisdiction of New Jersey and title to the western shore was in dispute. Baltimore claimed it as a part of Maryland, but the governors of New York exercised jurisdiction. Though the area lay outside the Duke of York's charter-granted boundaries, his governors claimed the area on the grounds of previous Dutch occupation and English conquest. After some hesitation, the duke leased the area to Penn in 1682. For about fifteen years the three counties of the Delaware were considered as a part of Pennsylvania. The residents of the area disliked this arrangement and in the first years of the eighteenth century a separation was effected by the creation of an independent legislature. The further arrangements were unusual. Penn appointed the governor and invariably he was also the governor of Pennsylvania. The appointment to the governorship of Delaware needed royal approval. Thus Delaware—or more correctly, the Lower Counties, as they were always described—stood somewhere between being a royal and a proprietary colony.

Penn went out to America in 1682, stayed about two years, and returned to America in 1699. In the context of his hopes, the story of the early years is one of the frustration of an idealist. Materially, the province prospered from the start. Penn saw Philadelphia laid out according to plan, saw a commerce develop, and witnessed the distressed farmers of England and Europe pour into and begin to cultivate the fine lands of eastern Pennsylvania. His ideal notions concerning government failed just as surely as Locke's theoretical constitution for the Carolinas. The day of the proprietor was done. The people of Pennsylvania quickly established the standard pattern of American colonial government, with the essential authority in the legislature. Within the assembly a group of prospering Quakers steadily wore away Penn's prerogatives. By 1700, the fact of Pennsylvania public life was a normal struggle for power rather than the Utopia that its founder had envisioned. In 1693 Penn wrote: "I abhor contention, nicetys, doubtful disputation, divisions, etc., and am for patience, forbearance, long suffering and all true moderation." In 1705: "I am a crucified man between Injustice and Ingratitude there and Extortion and Oppression here."[2]

2. *Op. cit.*, Andrews, III, 304.

Chapter 7

American Politics, Imperial and Domestic, 1660-1685

Imperial Policy in America, 1660-1685

*N*ews of the restoration of Charles II created attitudes in the American colonies that varied from genuine joy in Virginia to sullen disbelief in Massachusetts. For the dominions, the return of the Stuarts brought a restoration of the imperial prerogative that quickly forced latent conflicts into the open. The various agencies of English government turned immediately to the task of reorganizing the empire along lines of economic and political standardization and control. This effort defined the issues. In several New England colonies, Massachusetts particularly and to a lesser degree in New Hampshire, the conflict of interest went to the very heart of the imperial relationship and raised the question of ultimate sovereignty. In all of the mainland colonies, the efforts to implement the commercial code set out in the Navigation Acts brought on the first major English attempt to enforce law in America.

Four American colonies either regarded the Restoration as a positive good or saw in it an opportunity to strengthen their position. Virginia had settled into the pattern of a royal colony before the Civil Wars. Rigidly Anglican, strongly royalist, and potentially aristocratic in her outlook, she had received emigrating supporters of the defeated Stuarts. The Old Dominion had more trouble with the various governments of the Interregnum than any other colony. Though Virginians welcomed the return to the older forms, they had a time of anxiety in the early 1660's. As a part of the general scramble for privilege that came with Charles's return, a series of fantastic proposals were made to establish proprietary rights to huge tracts within Virginia. Though some of these grants were actually made, Virginia was able to prevent their execution, presumably through the agency of Sir William Berkeley, who represented their interests at London in 1660. Maryland had been a storm center during the Interregnum. Lord Baltimore was necessarily a strong Stuart supporter. As a consequence, he lost control of Maryland when a group of Puritans led by his implacable enemy, William Claiborne, staged a revolt. Though Cromwell later restored the proprietor's rights, Baltimore naturally felt more secure with the control of the central government in the hands of the Stuarts. Two New England colonies—Rhode Island and Connecticut—approached the Restoration opportunistically. Neither colony had ever been grounded on the solid base of a royal charter. Both had been involved in altercations with Massachusetts over boundaries and both were suspicious of their northern neighbor. The two colonies petitioned for charters. Rhode Island acted through its agent, Dr. John Clarke, who had been in England since 1651. Clarke put in the formal Rhode Island petition in January 1662.

At the same time, Connecticut was also seeking a charter, and her appeal showed a substantial part of the Narragansett Territory to be in dispute. Early in 1661, Connecticut had sent her governor, John Winthrop, Jr., to England to obtain a charter. This was a most fortunate choice because Winthrop not only had influential friends but was also a man whose merit commanded respect. The Connecticut charter had already been sealed when the fact of the overlapping boundaries became apparent. Winthrop agreed to submit the question to arbitration and a five-man board decided in favor of Rhode Island. With the boundary amendment, the Connecticut charter was issued and several months later the chancellor delivered Rhode Island's patent.

Both charters were extremely liberal. Neither made any reservation of royal power except on such obvious points as operating the courts in the king's name and a requirement for an oath of allegiance. In regard to government, the two colonies wrote their own provisions. Essentially the Connecticut charter adopted the Fundamental Orders whereas that of Rhode Island transposed provincial practice into the charter. For Rhode Island, Clarke obtained recognition of the cherished principle that had been the cornerstone of its policy. The charter specifically stated "that noe person within the colonie, at any time hereafter shall be in any wise molested, punished, disquieted or called in question for any differences in opinions in matters of religion." These charters had long lives. In each case, with minor modifications, they became the first constitutions of the states of Rhode Island and Connecticut during the American Revolution.

Why did the government of Charles II choose to create two corporate colonies at the very moment that its advisers were counseling a policy of consolidation and greater uniformity? Perhaps the best answer is to be found in Clarendon's concept of policy. For two years, information about the intransigence and ambition of Massachusetts had poured in. Clarendon saw that a strengthening of the two southern neighbors of Massachusetts would help to limit the growing power of the Bay Colony.

Massachusetts looked on the events of 1660 with a jaundiced eye. In Boston no proclamation for the king was read. On the contrary, the colony gave asylum temporarily to two of the regicides. While in London complaints against her piled up, Massachusetts fell back on her old policy of insulation and procrastination. The catalog of allegations, mostly true, was lengthy: she did not administer the oath of allegiance; her laws were repugnant to the English statutes; she coined money; she taxed freemen and made them liable to military service but would not permit them to vote; she was intolerant of all but Congregationalists; her charter was bad, or if good, had been extinguished by the *quo warranto* of 1635. In sum, the accusers charged Massachusetts with vastly exceeding her chartered powers and of aiming to establish an autonomous or independent state. In addition to such charges, the heirs of Mason and Gorges had constantly complained that Massachusetts' assumption of jurisdiction over New Hampshire and Maine violated their rights. Since the Mason-Gorges claims were specific and subject to adjudication, the English government tended to give them priority when it moved against the colony.

Late in 1660, Massachusetts sent a humble address to the king. Couched in general terms of submission, it surrendered no right. With the petition went instructions to the colony agents at London. Here Massachusetts outlined the tactics she would use to the end. Under no circumstances were the agents empowered to negotiate on the fundamental issues. Again and again English officials would be balked by the incompetence of the agents. In this way the colony took full advantage of the fact that the corporation of Massachusetts Bay was not resident in England. The law officers found the Puritan province an elusive target.

For two years Massachusetts sent agents and addresses and got royal letters in return. By 1662, the idea of sending a commission to America was being discussed, and in 1664 the Nicolls, Carr, Cartwright, Maverick commission was appointed. While the commissioners reduced the Dutch at New Netherlands—and before their full authority had been revealed—Massachusetts vehemently protested their presence to the home government. After Stuyvesant's surrender, all of the commissioners except Nicolls returned to Boston, where everyone made it abundantly clear that they were unwelcome. Their commission empowered them to survey the governments of New England and to pay particular attention to see that they operated within the framework of their charters. In addition, the commissioners were authorized to sit as a court to hear petitions and appeals. The whole business smelled of *quo warranto*.

Received with hostility at Boston, the commissioners decided to visit the other New England provinces before coming to grips with the Bay Colony. In Plymouth, Rhode Island, and Connecticut, the commissioners were largely successful in obtaining agreement concerning the oath of allegiance, religious toleration, and the repeal of any antiroyal legislation. When they returned to Boston, the magistrates cooperated at first by giving information about the state of the colony. There was, though, no meeting of minds on the oath or toleration. The open breach came when the commissioners attempted to sit as a court to hear appeals. Since this implied that the judgments of the magistrates were subject to review by a higher jurisdiction, the colony absolutely refused to admit the right. On the day appointed for the commissioners' court, the crier moved through the streets of Boston warning the citizens to stay away. At this point the commissioners gave up. They made a brief tour of the northern provinces. In New Hampshire they made no headway in gaining recognition of the Mason rights. In Maine they appointed a few officials. They then returned to Boston and wrote a report very critical of Massachusetts. A short time later, the king ordered the colony to send over new agents, but the colony stalled. The Dutch Wars, the fall of Clarendon, and the rise of the Cabal occupied the attention of English officials, and for a little longer the Puritans of the Bay Colony went their own way.

Through the early 1670's, Mason and Gorges intermittently pressed their claims, thus keeping the Massachusetts question before the government. In 1675 the crown decided again to demand that the colony send agents. Though the royal letter referred only to the northern boundary disputes, it is clear that the English officials intended to raise the whole question of government under the charter. The man who carried the order out to Boston proved to be Massachusetts' nemesis. Edward Randolph was an experienced officer who dedicated himself to the task of bringing Massachusetts to book. There is no case on the imperial record of a more ardent mutual animosity than that which Randolph and the Boston Puritans felt for one another. The charges and countercharges were so laced with hyperbole that the truth is hard to find. As soon as Randolph arrived in Boston, the sparks flew between him and Governor John Leverett. In a hostile atmosphere, Randolph gathered the materials for a hostile report, which, in addition to the older charges, put particular emphasis on Massachusetts' evasion of the Navigation Acts.

Early in 1677, new colony agents arrived at London. The government confronted them with the full dossier of charges that Randolph had prepared. The agents demurred, stating that they had been instructed to negotiate only on the Mason-Gorges claims. Randolph then went the whole way by recommending that government begin legal process to vacate the charter. The Massachusetts agents were detained in England until 1679. When they finally left they carried back with them a royal order to send out new agents within six months with full power to negotiate.

The next group of agents had some discretionary power, but they were not authorized to yield any of the colonial interpretation of the charter rights. English officials immediately informed them that their instructions were inadequate. In 1683, Randolph, who had become a transatlantic commuter, returned to England and summarized the charges in detail for the law officers. Shortly a writ of *quo warranto* issued, and indefatigable Randolph recrossed the ocean to serve it. For the last time, circumstances frustrated him; for, by the time he arrived, the date upon which the writ was returnable had passed. Randolph returned again to England where the attorney general advised vacating the charter by the expeditious writ of *scire facias*. By this summary process the English government nullified the charter that had made the Puritan commonwealth possible.

The status of the northern provinces of Maine and New Hampshire had long remained uncertain. During the negotiations that ended in the quashing of the Massachusetts charter, the colony agents had been able to purchase the Gorges rights. In 1677, the English attorney general and two judges of the common law courts wrote elaborate opinions concerning the Mason-Gorges rights in New England. In regard to New Hampshire, they ruled that Mason had a proprietary right to land previously ungranted. Since a grant by the old Council for New England could not have conveyed powers of government, the lawyers held that authority remained with the crown. On the strength of these opinions, New Hampshire became a royal province with land title vested in Mason.

If crown officials assumed that the vacating of proprietary rights of government would solve most of their problems in America, they were mistaken. The royal governors of the late seventeenth and early eighteenth century were forced to administer governments for a people who felt little attachment for

England. The notions of prerogative government which prevailed in England simply could not be applied in America. The first generation of English in America had developed governments in which the elected assemblies and colonial courts played important roles. These agencies, jealous of local rights, became the chief barrier to effective law enforcement by the royal governors. The early history of New Hampshire as a royal colony illustrates the conflict in exaggerated microcosm.

Two years after the lawyers had cut New Hampshire loose from Massachusetts, English authorities provided a provisional government by appointing John Cutt of Portsmouth to be president of the council. Richard Chamberlain, the first English officer to arrive, came out in 1680. As secretary to the council, Chamberlain soon came up against the stubborn determination of the Puritans to run their own affairs. The first assembly passed a typically New England code of law and settled local government in the town meetings. When Chamberlain protested that the law code deviated too far from the English statutes, the assembly and council simply ignored him. They set his fees at a very low level and refused to provide any salary at all.

In 1682, the first royal governor, Edward Cranfield, arrived at Portsmouth. Like all too many royally appointed officials, Cranfield seems to have regarded the office as an opportunity to enhance his personal fortune. The assembly suspected not only Cranfield's personal motives but also the authority he represented and the possibility that he would successfully back the Mason land claims. At each successive session of the assembly, the governor would ask that taxes be voted. The assembly would refuse; the governor would dissolve it. The result was an impasse in which the assembly maintained the stronger position. With practically no money in the treasury, and with little prospect of obtaining any, Cranfield struck out on a reckless course. He extorted fees, packed juries, hounded provincial leaders with criminal accusations, and ultimately tried to collect taxes on his own authority. Worst of all, he attacked the Congregational ministers by requiring that they administer the sacrament in the Anglican form to all who requested it. His excesses led to his recall in 1685. Osgood, an historian not given to sweeping generalizations, described Cranfield's career as "the most reckless and tyrannical course of policy which was ever followed by an appointee of the crown in the American continental colonies."[1]

Though the Cranfield incident was brief and exaggerated, it illustrated a basic dilemma of royal government: law enforcement cost money and the colonial assembly controlled the purse.

Between 1660 and 1673, Parliament laid the foundations of the imperial commercial code by passing the three navigation acts. The American colonists felt little inclination to obey these laws and quite openly evaded them. Through the 1660's they exported enumerated commodities directly to the continent in defiance of the act of 1660 and brought back European goods without clearing at an English port in violation of the statute of 1663. Colonial merchants and ship's captains interpreted the act of 1673 to mean that payment of the plantation duty freed them to clear for a European port. The three laws were as much breached as observed. This clearly apparent fact underlined the need of effective law enforcement.

The obvious place to locate responsibility for enforcement was with the colonial governors. This the Navigation Acts did without distinguishing royal, proprietary, or corporate governors. The royal governor could be instructed specifically to enforce the laws and this practice was followed in individual cases until in 1685 his obligations were codified and became a separate part of his formal instructions. The corporate and proprietary governors were less easily bound. Ultimately they were required to take a specific oath to uphold the code. From time to time English officials addressed special or general circular letters to the governors informing them of their obligations. General letters went out in 1663 and again in 1676 explaining the acts and mandating strict compliance. Gradually the governors began to delegate the responsibility for enforcing the commercial law and in course of time this executive agent came to be known as the naval officer.

The flow of evidence arriving in London concerning the effectiveness of enforcement all tended to prove that the governors were doing their jobs poorly and that the laws were flouted. This became particularly obvious after the act of 1673 required the

---

1. Herbert L. Osgood, *The American Colonies in the Seventeenth Century* (New York: Macmillan, 1904–1907), III, 338.

collection of duties at American ports. By the late 1660's government had been convinced of the need to appoint resident customs officials. Until 1671, collection of the trade duties had been arranged contractually with private businessmen, the farmers general. Since illicit trade depreciated their profits, they were as much concerned with the problem as the government was. Though the Treasury encouraged the farmers to send over provincial agents, they appointed few, probably because they had just as notorious problems with the British Isles. After 1671, a public board—the Commissioners of Customs—stood responsible to the Treasury for collection. In that year they appointed their first surveyor or collector of the customs, Edward Digges, for Virginia. In 1675 he was replaced by Giles Bland. In 1676, the commissioners appointed Christopher Rousby for Maryland and Thomas Miller for the Carolinas. In 1678, the most famous, or notorious, of the surveyors, Edward Randolph, came out to New England. The volume of business soon suggested consolidation and in 1683 the commissioners created the office of surveyor general of the customs in America and gave the office to William Dyer. The attempts of these officers to do their duty called forth violent resistance in America.

When Giles Bland assumed his surveyorship he was already in bad odor with Virginia government. The previous year he had been involved in a serious altercation with the local officials and had been fined heavily for insulting the burgesses and council. As surveyor he at once fell out with the cantankerous, imperious governor, Sir William Berkeley. The governor, a substantial tobacco planter, had protested the Navigation Acts as unfair to Virginia. There is evidence of a willingness on Berkeley's part to enforce the law leniently—if at all. He and Bland came to blows over the extent of the surveyor's authority. Bland insisted that he needed to see all ships' papers if he was to discharge his duty. Berkeley contended that the enforcement of the acts of 1660 and 1663 was none of Bland's business. The sole function of the surveyor, according to the governor, was to collect the plantation duty on tobacco. Bland accused Berkeley of obstructing the law and the governor removed him from office, at the same time referring the case to London. Before the Commissioners of Customs could review the case, Bacon's Rebellion erupted. Bland joined the insurgents and subsequently paid for his action on the gallows.

The resistance to Thomas Miller as surveyor in North Carolina was complicated by the longer struggle of the residents of the area against the Carolina proprietors. The Albermarle region had attracted a restless lot of men who regarded themselves as perfectly capable of running their own affairs. Thomas Miller identified closely with the proprietary interest and held office under their authority. In 1676 they obtained the surveyor's appointment for him. Miller went out to the province with a newly appointed governor who detoured into the West Indies for personal reasons. In North Carolina, Miller announced that he would act not only as collector but as governor. It is difficult to tell which the colonists resented most. Miller found a lively illicit trade, mostly driven by New Englanders, flourishing along the coast. He made seizures and levied fines in wholesale lots. Miller overreached himself when he imprisoned George Durant, the leader of the antiproprietary party. The country rose in revolt, imprisoned Miller and established a government. The new government made one John Culpeper collector of customs, hence the incident has since been known as "Culpeper's Rebellion." In due course Miller escaped from an inadequate jail and returned to England. The Carolina "rebels" then sent Culpeper to London to justify their action. The proprietors and English officials ruled the contest a draw, with dishonors just about even. They deprived Miller of his office for his highhanded conduct. Culpeper was tried before King's Bench on a technically correct but fantastic charge of high treason but was acquitted.

In Maryland, a violent altercation between the proprietor and royal agents ended in the murder of the collector, Christopher Rousby. Calvert, in residence as governor, charged Rousby with arbitrary conduct and malfeasance. The collector returned to England to defend himself. In the interval, Calvert precipitated a conflict with another royal official over the collection of the plantation duties of 1673. The central government upheld its agents, reprimanded Calvert and sent Rousby back to Maryland. Soon after his return, the president of the provincial council, in a drunken rage, stabbed Rousby to death.

In addition to his special missions that ended in the quashing of the Massachusetts charter, Edward Randolph acted as royal collector for New England between 1679 and 1683. He was, of course, *persona non grata* when he arrived and the New Englanders proceeded to frustrate him at every turn. Without a staff, Randolph had to rely on provincial executive and judicial agencies to assist him in enforcing the commercial code. They were not so minded. Again and again Randolph filed informations against violators. The colonial juries, refusing to convict, brought in a series of judgments against the king. To add injury to insult, the provincial courts forced Randolph to pay costs. Peremptory orders from London addressed to the local magistrates produced no result. Though the colony formally acknowledged the Navigation Act of 1660 and the Staple Act of 1663, it continued to evade the law. To expedite evasion, Massachusetts created the post of naval officer and empowered that official to clear vessels and register bonds. This took the responsibility for the inspection of vessels out of Randolph's hands and limited his function to that of tax collector. He found it impossible to inspect ships or even to see their papers.

Though the evasive tactics of Massachusetts Bay stood out prominently, perhaps because Randolph had been so articulate, the fact remained that down to 1685 the imperial code went largely unenforced in all of North America. The provincial form of government made little difference, for the southern proprietaries and royal Virginia evaded the law just as surely as the proud corporate jurisdictions of New England. The experience of the first royal collectors pointed directly to the central imperial problem, that of law enforcement. Randolph had seen clearly that the navigation system would not work so long as English agents had to rely on the American governments to get their job done. In a series of reports he recommended an expansion of the American customs service both in personnel and function. He asked the home government to arm its agents with special legal devices to facilitate the gathering of evidence. Finally, he urged the extension of vice-admiralty jurisdiction to America so that the agents would not need to prosecute before unfriendly colonial juries.

American Politics, 1660–1685

The political issues that agitated the English communities on either side of the Atlantic during the third quarter of the seventeenth century were essentially similar. Though the causes of specific disputes ranged from fear of popery to tobacco prices, at bottom the issue was constitutional. The imbalance of the constitution in favor of the executive power that the Tudors had created remained. The English executives—kings and governors, royal or proprietary—attempted to maintain and extend their prerogative. The communities attempted to arrest the thrust of executive power by consolidating and expanding the authority of the legislature. The combat in the political arena produced no definitive settlement in England until 1689. It followed that the primitive mirror of the American scene would reflect the indecisive result in the homeland.

In the English world, the constitutional base determined the character of political action. The unsettled constitution produced erratic, often violent, politics. In England, the Fifth Monarchy Men rose in London in a desperate, hopeless revolt; Titus Oates spun out the infamous lie of the Popish Plot; the Rye House conspirators narrowly missed assassinating Charles and James; Monmouth invaded England to try to topple the crown from the head of James II. In America, strong words and violent action flared out again and again on the political scene.

Though the causes of dispute were various, the opposition in America found a common denominator in resistance to executive authority. In the corporate colonies of New England, the resistance took the form of frustrating the efforts of English appointed officials such as Edward Randolph. In royal colonies such as New Hampshire and Virginia, the appointed governor and council became the targets. In the proprietary colonies, the attempts of the governors to put into action the sweeping powers granted in the charters called forth the opposition. Since each of the executive agents mentioned represented an external sovereign, all American resistance to their pretensions represented a uniformly held conviction: that Englishmen in America were competent to run their own affairs. This jealous zeal for local control of the process of government, nurtured for a century, ultimately became a basic cause of the American Revolution.

The quarter century following the Stuart restoration was one of trouble and anxiety in the province of Maryland. The major issues of English politics, coming to the colony in the form of half-truth and rumor, had special relevance for Maryland. The trend of Charles's policy seemed to be toward prerogative and popery, with the sun king of France the obvious model. Marylanders did not have to look for bogeymen in dark corners because a substantial Catholic minority lived among them and a Roman Catholic proprietor openly pushed his prerogative. However astute the policy of the Calverts in matters religious may have been, immediately under the surface of provincial life lay the deep antipathy of the Protestant majority to the Roman church. Lord Baltimore's subjects had other substantial fears. It was a time of economic depression. By 1660, Maryland had become an agriculturally specialized area committed almost exclusively to tobacco culture. Year by year production increased and as the volume soared, prices declined steadily. The prevailing low price of tobacco created real distress. Politically disturbed, religiously suspicious, and economically unsound, many of the people experienced the ultimate fear, that of physical extinction, for along the edges of settlement the Indians raided continuously and the general call to arms went out regularly. The conflict between the medieval prerogatives asserted by the Calverts and the claim to the rights of seventeenth century Englishmen advanced by the colonists must be seen in the context of these real insecurities.

The course of events in Maryland during the months immediately preceding and following Charles Stuart's restoration threw the basic constitutional issues into sharp relief. Just prior to that event, Josiah Fendall led an essentially Protestant group to the full repudiation of the proprietary rights. Speaking through the lower house of the provincial legislature, Fendall claimed for that body complete authority to make law and control its administration. He had taken the position of the English Long and Rump Parliaments at a singularly inauspicious time. Upon his restoration, Charles II restored the Calverts to their full rights. The Baron Baltimore, acting through his son Charles, whom he appointed as governor, set himself at once to the task of consolidating the proprietary position. For the Baltimores, the palatine powers of the Bishop of Durham were neither nominal nor moribund; they meant to use them in America.

All power emanated from the proprietary prerogative. As agent, the governor "was autocrat and dictator of the province." The executive authority was complete. The governor had the command of the military and naval forces. With the advice of his appointed council, he had full control of the administration. He had the patronage and appointed all local officials—sheriffs, justices of peace, and constables. The governor was at once the source of all judicial authority and the ultimate judge in all matters of law and equity. His legislative authority was extensive. He could proclaim law by ordinance. He summoned, prorogued, and dissolved the legislature at will. He had what amounted to a triple veto power. His council, as the upper house, could prevent the enactment of legislation; he could veto; ultimately all legislation was subject to the approval of the proprietor himself.

Power corrupts and it did so in Maryland, producing maladministration and substantial grievances. If on the credit side of the ledger it could be said that the Calverts took a personal interest in their province, the debit side reveals substantial nepotism. The Calverts built a tight oligarchy based on family. They appropriated virtually all of the positions of power, and pluralism was rife. The holding of five, six, or seven offices by one man was normal. If power was in office, wealth was in land. The family and its friends aggrandized themselves, creating vast estates in the process.

The abuse of power created many specific issues. For example, the proprietor misused his right to review legislation. On occasion he withheld his decision for as long as five years and then invalidated statutes that had created both real and personal rights. On other occasions the governor and council, on grounds of emergency, levied taxes without enabling legislation. At the local level, appointed officials operated a fee system that verged on extortion.

As best they could, Marylanders fought the proprietary power in the legislature. In the session of 1669, they impeached one of their own members, who, as a local official, had abused the fee system. The upper house refused to convict. In the same session, the assembly listed their grievances and presented them to the upper house. The Calvert-dominated council, reacting with indignation, reminded the assembly that it was no parliament and demanded that it expunge the offensive passages from its record. After parley, the lower house complied.

Through the 1670's the two sides jockeyed for position. A series of laws regulated the fee system at the central and local level; another limited the term of office and the authority of the sheriff. In its money bills, the assembly specified in great detail the purposes of the appropriations, thus strengthening the legislature in fiscal matters. The assembly also attempted to put its legislation on a more positive basis by demanding that the governor's approval of a law should not later be subject to the proprietor's veto. The assembly won the limited concession that the proprietor would approve or veto within eighteen months. On the whole, though, the proprietor had the better of the jousting. In 1670 he restricted the franchise to those holding fifty acres of real property or personal property worth forty pounds sterling. Six years later, he summarily reduced the size of the assembly by ordering the chancellor to issue writs for the election of two, rather than four, representatives from each county.

In the seventeenth century, the boundaries of legal political action were very constricted. Frustrated within that narrow area, aggrieved parties readily took up arms. In Maryland, tension generated by low tobacco prices, Indian raiding, and an exaggerated fear of popery grew year by year. In 1676, the poorer farmers of Calvert County met in arms and drew up a list of their grievances. Refusing to obey a peremptory order to disperse, they moved, apparently without clear plan, into the Delaware region. There the militia broke them up and arrested their leaders, William Davyes and John Pate. The government underlined with finality the grim nature of the business by taking the lives of Davyes and Pate.

The Davyes-Pate rising was a flash in the pan, little more than a riot. The sustained opposition of Josiah Fendall and John Coode was much more dangerous to government. Both men agitated in Charles County, the western fringe of settlement. Undoubtedly they were affected by, and probably they were in collusion with, the Virginia adherents of Nathaniel Bacon. In mass meetings,

Fendall stated and restated the grievances in the language of hyperbole. Again and again he suggested that the government would fall easily in a test of force. In 1681, he marched against St. Mary's where government forces easily defeated him. His trial remains something of a mystery, for the government contented itself with levying a large fine. Perhaps the governor feared that his execution would galvanize and unite the opposition. Fendall left the country, but Coode continued the agitation. Maryland politics remained in a turbulent state.

Underlying the Davyes-Pate and Fendall-Coode insurrections was a basic understanding that went to the heart of the Maryland problem. Both groups protested the anomaly of the feudal and seigneurial prerogatives of Baltimore and announced the aim of eliminating the proprietor so that the colony might come under the direct control of the crown. Whether or not they read the situation correctly, the Maryland rebels believed that they had a better chance to win the rights of seventeenth-century Englishmen under the king than under the Baltimores.

In New York, the Duke of York announced clear-cut policies for his American province. His often reiterated stand in regard to government was that fair and just law and administration could and would be established by executive and judicial officials responsible to himself alone. For legislative assemblies he had absolutely no use. The duke designated the governor as principal officer and to this post he appointed a series of four competent men. The provincial legislature clearly resembled the original medieval English Parliaments. When the governor, council, and the judges of the court of assizes sat together, the legislature was in session. On such a political base, the duke hoped to elect a profitable province. The chief regular revenues were to be derived from taxes on trade and the quit rents. In the political and economic pattern dictated by the duke lay the sources of grievance and resistance.

The native Dutch residents, well conditioned to executive government, gave the governors little or no trouble. In fact, they had little cause for complaint because the duke's agents handled them justly. Indeed, some of the English complained that the governors went beyond justice and preferred Dutch factors, particularly in regard to commercial privileges. The first complaints came from the Long Island towns. The settlers there, primarily New Englanders, resented the quit rents and demanded an elected assembly. To the Long Island protests were soon added those of English merchants from the city. They spearheaded the drive against the duke's customs duties and joined the chorus that demanded the political rights of Englishmen.

The first governor, Richard Nicolls, called a general meeting at Hempstead, Long Island, in March 1695. Making it clear that the body was in no sense a legislature, he used the occasion to proclaim what came to be known as the Duke's Laws. The code was reasonable. For example, it made a bow to the prejudices of the Long Islanders by including substantial portions of typical New England codes. But, at bottom, the Duke's Laws stood on prerogative. This is seen most clearly in the provisions establishing free and common socage as the basic land tenure and those which vested in the governor the power to lay and collect taxes. The Long Islanders opposed the proprietor's code continuously— by petition, address, and occasional violent resistance to local officials. On several occasions, the governors laid the demands for an assembly before the Duke of York. His answer came always as a patronizing negative. The third governor, Edmund Andros, again brought the protest to his attention. The duke responded with this injunction:

> I have formerly writ to you touching Assemblyes in those countreys. . . . I cannot but suspect they would be of dangerous consequence, nothing being more knone than the aptness of such bodyes to assume to themselves many priviledges wch prove destructive to, or very oft disturbe, the peace of ye governmt wherein they are allowed.[2]

While the Long Island countrymen remonstrated, the city merchants set another pot to boil. Information regularly came back to the duke that the governors cheated him of his customs revenues. In 1680, he sent out an auditor to check the accounts, and Governor Andros returned home to defend himself. The executive authority devolved on a deputy. At this precise junc-

2. Edmund B. O'Callaghan and John R. Brodhead (eds.), *Documents Relative to the Colonial History of the State of New York* (15 vols., Albany: Weed-Parsons and Co., 1853–1887), III, 235.

ture, the customs duties, normally limited to a three year period, expired. The merchants immediately informed the deputy that they would not pay the duties and did stop payment. The collector, William Dyer, perhaps motivated by possibilities of lucrative graft, unwisely continued to try to collect the taxes. Before a special session of the general court of assizes, the merchants brought an incredible charge of high treason against Dyer. They charged that he had collected taxes contrary to Magna Carta and the Petition of Right. At the same session, an ex-mayor of New York, Francis Rumbouts, was also indicted for high treason for having jailed and then fined a gambler without jury trial, again contrary to Magna Carta and the Petition of Right. On their face, these proceedings appear ridiculous and seem to be evidence of a colossal ignorance of English law. More probably, these transplanted English jurors made the incredible charges to bring the grievances before the duke in dramatic fashion.

The merchant agitation, backed by the steady flow of rural petition, succeeded. In 1682, the duke informed the acting governor that he intended to permit an assembly. In 1683, a new governor, Sir Thomas Dongan, went out with instructions to summon a representative assembly. The writs to the sheriffs ran, and in October 1683, the first New York general assembly met in the fort at the tip of Manhattan. Though most of its record has been lost, its famous "charter of liberties" survives. This document, English to its very marrow, born of protest, was yet profoundly conservative. Englishmen on the American frontier chose to define their rights exclusively in terms of the landmarks of the English constitution. For example:

NEW YORK, 1683	ENGLAND, 1215–1641
. . . a sessions of a General Assembly be held in this province once in three years at least.	. . . in case there be not a parliament summoned by writ under the great seal of England and assembled and held before the 10th day of September which shall be in the third year next after the last day of the last meeting and setting in this present parliament . . . and so from time to time and in all times hereafter . . . that then . . . parliament shall as-

semble and be held in the usual place at Westminster.

[Triennial Act (1641), 16 Ch. I, c. 1.]

. . . representatives are the sole judges of the qualifications of their own members, and likewise of all undue elections, and may from time to time purge their house.

The king said . . . that our privileges were not in question. . . . He granted it was a court of record and a judge of returns.

[*Goodwin's Case* (1604)]

That no member of the General Assembly or their servants during the time of their sessions and while they shall be going to and returning from the said Assembly, shall be arrested, sued, imprisoned, or any ways molested or troubled.

Sir Thomas . . . affirmed that the arrest was made . . . he wished the serjeant to take knowledge . . . that he was elected a burgess . . . for the borough of Steyning . . . the house agreed . . . whether Sir Thomas Shirley shall have privilege; . . . resolved in the affirmative.

[*Shirley's Case* (1604)]

. . . no freeman shall be taken and imprisoned or be disseized of his freehold or liberty of free customs, or be outlawed or exiled, or any other ways destroyed, nor shall be passed upon, adjudged, or condemned but by the lawful judgment of his peers *and* by the law of this province.

No freeman shall be captured or imprisoned or disseized or outlawed or exiled or in any way destroyed, nor will we go against him or send against him, except by the lawful judgment of his peers *or* by the law of the land.

[Magna Carta (1215), c. 39.]

Justice nor right shall be neither sold, denied, or deferred to any man within this province.

To no one will we sell, to no one will we deny or delay right or justice.

[Magna Carta, c. 40.]

. . . no aid, tax, tallage, assessment, custom, loan, benevolence, or imposition whatsoever shall be laid, assessed, imposed or levied on any of his Majesty's subjects . . . but by the act and consent of the Governor, Council, and representatives of the people.

. . . by a statute made in the time of King Edward the First . . . *Statutum de Tallagiao non Concedendo* . . . your subjects have inherited this freedom, that they should not be compelled to contribute to any tax, tallage, aid or other like charge not set by common consent in parliament.

[Petition of Right (1628)]

... no freeman shall be compelled to receive any mariners or soldiers into his house and there suffer them to sojourn against their wills, provided always it be not in time of actual war within this province.

... of late great companies of soldiers and mariners have been dispersed into divers counties of the realm, and the inhabitants against their wills have been compelled to receive them. . . . They do therefore humbly pray . . . that your majesty would be pleased to remove the said soldiers and mariners.

[Petition of Right]

... a widow after the death of her husband shall have her dower and shall and may tarry in the chief house of her husband forty days after the death of her husband.

And after his death she shall remain in the house (principal dwelling) for forty days, within which time her dowry shall be assigned to her.

[Magna Carta, c. 7]

... a freeman shall not be amerced for a small fault, but after the manner of his fault, and for a great fault, after the greatness thereof, saving to him his freehold; and a husbandman saving to him his wainage; and a merchant likewise saving to him his merchandise. And none of the said amercements shall be assessed but by the oath of twelve honest and lawful men of the vicinage.

[Charter of Liberties]

A freeman shall be amerced for a small offence only according to the degree of the offence; and for a grave offence he shall be amerced according to the gravity of the offence, saving his contenement. And a merchant shall be amerced in the same way, saving his merchandise; and a villein in the same way, saving his wainage. . . . And none of the aforesaid amercements shall be imposed except by the oaths of the good men from the neighbourhood.

[Magna Carta, c. 20]

In the short run, the New York assembly of 1683 had no effect. Soon after James came to the throne he incorporated his province into the Dominion of New England. With the collapse of the Dominion, New York regained its assembly and remained committed to the concept of rights expressed in the charter of liberties.

In 1675, the Old Dominion became the scene of the most widespread and violent revolt of the whole colonial period. Sir William Berkeley returned to Virginia as governor in 1660. He had held the post previously between 1641 and 1652. He had been a good governor, even "the darling of the People." Perhaps he was a good governor during his second tour of duty, but this, like practically every other judgment connected with Bacon's Rebellion, remains in dispute.

During the Interregnum, Virginia had experimented with a democratic government in which all freemen voted. With the re-establishment of the royal forms, the colony returned to the normal pattern of a franchise restricted by property qualifications. The assembly elected in 1660 was not dissolved until the crisis of the revolt fifteen years later. Certainly it had ceased to be representative. If the legislature was static, the executive branch was rigidly so. Berkeley built a tight oligarchy that monopolized the offices of central government. Through the patronage the same group controlled the counties. Whether or not Berkeley and his coterie were guilty of maladministration and corruption is beside the point; Virginians believed that they were. Specifically, Berkeley was suspected of misappropriation of public monies, speculation in land and of manipulation of the Indian trade for his own advantage.

As in Maryland, the years 1660–1675 were a time of severe economic depression for Virginia. Tobacco prices sunk to an all-time low. As prices skidded, the Navigation Act of 1660 began to operate and in so doing denied the planters direct access to their European markets. While personal income dwindled, taxes increased. The Dutch Wars had mandated costly preparations for defense and the colony built several expensive but ineffective forts at the river mouths. The government relied on a poll tax to meet its ordinary and extraordinary expenses. Such a tax fell with unequal weight on the persons pinched most by the general depression. Between 1670 and 1675, first the fear and then the fact of Indian war caused further increases in the poll taxes. It was a combustible situation.

Disagreement about Indian policy ignited Bacon's Rebellion. In 1646, the tribes had signed a treaty which expressed Virginia's policy. The underlying assumptions were that the Indians had a valid title to land and that they could not be assimilated into a white civilization. The races were to be segregated. Essentially, the treaty established a policy of reservations for the Indians. The legislature extended the principle of segregation in a series of laws that licensed the Indian trade and severely restricted the natives' freedom of movement off the reservations. But treaty and statute could no more contain the thrust of expansion on the Virginia frontier than they did on any other. Seeking land and furs, the traders and planters intruded into the reserved areas. The policy of insulating the races failed and the inevitable incidents and atrocities followed.

The murder of a planter set the chain of events in motion. The militia pursued the Indians, whom they assumed to be the guilty party, into Maryland and took their revenge in blood. The blood they drew was that of the Susquehanna, a warlike tribe that had been pushed southward by the potent Seneca. The tribe retaliated with sporadic raids all along the northern Virginia frontier. In the fall of 1675, Maryland and Virginia combined their militia and went against the Susquehanna. The main result was the perfidious murder of five chiefs. After that the tribes hit the war trail in earnest.

Berkeley, an old Indian fighter, appointed a commander and made plans for a vigorous offensive. The force had no more than been mobilized when the governor inexplicably called it off and fell back on a policy of defense. Arguing that the enemy Indians would strike and then fade into the inaccessible forest, he announced a plan for a ring of spaced forts to be manned by rangers. As a corollary he urged that the remnants of the pacified tribes be dealt with as allies. The exposed planters responded with the opinion expressed on every frontier that the only good Indian was a dead one and demanded massive retaliation.

The murder of his foreman projected Nathaniel Bacon to the leadership of the distressed planters. His character is as difficult to define as that of his antagonist, Berkeley. On the Virginia scene he appeared as a headstrong, moody, violent, and eloquent man. He had arrived but recently from England, where, after receiving a good education, he had proved to be an inconvenient, even a disreputable, son of a prosperous and proper county squire. Berkeley recognized Bacon's social standing by appointing him to the council, but the young gentleman took up land on the frontier and rarely visited Jamestown.

In command of several hundred eager volunteers, Bacon asked the governor for a commission. This Berkeley refused, arguing that it was not clear which tribes were hostile and that, in any event, the policy of fort defense would adequately protect the frontier. Bacon decided to act without authorization and proceeded to put into action the policy of no good Indian but a dead one. On an island in the Roanoke River he found a group of Occaneechis and a smaller band of Susquehanna. Probably employing treachery, Bacon's men annihilated both groups. It was Berkeley's move and he countered with a series of proclamations which branded Bacon a rebel. An unsuccessful attempt to arrest Bacon showed the governor the widespread unrest in the country. Berkeley then dissolved the Long Assembly, and writs for a new election ran. Bacon's neighbors returned him as a burgess and he proceeded down river to Jamestown with a small armed guard. The governor arrested Bacon, then pardoned him and restored him to the council. The purpose of the last move was probably to keep Bacon out of the lower house.

The legislature, misleadingly styled by historians "Bacon's Assembly," turned to the work of reform. The measures passed were neither Baconist nor Berkeleyite. The most important measures struck at the abuses in the counties and in large measure restored home rule. While the burgesses debated, Bacon apparently convinced himself that Berkeley was not acting in good faith. He returned to his home county and mustered a large force which escorted him back to Jamestown. Again he demanded a commission. It was here that Berkeley played out the little drama of baring his chest to Bacon, asking that he be shot on the spot if he had harbored designs against the liberties of Virginia. This Bacon declined to do. Under threat of force, Berkeley issued the commission and Bacon led his men back to the frontier where he intermittently skirmished with the Indians.

With Bacon in the west, Berkeley canceled the commission on the ground that he had been under duress when he issued it and again proclaimed Bacon a traitor. An attempt to raise the eastern counties against Bacon produced nothing but apathy. When informed of the governor's moves, Bacon returned to the settled area and called a meeting at Middle Plantation (Williamsburg). In a flaming speech, "The Declaration of the People," he justified himself and indicted Berkeley. Bacon's next move created the insoluble riddle of his intent. In addition to an oath binding to himself those who approved the declaration, he proposed another oath that obligated the juror to support him even against royal troops should they be sent. This was treason without qualification.

Historians disagree violently in their interpretations of Bacon's intent. Was he, from this point out, "The Torchbearer of the Revolution"? The implication of a positive answer to this question is that Bacon understood that there could be no reform, certainly no democracy, so long as the power of England stood behind the provincial oligarchs. The further inference is that he believed that a union of Maryland, the Carolinas, and Virginia could be effected and that so united, the southern colonies could successfully resist England. Or was he merely a desperate opportunist, an irresponsible demagogue, who would drag as many as he could with him to ruin? That Bacon was desperate there can be no doubt. That he considered, but rejected, the possibility of armed resistance and independence is probable. The best explanation of his intent is the one that he advanced at the time. He was convinced that he was right; he thought that he had the power to maintain himself against whatever forces Berkeley could muster; he knew that the electric words traitor and rebel would involve the central government, and he believed that a fair hearing in England would discredit Berkeley and bring reform.

Soon after the Middle Plantation meeting, Bacon marched against Jamestown. The governor abandoned the village and Bacon, fearing a counterattack, burned the town. He retired, regrouped, and then launched an attack against the eastern shore counties. On this campaign he died. Whatever else Bacon's Rebellion had been, it had been *his* rebellion. With the loss of its leader, the resistance faltered and the organization fell apart. Berkeley easily re-established his authority and then conducted his notorious judicial reprisal, dispensing drumhead justice in courts martial and prejudiced special civil courts. Whether or not Charles II actually spoke the words, the reaction to the last act of the tragedy attributed to him is just: "That old fool hanged more persons in that naked country than I did for the death of my father."

Chapter 8

The Rise and Fall
of the Dominion
of New England

Transatlantic Reaction, 1681–1688

*I*n the late 1670's, Charles II rode out the crisis of his reign. Tempestuous politics produced the crude beginnings of political parties—Tory and Whig. The Tories, standing with the king, committed themselves to Anglican uniformity and the royal supremacy. Shaftesbury organized the Whigs. They opposed the growth of royal power and argued for further guarantees of the subjects' liberties. Deeply suspicious of Stuart religious policy, they regarded it as an attempt to subvert Protestantism and bring back the Roman church. The popular wing of the Whigs rallied to the cry, "No popery, no slavery." The Whigs had a specific program. They urged that the regular succession be interrupted and that James be barred from the throne. In his place they would have put the Duke of Monmouth, the incompetent, but Protestant, bastard son of Charles. The Whigs carried their program into the last three Parliaments of the reign in the form of Exclusion Bills.

The temper of London had been so violently Whig that Charles summoned his last Parliament to meet at loyalist, Tory Oxford. When it became apparent that the Commons would again push for exclusion, Charles dissolved it and turned, as his father had in 1629, to an experiment in personal government. His hope of success lay largely in the fact that Louis XIV had promised to support him with annual subsidies. Charles then launched an attack on the Whig leaders. The first to go was Shaftesbury, off to exile after an attempt to try him for treason failed because a London grand jury refused to indict. For their part, the leaderless Whigs turned to desperate measures. A small group planned the assassination of the king and duke. They were to be murdered at the Rye House as they returned from the Newmarket races. By accident, the scheme failed and later an informer revealed the plot. Many of the great Whigs who had been indirectly involved fled the country. In the wake of the plot, two scions of great families, Algernon Sidney and Lord Russell, suffered the penalty for treason merely for having maintained that under certain circumstances resistance to an anointed king was justifiable. Sidney and Russell became the martyrs of the Whig cause.

After 1681, Charles moved to nail down his triumph. The leaders of the opposition had been exiled, executed, or driven underground. There remained, however, enclaves of potential resistance in the form of the municipal corporations. The cities had returned the violent Whigs to the later Parliaments. In addition, their juries, grand and petty, had frustrated crown law officers again and again by refusing to indict or convict opponents of government charged with crimes of disloyalty. London, a seedbed of resistance, was particularly obnoxious. In 1681, the law officers began to examine the city charters to determine if the franchises granted had been exceeded. The next year, subservient courts vacated the charters of several of the lesser cities. In 1683, a *quo warranto* ran against London with the inevitable result that the charter was quashed. After the defeat of London, the smaller boroughs paraded into chancery to resign their charters. Though no direct connection between the assault on borough rights in England and the attack on the charters of the American colonies can be proved, the parallels are so obvious as to suggest *ipso facto* a double-barreled attack on transatlantic incorporated rights.

Charles enjoyed his long-delayed triumph but a short time. He died in 1685, proclaiming himself a Roman Catholic by accepting the last rites. With a pledge to uphold the constitution and the subjects' rights, James II came peacefully to the throne. The first Parliament, elected placidly enough, showed itself not ill-disposed to the new king. While the Parliament assembled, two piddling invasions were launched. The Earl of Argyle tried to raise the North, but was captured in what was little more than a police action. The Duke of Monmouth landed in the west and was quickly defeated at the battle of Sedgemoor. The king grimly underlined the folly of resistance. The Lord Chief Justice Jeffreys moved through the western circuit where he wrote a record of judicial violence which has left his name a synonym for repressor and indelibly labeled the whole proceeding as the "Bloody Assize."

After Monmouth's Rebellion, James asserted his power. He refused to disband the military forces that had been assembled, and for the first time in her history, England witnessed the possibility of a standing army to uphold royal pretensions. In a menacing fashion, James posted the force on the environs of London. In the context of creating the new army, James revealed a main line of his policy—the removal of the Roman Catholic disabilities. The Test Act, with its requirement of Anglican communion and oath, had effectively barred Catholics from military and civic office. James dispensed with the act in an individual instance and won a victory for the principle in the courts in the colluded action of *Godden v. Hales*. On the basis of the decision he began to fill the lists with Catholics. Having dispensed with the statute in individual cases, he moved in 1687 to a general suspension of the religious penal laws with his first declaration of indulgence. The next year, the king reinforced his first declaration with a second. He ordered it read out in the churches. Several of the great men of the church, including the Archbishop of Canterbury, protested in a petition to the king. The law officers caused them to be indicted for a seditious libel. When the seven bishops pleaded to their indictment at King's Bench, the Stuart despotism had reached its apogee.

Inevitably, America felt the backwash of the rising tide of Stuart absolutism. In England, Edward Randolph rode the crest of the tide and brought in a comprehensive and extraordinary program for the reorganization of New England.

The charter of Massachusetts Bay had been vacated in October 1684. The act was consistent with the larger plans of the Lords of Trade who were urging that the American dominions be forced into a greater dependence on the crown. Randolph, the American expert, was at hand with a plan of reorganization. Apparently he had convinced some New Englanders of the inevitability of a closer connection with the central government. His projected scheme would have preserved some measure of American home rule. Into the bargain it would have promoted to prominent positions in the new government those subjects in the Bay Colony who had seen the light as revealed by Randolph. As an incident of the conversion to the new system, Randolph would obtain several lucrative offices. The plan would have created a confederation of the New England colonies. Existing patterns of local government were to be continued. The government of New England would consist of a governor-general and a council and assembly in which the colonial units would be represented roughly in proportion to population.

Before the Lords of Trade had come to a decision, Randolph's immediate superiors, the Commissioners of Customs, sent him to the Netherlands on a minor mission. During his absence, the lords decided to combine Massachusetts Bay, Maine, New Hampshire, and King's Province (the disputed Narragansett territory) into a single dominion. The lords consulted the king himself concerning the policy for the new dominion. Responding to a series of questions, Charles stated that the Anglican Church would be introduced into New England. The rights of the crown to ungranted land were to be resurrected and all future grants were to be subject to an annual quit rent. Charles said nothing about a representative assembly and the inference was that there was to be none. For governor, Charles nominated Percy Kirke, a man who had written a stern record as governor of Tangier and who would soon make himself notorious in the repression of Monmouth's Rebellion. By these decisions and this appointment, the imperial bureaucracy committed itself to a policy of consolidation and repression in America.

Before Kirke could be sent out, Charles died. The accession

and coronation of James, the summoning of a Parliament, and the risings of Monmouth and Argyle pushed American matters into the background temporarily. Randolph returned to London to oppose vigorously the Kirke appointment. To his confidants, Randolph wrote that a man like Kirke would incite armed revolt in New England. Randolph again advanced his plan. The new king accepted the idea of a federation in which the constituent units would be represented in a grand council. He also approved the unified executive in the person of a governor general. He flatly rejected the proposed assembly that was essential to Randolph's scheme of moderate compromise.

With Kirke on a military campaign in the west country, the Lords of Trade decided on a provisional government. They appointed as president of the council Joseph Dudley, a New Englander who had previously indicated his acceptance of a new order. Randolph obtained a series of important and potentially lucrative positions. He was to be secretary and registrar, collector of customs, postmaster general, surveyor of the woods, and the deputy of William Blathwayt, who was auditor general of the plantations.

When Randolph sailed for Boston in the spring of 1686, he carried with him, in addition to the commission for Dudley, documents that revealed the full scope of the Stuart plan for America. During the months that Charles and James had considered reorganization of New England government, the law officers had obtained writs of *quo warranto* against Connecticut, Rhode Island, Pennsylvania, Delaware, and the proprietors of East and West New Jersey. Randolph had the Connecticut and Rhode Island writs with him. Clearly, the intent was gradually to amalgamate the northern colonies into a single, highly centralized dominion. It seems most probable that, had the northern dominion succeeded, the plantation colonies of Maryland, Virginia, and the Carolinas would have been combined into a southern dominion. Had these plans come to fruition, English America would have resembled French Canada and the Spanish kingdoms of New Spain and Peru. Such a development would have tipped the balance of the imperial constitution permanently to the side of executive power. Infant America, with its infinite promise, would have been stillborn.

Dudley's provisional government lasted seven months, from May to December 1686. Though the new government lacked legislative power and therefore could undertake no sweeping change of the law, it used its executive and judicial authority in ways that shocked the Puritan community. With Randolph aboard the frigate *Rose* came an Anglican minister, Robert Ratcliffe. When, clad in the surplice, he first held service according to the Prayer Book, he aroused the incipient fear of popery. While Ratcliffe prayed, Dudley and Randolph did the business nearest the collector's heart along the waterfront. With amazing suddenness they clamped down on the illegal traders. Dudley had been commissioned vice admiral and immediately Randolph began to prosecute before his court. In a short time, six or more vessels had been condemned, with the result that the channels of illicit commerce dried up. To have introduced Anglicanism and enforced the Navigation Acts in less than a month was proof of the effectiveness of the new executive government.

Dudley, Randolph, and the councilors who supported them expected to profit personally from the new order. As surveyor of the woods, Randolph launched a large commercial venture. He let contracts to loggers reckoned in the thousands of pounds sterling, and they began cutting out huge trees that were to be masts for the ships of the royal navy. As registrar, Randolph turned to the pleasant task of exacting fees on a large scale. Every military and civil commission had to be reissued, and as he sealed the new documents the registrar took his fees. When the rush of reissuing was over, Randolph claimed that all deeds and legal documents had to be registered in his office. This was too much, even for Dudley. The president refused to admit the interpretation. This marked the beginning of the break between Randolph and Dudley. Soon Randolph complained of being cheated of the fruits of his perquisites and criticized the president for backsliding to Puritan ways. Dudley and several members of the council also sought personal gain, largely through their power to grant lands. Of the many projects launched, by far the most spectacular land grab was the Million Acre Purchase. Enlisting the support of officials in England as well as America by giving them shares in the company, they pieced together a huge tract in the Merrimac River region.

Edmund Andros, recently knighted for his service to the Stuart cause in England and America, arrived at Boston in December 1686. With him came two companies of regular infantry, red-coated symbols of the fact that the central government was deadly serious in its intent to alter the New England society. Andros' commission gave him full executive, judicial, and legislative power, subject only to the need to obtain the advice and consent of an appointed council in legislative matters. In practice, Andros swept away even that limited restriction. In the context of his intent, James had chosen his man well. If any man could overcome New England, stern, experienced, Anglican, military-minded Sir Edmund was that man.

The despotism of Andros, and it may fairly be called that, developed along three lines—religious, economic, and political. Under Dudley and Randolph, the Anglican cause had not prospered. Only a handful of the official group attended Ratcliffe's services in the town house. Andros forced the issue by demanding that the South Meeting House of the Congregationalists be made available for the Anglican services. By threat of force, he obtained the keys, and then made an arrangement that the Anglican services would be held first each Sabbath, with the Puritan worship following. This worked poorly and became a standing source of friction. Finally, an exasperated Andros seized a lot on the Boston Common and began to construct King's Church. In many lesser ways the governor offended the Puritans. He celebrated Christmas with a show. He permitted the erection of a Maypole. He forced the saints to swear their oaths on the Bible. He made it inconvenient to be married anywhere but in the Anglican church. He violated the boundaries of New Canaan.

In matters religious, the Puritans were sure that the worst was yet to come. They feared Andros as the agent of a king determined to reunite England with Rome. They regarded the promise of general toleration in James's declarations of indulgence as a ruse and a temporary tactic designed to weaken Anglicanism and lull the Protestant noncomformist. They saw in the declarations the ultimate aim of a Catholic triumph. The fear aroused by Andros' Anglicanism and James's presumed duplicity was intensified by French activity in Canada and the stirrings of the Indians on the northern frontier. As the Puritan read the evidence, it all pointed to a monstrous conspiracy to subvert true Protestantism. The depth of their suspicion was illustrated in the winter of 1688–89. French agents had been active among the Abenaki Indians along the coast of northern Maine. To check the threat of an Indian war, Andros undertook a difficult and successful winter campaign in that region. In his absence, rumor flew through southern New England. The Puritans genuinely believed that Andros was a covert Catholic, that he was arming and raising the tribes against them, and that he had matured plans to deliver New England to France.

The seventeenth-century New Englanders organized their economic life on the base of a family-operated subsistence farm and a self-sufficient town. The security and well-being of the community was rooted in the land—in the right of the town to grant and the right of the individual to hold. Under the charter, the general court had given lands to the towns; in turn they had passed a fee simple title with no encumberance to the individual farmer. The whole process was unknown to the English law of conveyance. The general court grants were often based on titles derived from Indian cessions; in any event, they never mentioned the pre-eminent rights of the crown. Because the towns were unincorporated they had no right at law to pass on a title. The Puritans had established their whole rural economy on an inadequate legal base, and both Andros and Randolph quickly recognized the fact. Each township had reserved land for common use. Either because such land had been improved or simply because it was within a developed area, its value had been enhanced. In addition, there were scraps and parcels and offshore islands within the settled areas that had never been granted. Randolph cast a covetous eye on the commons and ungranted enclaves. His demands show clearly the dreams of a minor official for social status and economic security. A house lot on Boston Common, a substantial farm on the coast, and seven hundred acres for speculation would have done the trick. Because Andros mistrusted Randolph, nothing came of the collector's requests. The fact that Randolph failed and but a few others succeeded reveals the underlying purpose of Andros' land policy.

However rigid Andros may have been, he was no corruptionist; nor would he be privy to the selfish schemes of others. At the very beginning he let it be known that he had the authority to recall all grants, inspect their validity, and, if he thought it should be so, regrant the land subject to an annual quit rent after the land had been resurveyed. With this open threat he tried to "fix a man's allegiance by fixing his interest." The king and Andros, not the general court and the town, were to be master. To give substance to his threat, Andros caused writs of intrusion to be issued against a dozen or more titles. In the ensuing process the governor made two things clear; neither Indian titles nor town grants had any validity. When one Yankee put an Indian deed in evidence, Andros described it as having no more legality "than a scratch with a Bear's paw." Another cited general court and township grants in support of his title. Andros responded that he knew of no such things. The threat was explicit: submit to the Stuart prerogative or lose your land.

The economic and religious communities of New England had been erected upon a set of specific political assumptions. In spite of indigenous tendencies toward consolidation, the right of the separate units to exist on the constituent base of charter or compact had been recognized. Certainly the New England Confederation had acknowledged the autonomy of the units. Each jurisdiction, in turn, claimed the right to make law, enforce it, and render judgment. With variations, the process of law from creation to judgment was controlled by two further assumptions: the people, under restrictions that varied with the aims of the communities, were to be represented in the governmental process; and the American freemen held all of the common-law rights of Englishmen. Andros assaulted each of these assumptions and in so doing voided the results of three-quarters of a century of experiment.

In the summer of 1686, Randolph had moved toward consolidating the northern colonies into a single dominion by informing Rhode Island and Connecticut that he had in his possession writs of *quo warranto* against their charters. Actually the writs had expired. Rhode Island, aware of the inevitable result of the process, submitted without attempting a defense. Connecticut adopted the tactics that Massachusetts had previously. She stalled, looked for technical flaws in the process and prepared to make a legal defense in England. About the time that Andros took ship for America, the law officers obtained another writ against Connecticut. Randolph served it early in January 1687. The Connecticut general court then wrote to one of the secretaries of state. In the letter they stated that they preferred to remain under their charter, but that they would submit if the king was determined that they should. With this informal submission in hand, the Privy Council instructed Andros to assume the government of the colony. He went to Hartford for this purpose in October. The legend of the charter oak was born of the governor's meeting with the Connecticut general court. The tale is that, as the negotiations stretched into the evening, the lamps were lighted. Suddenly someone snuffed them out, and when they were relighted the charter had disappeared, to be secreted, we are told, in the trunk of a hollow oak tree.

The following summer the home government added additional territory to Andros' jurisdiction. At James's accession, New York had automatically become a royal province. In August 1688, the Privy Council removed the governor of New York. The proprietary rights in the Jerseys had been vacated previously. A new commission to Andros added these colonies to "our territories and dominion of New England." The plans of the earlier Stuarts, announced in the Virginia Charter of 1606 and in the patent to Gorges for the Council for New England, had been realized. A single dominion stretched from the Delaware River to the St. Croix. Within it Andros went about the business of establishing a single executive government.

Both of Andros' commissions had authorized him to make law with the advice and consent of the appointed council. In this way a vestige of the representative principle would have been preserved. Though the council was a large body, five members constituted a quorum. In practice not many more than five attended sessions. Andros would not submit even to the weak restraint of the appointed council. Permitting little debate, he dominated what discussion there was. On several occasions he simply signed important measures without asking for a vote. To avoid inconvenience he would call the council into session on very short notice and would cause it to meet in unusual places.

By such tactics Andros subverted the principle of representation and made himself the virtual dictator of the Dominion of New England.

In a famous case, he and Dudley, who had been made chief justice, spelled out the legal status of the individual. In its spring session, 1687, the council had debated a comprehensive revenue bill. The opposition was considerable and after the second reading, the governor made it law with his signature without calling for a division. Many of the towns refused to collect the taxes. The town of Ipswich made the resistance specific with a resolution sponsored by their great pastor, John Wise. The assessment infringed "their Liberty as Free borne English subjects of his Majestie." They would pay no rates until they had been voted by a general assembly. Andros thought otherwise. His agents arrested Wise and five others. An appeal for the writ of habeas corpus proved useless. Before Dudley and what was alleged to be a "Packt and pickt" jury, the accused cited Magna Carta, the English statutes, and the practice of the colony in their defense. No defense would have been effective. From the bench Dudley informed them that the rights of Englishmen would not follow them to the ends of the earth and that they differed from slaves in the sole particular that they could not be bought and sold. Found guilty, the Ipswich men were fined heavily and barred from public office.

Andros, like Lord North ninety years later, saw the New England town meetings as cells of sedition. The whole policy of intruding into the commons and challenging land titles had as a major part of its intent the bringing of the townships to heel. But the Ipswich incident had proved that economic sanctions would not bring them to heel. Andros took the logical step of repressing the town meetings by direct legislation. In March, 1688, a law passed which restricted the towns to one annual meeting. The business of the single meeting was to elect a board of selectmen and a commissioner to act as tax assessor and collector.

Sir Edmund Andros had proved himself an effective agent. In less than two years he had introduced Anglicanism, enforced the Navigation Acts, and established the crown's right to the land. He had ridden over the vested rights of charter and covenant and combined diverse jurisdictions into one dominion. Within the dominion he had circumvented the representative principle and made himself the master legislator and executive. Speaking through subservient judges, he had denied the subject the common law rights. He had dug out New England autonomy at its roots by suppressing the town meeting. He had, in fact, translated the theories of the imperial constitution into real policy.

The rising fortunes of English America had plunged to their absolute nadir in the summer of 1688. Just when all seemed lost, the electrifying news arrived from England that William of Orange had invaded the kingdom and that James had fled his realm. The integrity of the American experiment was saved by an English revolution.

The Glorious Revolution in England and America, 1688–1689

The eyes of the nation were on London when the seven bishops came to trial for their petition to James protesting his declaration of indulgence. Departing from normal procedure, the chief justice and three of the puisne justices charged the jury separately. The chief justice and one of the judges regarded the fact of publication of the petition to be sufficient to bring the case within the restrictive rules of the law of seditious libel. Two of the judges disagreed, arguing that there had been no bad intent. The jury agreed with the latter justices and brought in a verdict of "not guilty." London and most of the nation went wild with jubilation. Clearly the sentiment of the nation was overwhelmingly Protestant and hostile to James's Catholic policy.

While the bishops had been confined in the Tower, a separate event had startled England. The queen, Mary of Modena, gave birth to a son. The Protestants had tolerated James largely because he had no heir. The alternative to his succession had been the desperate one of civil war. Until the birth of the son, the heir apparent had been Mary and her staunch Protestant husband, William of Orange, Stadholder of the Netherlands. The birth of the prince threatened to rivet a Catholic succession on the nation.

William of Orange had been interested continuously in English affairs. In part, his interest derived from his concern for Protestantism. His chief interest, though, was the diplomatic situation in Europe. In two wars William and the Netherlands had borne the brunt of the aggression of Louis XIV. It was apparent that the French king would go to war again to achieve for France her "natural" boundaries. In 1686, William had constructed the League of Augsburg, but it appeared to be inadequate for the job of containing Louis. Though the diplomacy of England had been largely a cipher, James's Catholicism, plus the on-again off-again relationship with Louis seemed to indicate that at best, England would remain neutral and at worst, would go to war on the French side, in the event of a new Franco-Dutch war. The desire to draw England into the League of Augsburg was paramount as William anxiously watched developments across the Channel.

From the beginning William made it clear that he would not intervene in England unless he was invited to do so. In July 1688, the invitation came. It had been signed by responsible men representing a broad part of the spectrum of English opinion. William gathered his forces, recruited additional men in the Germanies and prepared the ships. In November, a great fleet of two hundred and fifty vessels, with fifteen thousand men aboard put out into the Channel. The "Protestant Wind" carried it safely past the English squadrons to a landing in the west country.

William took the position that he had come only to guarantee a free Parliament in which policies in regard to religion and the succession could be settled. His military campaign was a masterpiece of restraint. He moved slowly toward London, encountering virtually no opposition. Gradually James's support melted away as one after the other of his civilian and military officers defected to William. A few days before Christmas, James fled to France. William came on rapidly to maintain order in London. Writs for the election of a convention ran immediately. Opinion among English leaders divided as to what William's status should be. He resolved this cleanly by saying that he would be nothing but king. When the convention assembled, it drafted the Bill of Rights and imposed it upon William as a condition of his accession. A typically English constitutional document, it declared illegal the specific abuses of the later Stuarts. Left to the future were such important questions as religion and public finance.

Louis XIV had reopened the war with the Dutch; he now declared war upon England. In the turmoil created by the bloodless revolution, the reorganization of government, and the preparation for war, the American dominions were all but forgotten. The transatlantic subjects needed no mandate to act. When they heard of William's invasion of England, they pulled down James's Dominion of New England as if it had been a house of cards.

By the spring of 1688, the various lines of Andros' policy had been made crystal clear to the Massachusetts Bay Puritans. They decided to take their case directly to the king and chose as their agent Increase Mather, a powerful minister and president of Harvard College. After a flurry with Randolph in which the collector tried to have Mather arrested on a trumped-up charge, the preacher escaped in disguise and took ship for England. Between May and October, Mather had six interviews with James. Mather, of course, made his brief out of colonial grievances against Andros. Mather's ultimate aim was either a restoration of the old charter or the issuing of a new one that would guarantee the rights of Massachusetts Bay. In the interviews the king always spoke vaguely and in generalities. He continued to try to win support from the Protestant Nonconformists with promises of general toleration. The insincerity of the offer and its obvious political purpose should have been apparent. The king heard the indictment of Andros but made no comment.

By the early summer of 1688, the great English Whigs had begun to lay the groundwork for the overthrow of James. It was a time for speculation. That James would be more energetic in the defense of his crown than events proved him to be would have been a fair assumption. There were rumors that the king would restore the municipal charters, and Mather hoped that the restoration of the American franchises would be included in a general measure. When James finally made his offer it was too late; Mather had to await the results of the revolution and make his case before William III.

Rumors of a possible invasion of England by William arrived in America in the winter and early spring of 1689. The subsequent course of events makes it apparent that the old leaders of Massachusetts Bay then began covertly to plan their own revolt. Direct news of the invasion reached Boston on April 4th. Exactly two weeks later the Boston insurrection came off. At the North End boys spilled into the streets crying, "The South End is risen!" Simultaneously the South End boys shouted the news that the North End had risen. Then, "immediately the drums began to beat, and the people hasting and running, some with and some for arms." The multitude began securing Andros' agents. With things going according to plan, the insurgents flashed the signal to a thousand waiting country militiamen that their services were not needed. By evening the fort had been surrounded. The Bostonians must have relished the fact that Randolph made the formal surrender. The next day, the militia completed the military revolt. They immobilized the frigate *Rose* and accepted the surrender of the Castle and of Andros and the councilors.

The military goal of the revolt had been obvious and easily achieved. The political aims were not nearly so clear. Even to be acknowledged a leader of the resistance was dangerous. The overthrow of Andros had presupposed the success of William's invasion of England. Had it failed, the Bostonians would have been traitors, subject to the ultimate penalty of the criminal law. This was a specific risk, to be calculated and taken. The larger question was, what political demands should be made? An obvious course was to go the whole way and petition the king for a restoration of the charter. Many doubted that the central government would accept such a proposal. A moderate party, probably representing a minority of the total population, but a majority of Boston leadership, realized that the whole trend of imperial policy since 1660 had been away from particularism and local autonomy. They realized that the best they could expect would be a compromise. Most of the moderate leaders also understood that the old oligarchy, which was based on religious restriction, had come to be an anachronism.

On the morning of the first day of the rising, while some Bostonians were arresting Andros' agents, others gathered up men who had held office under the charter. From the town house the people listened to the reading of a document that must have been prepared days or weeks earlier. "The Declaration of the Gentlemen, Merchants and Inhabitants of Boston and the County Adjacent" indicted Andros vigorously. Beyond this it did not go. Significantly it was addressed neither to William nor James, but to "his Highness" whoever he might be. The declaration committed Massachusetts Bay to no specific future course. As a reflection of their indecision, the assembled Bostonians created a council of safety to act as a provisional government. At its head they placed a venerable patriarch, Simon Bradstreet, who had come out to the colony in 1630. By the fact of his advanced age, Bradstreet had no political future.

The council of safety went to the towns for a mandate. On May 9th and again on May 22nd, representatives met in convention. By about a three-quarter majority, the convention recommended a return to government under the old charter. The re-established magistrates turned to the difficult job at hand, the prosecution of the Indian war that had come inevitably with the outbreak of the War of the League of Augsburg in Europe. Everything remained unsettled. The advocates of Massachusetts autonomy had hoped to strengthen their position by standing on the charter and presenting the new sovereign with an accomplished fact. The moderates had thought the wiser course to be to open negotiations for compromise. Both parties realized that the decision would be made in England.

Across the Atlantic, Increase Mather continued to represent the colony. By the force of his personality he commanded respect. He had an early audience with William III. Mather decided to present his case directly and argued in his first petition that the old charter should be restored because the process by which it had been vacated was illegal. Harassed by the need to produce a general constitutional settlement as well as the need to organize the English war effort, William referred the petition. A committee of a reconstituted Privy Council considered the case. From the beginning, the logic of imperial consolidation, persistent since 1660, argued against the Massachusetts claim. To complicate Mather's job, conflicting reports of Andros' administration and the rising in Boston poured in from America. The petition for the restoration of the charter was further weakened by reports of mismanagement of the Indian war in New England.

Mather's attempts to revive the old charter illustrated both the confusing complexity of the imperial administration and the general agreement in England that colonial particularism had to yield to centralization. Mather succeeded in having a bill introduced in Commons reversing the process in chancery that had vacated the charter. The bill passed Commons but failed in the Lords. He next moved for a writ of error to get a review of the chancery process before King's Bench. Again he failed. Checked by the legislature and the courts, he petitioned the king who again referred the matter to the Privy Council. The councilors, in their turn, referred the request to the Lords of Trade.

Mather and the other Massachusetts agents argued step by step with the Lords of Trade as successive drafts of a new charter were proposed. Finally the king threw his decisive weight with the lords and the charter of 1691 proceeded to the seals. The new charter represented a compromise. The king appointed the governor and his deputy. The provincial executive had the veto and the judicial patronage. The right to vote was controlled by a property qualification rather than a religious one. The elected general court, in its turn, elected the council, which acted as the upper house of the legislature.

The charter of 1691 attempted to compromise the basic issues of federalism that were inherent in the empire. The governor, aided by executive officials and the judges, stood as guardian of the imperial interest. The general court, elected council, and restored townships represented the local American interest. Because the elected councilors were responsible ultimately to the freemen of the colony, the governor stood in a weak position in time of real conflict of interest. Eighty-four years later, the North administration showed that it understood that the elected council was the weak link by including in the Coercive Acts a provision for the mandamus or appointed councilors. Yet the imperial compromise did last for eight-and-a-half decades. Like all such constitutional compromises, it would endure just so long as the political system it created could provide a common ground upon which the diverse imperial and provincial interests could be accommodated. When the interests of either party or both parties could no longer be accommodated within the system, the only alternative would be an appeal to force.

The Boston rising had determined the issue for the whole Dominion of New England because its centralizing principles had concentrated the leaders there. Rhode Island, Connecticut, and Plymouth returned immediately to their old forms of government. Plymouth's separate existence was soon ended when it, together with Maine, was incorporated into the jurisdiction of Massachusetts Bay. For a time it seemed that New Hampshire would also be attached to the Bay Colony. Instead of this, the Privy Council made it a separate royal colony. To the south, the proprietors of the Jerseys were able to re-establish their rights. In New York, the fall of the Dominion had bloody and tragic consequences.

Andros had governed New York through an appointed council and a deputy governor, Francis Nicholson. The council represented an aristocracy that dominated the province. Along both banks of the Hudson, the oligarchs had obtained large estates in land. They also controlled the commerce of the colony. These great families—the Bayards, Van Cortlandts, Schuylers, Phillipses—had prospered through the generation of James's rule. The news of William's invasion of England arrived at New York in February 1689. Though there can be no doubt that the New York aristocrats would ultimately have proclaimed William and Mary, they were naturally reluctant to abandon James. Lacking definite orders from London, lacking, in fact, positive evidence of the outcome of the invasion, they waited. They picked a poor time to do so.

Local and imperial issues combined to create an active and articulate opposition to the New York aristocrats. The desire for a representative assembly was revived. The general resentment of the oligarch's monopoly of land and trade came into the open and produced individual acts of defiance. Rumor revived and gave new force to the fear of Catholicism. Ex-governor Thomas Dongan had remained in the province and a credulous population saw him as the master mind of a popish plot. Everyone assumed that England and France either were at war or soon would be. War in Europe would mean war along the northern frontier of New York. The speculation that Andros had defected and would swing the pro-English Iroquois over to the French circulated as fact.

The possibility of war, plus the news of the overthrow of Andros at Boston, caused Nicholson to call out the militia in order to strengthen the tiny garrison of regular troops in the fort. Among the captains of the city militia was a German immigrant,

Jacob Leisler. Though he had prospered as a merchant and had married into the aristocracy, he had not been admitted to the inner circle. Leisler had also been involved in a bitter law suit with one of the councilors, Nicholas Bayard. A minor altercation between a militia officer and a regular army captain triggered Leisler's revolt. The militia mutinied and demanded the keys to the fort. Nicholson, a weak man, surrendered. For about a week the captains of militia rotated command of the fort. Gradually Leisler emerged as the leader. In June, news of the coronation of William and Mary arrived and Leisler immediately declared for them. Inexplicably, Nicholson failed to, preferring to return to England to report.

With Nicholson gone, Leisler usurped the powers of government. He imprisoned some of the aristocrats, called a convention and proceeded to act as governor. Leisler maintained himself in power for about two years. His government, based on the sword, was arbitrary within the province and militant in the larger community of English America. Within New York he regarded any opposition as seditious or treasonable. Seeing traitors and papists lurking everywhere, his correspondence bristled with "hellish conspiracies." His officers rode roughshod over procedural rights. If they were asked "by what warrant they committed this violence they would usually answer (clapping their hands upon their Swords) 'Here is our warrant!' "

Sharing the popular fear of France and Rome, Leisler was most concerned about defence. He corresponded with neighboring governments, imploring them to share the responsibility. Though offensive action by the Iroquois had frustrated French plans for an invasion of New York, Count Frontenac's Canadian forces raided all along the border. In February 1690, they sacked Schenectady, thus heightening the fear of invasion. Leisler was largely responsible for the intercolonial congress, which met in May 1690 to organize counterattacks against Canada.

While Leisler tried to organize the military forces of the northern colonies, the New York factions dispatched a voluminous correspondence to England. Each tried to outdo the other in protestations of loyalty and vituperative condemnation of their rivals. Late in 1690, the king appointed Harry Sloughter to be governor. Sloughter was delayed en route and Major Richard

Ingoldesby came on ahead in command of a complement of troops. The major demanded the surrender of the fort. Leisler refused. Several weeks later, Leisler's men fired on the regulars and killed two men. Sloughter arrived late in March, and Leisler surrendered to him.

With Sloughter's arrival the aristocrats again had the whip hand. The old councilors proceeded to make an example of the man who had humiliated them. Sloughter issued a commission creating a special court and a grand jury indicted Leisler and his chief lieutenant for the treason of levying war. Both men refused to plead to their indictment and were condemned as mutes. Under heavy pressure from Bayard and the other councilors, Sloughter signed the order that brought Leisler and Jacob Milborne to the gallows. Increase Mather's judgment of this judicial murder stands: "I am afraid that the guilt of innocent blood is still crying in the ears of the Lord against you."

Sloughter died late in 1690 and the Privy Council replaced him with Benjamin Fletcher. Under Fletcher, New York became "a perfect sink of corruption." He all but gave the province away in a series of extravagant land grants. Under Fletcher, the Navigation Acts went largely unenforced. He threw the port of New York open to pirates and they docked there with impunity. That the governor enriched himself from such activities cannot be doubted. In politics, Fletcher unequivocally threw his lot in with the old aristocrats. The hard-pressed Leislerians were pressed still harder.

Fletcher abused his power so flagrantly that the central government replaced him in 1695 with the Earl of Bellomont. He espoused the Leislerian cause and soon had the spirit of faction raging anew. During his six-year administration he reversed many of Fletcher's acts and caused the remaining legal disabilities of the Leislerians to be removed. Bellomont died in 1701, and rumor immediately had it that Edward Hyde, the Viscount Cornbury, would be the next governor. The aristocrats, hoping that Cornbury would support them, sent a new stream of petitions and addresses back to London. Nicholas Bayard opened one of these petitions for signatures at a public tavern. Each man who signed got "a double tankard of March beer." The Leislerians decided to act before Cornbury came out. They caused Bayard to be indicted under a statute that the aristocratically controlled Fletcher assembly had aimed at the Leislerians. Revenge nourished the desire for revenge. The Leislerians hurried Bayard to trial and conviction as a traitor—for having circulated a petition! Fortunately, Bayard's London agent prevented execution of the sentence by asking the Privy Council to review the proceedings.

The Leislerian revolt, rooted in religious bigotry and class animosity, split New York into two irreconcilable factions. It illustrated again the rigidity of the English political process, which provided little ground upon which a political opposition could stand. A group out of power was expected to comply. The group in power regarded noncompliance as illegal and applied the extreme penalties of a rigorous criminal code. The concept of a legitimate political opposition remained a long way in the future but the fantastic reprisals of factions like those of Leisler and Bayard added to the experience of America and helped ultimately to produce the principle of political toleration.

Chapter 9

The Empire
at the End of
the First Century

The Problem of Law Enforcement

*T*he central problem of the first British empire was that of law enforcement. The comprehensive set of statutes passed in the 1660's and 1670's made a blueprint for trade that put English interests in a position to dominate the imperial economy. But Parliament's master plan of trade had been realized imperfectly. The continuous efforts at strict enforcement had been met with stubborn resistance and the collapse of the Dominion of New England had symbolized the failure of an extraordinary effort to compel a large component of the empire to trade within legal limits.

William III did not immediately reveal his attitude toward the dominions. For him, the overriding consideration was to wage war against France. With the king so occupied, it appeared for a brief time that the drive for consolidation of the colonial units might be stopped. In William's first Parliament a bill was introduced in the Commons for the restoration of the charters. Though its sponsors were concerned primarily to re-establish the corporate rights that had been extinguished within the realm, the bill contained an item restoring the American charters. The bill passed in Commons, but failed in the Lords. It failed because of its ulterior political purpose. One clause provided that any official who had participated in any of the *scire facias* or *quo warranto* proceedings that had led to the quashing of the charters should be barred from public office for seven years. As an antiprerogative weapon, the bill cut too wide a swath. Prior to defeating the whole measure, the lords amended the bill by striking out the clause that would have restored the American charters. These were to be considered separately, if at all. By eliminating the American phase of the bill, the lords made it clear that dominion rights stood on a footing inferior to the franchises of the realm. In a sense, this casual action by the House of Lords was a harbinger of the continuation of the policy of colonial consolidation.

By a series of unconnected acts, William made it clear that there would be no change in imperial policy. He refused to be concerned with or to support those groups in America that had overthrown the government established by James. For political reasons he appointed new men to the Lords Commission of Trade and Plantations, but this made little difference because the working personnel of the committee remained. The reappointment of William Blathwayt as secretary guaranteed the continuity of policy. Other administrative agencies made it plain that the Revolution had not changed their concept of policy. The Commissioners of Customs, for example, sent Edward Randolph back to America, this time as surveyor general of the customs. Immediately, Randolph began playing his old theme of the need for centralization.

Randolph's tour as surveyor general extended from 1692 to 1695. Though he visited all of the mainland colonies from New England to the Carolinas, he spent most of his time in Virginia and Maryland. His correspondence and reports bristled with accusations. Officials, from governors to tidewaiters, were in collusion with illegal traders and accepted bribes. Plural office-holding in the American customs service was the rule, and the positions were regarded as sinecures. Accounts were kept irregularly, if at all. Colonial juries would not convict in cases involving evasion of the Navigation Acts. In sum, the laws of trade went unenforced.

In 1695 Randolph asked the commissioners of customs for permission to return to England. He came back to a London extremely upset about the general state of trade. The war with France dragged on into its sixth year. Though the combined Dutch and English flects had established their superiority at La Hogue, warships continued to take a heavy toll of shipping. As an incident of war, piracy flourished and the black flag threatened the merchant marine of all nations. With trade dislocated by war, the merchants were restive, disgruntled, and sharply critical of government.

During the war, the Scots made a determined effort to break the English monopoly of the imperial trade. The political and economic arrangements that had made Scotland a coordinate realm of the English king but had placed it outside the walls of the English mercantile system had never been satisfactory. Resentful of England's exclusive policy, individual Scottish traders had developed a large scale illicit trade with the colonies. In 1693, the Scots Parliament attempted to make the interloping trade a matter of national policy by passing a navigation act of its own. The act permitted individual Scottish traders to import Asian, African, and American goods free of any customs. This tax relief put the Scots in a strong competitive position in the re-export trade to Europe. It also threatened the English merchant's monopoly of the domestic market. A substantial clandestine trade had flourished overland along the northern border and it promised to swell in volume.

Through 1693 and 1694, petitions from London and outport merchants protesting the Scottish intrusions poured into the Commissioners of Customs, the Lords of Trade, and both houses of Parliament. Before government could act, the Scots Parliament moved again. In 1695, it chartered a joint stock company, the Company of Scotland trading to Africa and the Indies. The company had three aims and all were antithetical to established English interests. It hoped to find African and American markets for Scots textiles. It aimed to establish a colony in Central America that would become an entrepot of the West Indian trade. From its single, disastrous venture in colonization it derived its popular name, the Darien Company. Perhaps its most ambitious plan was to challenge the East India Company monopoly of the oriental trade. This interest drew in many London investors who resented the preferred position of the English company.

William III, absent on continental campaigns on the occasion of the passage of the Scottish acts, gave his consent to both bills through a deputy. The royal agent did so under a general instruction to approve measures for the improvement of trade and navigation. The royal approval of the Scottish acts added to the growing feeling that the king was neglecting English interests. When informed of the scope of the measure, William commented laconically that he had been "ill-used" by his ministers.

Parliament reconvened in December 1695 to a chorus of merchant discontent. The session of 1695 marks a decisive point in the role the legislature played in matters colonial and commercial. Beginning in that year, Parliament concerned itself continuously with trade and empire. The House of Lords turned immediately to the general question of the state of trade and to the specific issue of the Darien Company. In the context of Parliamentary concern, Edward Randolph had a busy and gratifying time. Legislative committees and executive agencies turned to him as the English agent best informed about American affairs. He had reported to his immediate superiors, the Commissioners of Customs, soon after his arrival. He repeated his theme of the need for stricter law enforcement and colonial consolidation for the benefit of the treasury lords, the Privy Council and the House of Lords. The reforms of 1696 were based directly on his recommendations.

Simultaneously the Parliament dealt with three related questions—Darien, the need for a new committee for trade and plantations, and the reform of the American customs service.

The threat of the Scottish company could not be ended by a single stroke. Parliament and the crown cooperated to harass and weaken the company. They forced English investors to withdraw their capital with threats of criminal proceedings and impeachment. Having intimidated individuals, Parliament would later move to exclude the Scots from the colonial trade by tightening enforcement procedures under the statute of 1696.

The Lords of Trade had been the subject of criticism and

ridicule for years. They deserved to be; they had proved themselves completely incompetent to oversee the affairs of the empire. A kind of administrative rigor mortis had set in. Since 1689 a rash of mercantilist pamphlets had appeared. Many of them pointed to the weakness of the Lords of Trade and recommended reform. A growing group of responsible and articulate persons expressed the opinion that Parliament should assume responsibility for imperial administration. The House of Lords began to act on this assumption in December 1695. A bill was introduced which created a new committee, appointed by and responsible to the Parliament. The proposed committee would have had a very extensive jurisdiction. In addition to the general oversight of mercantile matters, it would have been responsible for the protection of shipping in time of war. By February, the bill had proceeded to its second reading. Then the king threw his political weight against it. The Parliamentary debate made it clear why he did so. The bill, the debaters said, would effect "a change of our constitution in a very essential point." Since time out of mind the administration of dominion affairs had been His Majesty's business. William III intended to tolerate no such diminution of his prerogative. Particularly obnoxious were the provisions of the bill giving the new committee the control of wartime convoys. This broke violently into the sphere of the Lord High Admiral. An opponent of the bill argued that by such measures the "king would soon grow to be a duke of Venice." The bill disappeared after its second reading.

Though the prerogative in matters imperial had been upheld, the moribund state of the Lords of Trade remained a fact. The king had assured Parliament that changes would be made. Executive officers, fully aware of merchant discontent, moved rapidly to replace the Lords of Trade. In May, 1696, the documents creating the Lords Commissioners of Trade and Plantations, or the Board of Trade, passed the great seal. The board was an agency of the Privy Council. Its membership consisted of experienced administrators like Blathwayt. Though the board had no legislative or police power, the Privy Council normally translated its decisions into administrative orders. Its influence reached out in two main directions. Board of Trade recommendations carried great weight with the king and Parliament. Across the Atlantic it made its power felt through its instructions to the royal governors and circular letters to all colonial executives. Throughout its career the board was extremely sensitive to the demands of the English commercial and industrial community. The board became the mouthpiece of orthodox mercantilism, its members the priests who "sacrificed the colonies on the altar of England's moneyed prosperity."[1]

While the question of the Board of Trade was being resolved, a new navigation act proceeded through Parliament. The "Act for preventing Frauds and regulating Abuses in the Plantation Trade" became law in April 1696. The bill had been drawn by the Commissioners of Customs and was based on Randolph's recommendations. Essentially an administrative and procedural measure, it extended the rules of the English customs service to the dominions. The law reaffirmed the shipping provisions of the Navigation Act of 1660 by requiring that ships engaged in the empire trade be English-owned, be commanded by an English captain, and be manned by a crew at least three-quarters English or colonial.

A second group of provisions fixed the responsibility of American officers and agencies of government. All governors—corporate, proprietary, and royal—were required to take an oath to enforce the laws of trade. Failure to take the oath or negligence in service was punishable with removal from office and a £1,000 fine. The colonial naval officer, an agent of the governor, had often obstructed the efforts of the customs agents. The law required that they post bond in London with the Commissioners of Customs for the faithful performance of their duties. Because it had been reported that there were on the colonial statute books laws contrary to the navigation system, the statute of 1696 swept these away with a blanket nullification of all such dominion legislation. A third block of clauses strengthened and regularized the American customs service. The Treasury was authorized to appoint any and all necessary agents for the dominion establishments. The American customs officials were placed under the same rules that governed the English service by a provision that extended the Statute of Frauds of 1662 to the colonies. Other

1. Charles M. Andrews, *The Colonial Period of American History* (New Haven: Yale University Press, 1934–38), IV, 295.

sections of the law were aimed directly at the Scots, the "ill-disposed" persons referred to in the preamble of the act. On the assumption that Scots and other non-English nationals had infiltrated the American governments, the law barred all such persons from holding judicial or treasury offices in the dominions. They were also excluded from jury duty. To prevent the establishment of Scottish trading posts in America, the law forbade the sale or other conveyance of land to all but natural-born subjects of England, Ireland, or America.

The Navigation Act of 1696 was the capstone of the series of laws establishing the commercial system of the old empire. The statutes of the eighteenth century would either be restricted to the clarification and elaboration of the older laws or would deal with specific economic interests.

After a long career of frustration, Edward Randolph had had his day in court. For him the creation of the Board of Trade and the passage of the Navigation Act of 1696 was not enough. He pushed for additional reforms. Convinced that the law would remain unenforced if the king's agents had to prosecute in common law courts before colonial juries, he urged the establishment of a series of American vice admiralty courts.

Between 1697 and 1700, the crown extended the jurisdiction of the Lord High Admiral to the American dominions on a regular basis. The law administered by the English High Court of Admiralty had its origins in the maritime codes of the Mediterranean city-states. The court itself was created in the fourteenth century and attained its largest jurisdiction and greatest prestige during Tudor times. In the early seventeenth century, Sir Edward Coke waged legal war on the admiral's high court as a part of his effort to weaken or destroy the prerogative courts. The trend of the century was toward a limitation of the influence of the high court and a restriction of its jurisdiction to a true sea law.

There had been rights of admiralty jurisdiction in America prior to 1696. The charters to the proprietors had conferred such rights either explicitly or by implication. For example, Lord Baltimore's charter gave him full judicial power "within that land, and the sea of those parts." The Pennsylvania charter authorized the proprietor "to do all and every thing or things . . . unto the complete establishment of justice." In royal colonies, the commission to the governor empowered him to erect courts, though the specific commission to be vice admiral and the warrant to establish the courts came from the high admiral. In 1660, Charles II appointed the Duke of York to be Lord High Admiral of England and extended the commission to include the dominions in 1662. Though the duke's refusal to take the test oath forced him to resign his English commission in 1673, he retained his dominion warrant. As duke and king, James issued several commissions of vice admiralty. In spite of this, the bulk of maritime cases in the colonies were tried in common law courts.

The Navigation Act of 1696 did not establish colonial vice admiralty courts. It approached the matter obliquely by stating that violation of the acts of trade might be tried in such courts. The act thus assumed that these courts either already existed or would soon be created. For about a year, Randolph pressed for the actual establishment of a series of courts. The question of the courts became involved with that of the appointment of royal attorneys general and advocates who would have prosecuted all crown cases. The chief objection to the new legal officers and courts came from the proprietors, particularly William Penn. He argued that the office and the jurisdiction had been given to him by his charter. In March 1697, Randolph won his point. From lists submitted by him, the admiralty appointed the judges, registrars and advocates for eleven courts on the American continent and in the West Indies.

The colonial vice admiralty courts had a broad jurisdiction. Together with their English counterparts, they had cognizance of certain civil actions for damages, of prize cases, and of admiralty droits. The category of civil actions included disputes over certain forms of contract and salvage, disagreements among owners, masters, and mariners (usually over wages), and the mortgage of ships. The bulk of the business coming before the courts came within the class of civil actions. Here they performed a real service, for they dispensed a fair and appropriate law by an expeditious process. The prize jurisdiction was, of course, limited to time of war. The courts determined whether or not enemy vessels and cargoes captured by the public ships of England, the colonies, and allies were legal prize. The droit jurisdiction protected the royal right to great fishes (whales, sturgeon, and porpoises) when beached, flotsam and jetsam, and certain types of salvage. In addition to the traditional jurisdictions, the colonial vice admiralty courts heard and determined cases involving violation of the laws of trade. In England, the crown prosecuted cases of illegal trading at common law in the Court of Exchequer. Proposals to establish exchequer courts in America had been made, and for a time Randolph had favored such courts. Though Parliament passed this alternative by, it did not give the colonial vice admiralty courts exclusive jurisdiction in matters touching the trade laws. Since the provincial common law courts could also try cases involving illegal traders, a conflict of jurisdiction resulted. Colonial judges adopted the practices of English common law courts and issued prohibitions that stopped the proceedings in vice admiralty courts on grounds of lack of jurisdiction.

The procedures of the vice admiralty courts were simple and direct. They were well suited to the needs of the commercial and maritime community whose members had to move to meet the demands of time, tide, and market. Unlike common law courts, those of the Admiralty could easily be called into session at any time. An action began when an aggrieved party made his charges in the form of a libel. The court then proclaimed the charge and in the normal course of events the defendant appeared and formally answered the libel. The briefs of the contending parties were presented to the court. The judge then rendered his decision, the decree. All proceedings were *in rem*, that is, they were directed against things, either vessels or goods, rather than persons. If the decree led to the forfeiture of property, it was sold and the proceeds were divided equally among the king, the governor, and the individual who had made the charge. Though the process of the vice admiralty courts was efficient, it was alien to the American experience. Because these courts proceeded without a jury, Americans could and did raise the issue of violation of fundamental rights.

By intruding into some colonial jurisdictions and by keeping the question of jury trial alive, the American vice admiralty courts acted as a minor but continuous irritant. Their presence must be regarded as an ancillary cause of the American Revolution.

The Restriction of Colonial Manufacturing
and the Problem of Returns

In 1699 Parliament passed the Woolens Act and by so doing announced a new policy that further restricted colonial economic activity.

Through the seventeenth century the woolen industry had continued to dominate the English economy. At all times king and Parliament protected the industry. It was politic for them to do so because the manufacture of cloth affected the interests of every major economic group. The industry demanded and got a monopoly of the imperial market. The most significant law was the Staple Act of 1663, which, in effect, threw a protective tariff wall around the empire.

The main threats to the textile monopolists came from oriental fabrics which were imported by the East India Company and from the developing Irish woolen industry. The English woolen interests conducted a continuous battle to restrict or forbid the use of Indian textiles, and they were largely successful. Parliament also maintained a strict surveillance of the Irish economy. As the English cloth-finishing industries expanded, Irish production of raw wool was encouraged. Inevitably some of the wool was worked up into cloth. Though the Irish textile industries were never large, the English interests became alarmed and poured petitions into Parliament demanding repression. The Board of Trade struck the keynote by describing the Irish industry as "wholly incompatible with the fundamental trade of England."

In December 1698, Sir Edward Seymour brought in the Irish woolen bill. It accomplished its intent by restricting the export of Irish cloth. As the bill proceeded through Parliament, someone tacked on an American provision. The clause forbade the exportation of any "wool, wool-fells, shortlings, mortlings, wool-flocks, worsted, bay, or woolen yarn, cloth, serge bays, kerseys, says, friezes, druggets, cloth-serges, shalloons, or any other drapery stuffs or woolen manufactures whatsoever." These nonexportation provisions guaranteed that Irish and American woolen cloth would not compete with the English product. The English manufacturer sold in an expanding world market. This made it possible to invest larger amounts of capital and thus produce goods more cheaply. With a restricted market the Americans and Irish could not afford the capital investment that would have made economical, large-scale production possible.

For decades prior to the passage of the Woolens Act, English agents and commissions had expressed alarm about the growth of the American textile industry. How real was the threat of American manufacturing? From the beginning, those colonists who were able had made yarn and cloth in their homes. This practice continued, and the overwhelming proportion of American manufacturing remained in this primitive homespun stage. There is scattered evidence of the creation of fulling mills, but such industry never went beyond the domestic-commercial state and it supplied only limited and local markets. Several general economic factors worked against the expansion of provincial industry. Throughout the colonial period, the shortage of labor kept wages in America at substantially higher levels than those prevailing in Europe. Capital for investment was limited and difficult to concentrate. Credit facilities essential to large-scale production and distribution were nonexistent. Given the facts of American production, the fear of colonial competition was vastly exaggerated.

A basic tenet of mercantilism was that England would manufacture and the colonies would produce raw materials. The great problem was that of returns—that is, the development of colonial commodities that were acceptable in exchange for manufactured goods. The southern mainland colonies had developed a pattern of trade that was workable if not satisfactory. Specializing in tobacco, they exchanged it for wanted manufactured goods. The balance of trade ran against the planter but was redressed by British investments in the expansion of the tobacco plantation system. The planter was reduced to the position of permanent debtor. The normal produce of the northern colonies—grain, meat, and lumber—was not acceptable in England for direct exchange for manufactured goods. Those colonies had developed the triangular trades through which their unwanted surplus was converted into money or commodities that were acceptable in England as returns. These trades pivoted in the West Indies. They posed a problem for the mercantilist planner because they led the colonial merchant outside of the empire into a trade with the Spanish and French West Indies. In effect, the northern provincials' capacity to buy English goods depended on the success of his trading ventures with the foreign West Indies.

The War of the League of Augsburg and the War of the Spanish Succession interrupted the triangular trades and seriously reduced the purchasing power of the northern colonies. This meant that they would turn increasingly to home manufacturing to supply their needs unless acceptable returns were found. Faced with this dilemma, the home government attempted artificially to develop returns, specifically naval stores. England was dependent on foreign sources for her supply of naval stores—lumber, tar, pitch, rosin. Sweden and Russia were the main suppliers. This dependence on foreign supply in an area so vital to maritime commerce and naval security did not square with mercantilist principles. A naval stores industry in the northern colonies would solve two problems, that of returns and dependence on foreign supply in a critical area.

Parliament passed the Naval Stores Act in 1705. The law recognized the relationship of naval stores to markets with the statement that it would increase the "Trade & Vent" of English manufactured goods. The statute placed all naval stores on the enumerated commodity list. It also provided a bounty to encourage colonial production and to make it possible for the American products to compete with the stores from northern Europe. The home government went to great lengths to stimulate the industry. For example, it sent special agents to New England to instruct persons in production and it encouraged and aided the emigration of the Palatines to New York to create a naval stores industry there.

In spite of the bounties and other encouragements, the industry never flourished. Production costs were high. In England, the Admiralty took a dim view of the colonial products that were of inferior quality. They refused to purchase American naval stores. When reminded that the consumption of the American product was essential to the general economic welfare of England, the naval officers responded that they could not care less. In America, the merchants also opposed the development of naval stores. They preferred, legally or illegally, to obtain their returns in the West

Indian trade. The policy of stimulating naval stores failed to solve the problem of returns.

In subsequent years, Parliament showed itself willing to extend the principle of protection. In 1732 it restricted the growth of the colonial hat-making industry. The Iron Act of 1750 arrested the development of American metal-finishing and -fabricating industries. The Privy Council also aided English manufacturers. On numerous occasions it disallowed laws of colonial assemblies which had been designed to stimulate manufacturing. The policy of monopolized markets created a real economic grievance, which became aggravated as the coming of the industrial revolution made it clear that manufacturing was the prime area of profitable investment. A distinguished English economic historian has written, "It was a mistaken policy on the part of the mother country to exhibit this jealous spirit towards American industries . . ."[2] Perhaps most important, the policy of restriction was a standing reminder of the economic inferiority and dependence of the American colonies, ever-present evidence that "the *pacte colonial* had been settled by only one of the parties concerned with the agreement."

The Attack on the Private Colonies

For Edward Randolph the ultimate imperial issue was that of colonial consolidation. In the late 1690's he once again mounted his attack on the proprietary and corporate colonies. His many reports continued to be sharply critical of the management of the private colonies. Late in 1695, the House of Lords became interested and asked the Commissioners of Customs if the laws of trade could be enforced in the private colonies. The commissioners answered that they doubted it. Sometime later the Lords requested a list of such colonies. Randolph not only supplied the list, but also furnished an indictment and a plan of reform. He repeated the old charges that their governors were weak, that they harbored pirates, that they violated the laws of trade. Again he charged that they aimed at independence. They wanted, he

2. Ephraim Lipson, *The Economic History of England* (London: Adams & Charles Black, 1948), III, 193.

alleged, "to break loose and set up for themselves." He then recommended royalization and consolidation of the continental colonies. South Carolina was to be royalized; North Carolina annexed
to Virginia; Delaware added to Maryland; West New Jersey
attached to Pennsylvania; East New Jersey and Connecticut combined with New York; Rhode Island with Massachusetts Bay.

The Lords apparently never seriously considered Randolph's
entire proposal. Rather, they chose to single out one proprietor
and carefully scrutinize the operation of the trade laws within
his province. They chose William Penn, and for several weeks
Randolph made his accusations before a committee of the Lords.
In the end they let Penn off with a sharp reprimand. It would
appear that the Lords had used the Penn hearings to warn the
proprietary and corporate colonies of parliamentary interest in
their affairs. The threat was explicit—enforce the laws of trade or
lose the charters. To give force to the lesson, the Lords addressed
the king and requested him to put the governors of the private
colonies under bond. Vigorously worded warnings were sent to
the governors of all private colonies. Though Randolph and the
Board of Trade continued to be concerned with the status of
the nonroyal colonies, they abandoned the overt attack for five
years.

Though the attempt at a wholesale vacating of the private
charters failed temporarily, the wars with France gave urgency to
the need for some form of unity. The Board of Trade turned toward more limited attempts to install a uniform administration in
the American colonies. The board concentrated its efforts on the
colonial governors. As a consequence of the Glorious Revolution
the crown had assumed the authority to appoint the governors in
Pennsylvania and Maryland. Though the board attempted to
convert these units into royal colonies it failed and the proprietors
were restored. In the Jerseys the board was more successful. Under pressure, the Jersey proprietors, who had never had a firm
title, surrendered their rights in 1702. Along another line of policy, the board backed the appointment of one man to several
governorships. For example, Benjamin Fletcher was for a time
governor of New York, Pennsylvania, and the Jerseys. Later, the
Earl of Bellomont acted as governor of New York, Massachusetts,
and New Hampshire. The French wars created the demand for

intercolonial military commands. Sir William Phips, as governor of Massachusetts, had a commission to command the militia of Connecticut and Rhode Island. The commissions of both Fletcher and Bellomont extended their military authority into colonies other than those where they were actually governor. The attempts at limited union through multiple appointments and consolidation of militia commands worked poorly. The private colonies stood on their charters and resisted every effort to intrude within their jurisdictions.

The board might have turned back to the policy of instituting legal process against each private colony under the writ *quo warranto*. Apparently it gave no serious consideration to this possibility. The use of the *quo warranto* during the seventeenth century had not been fruitful. The many attempts to obliterate charter rights had succeeded only in Virginia and Massachusetts and it had taken over a half a century to obtain the judgment against the Bay Colony. Crown lawyers would have been horrified by the burden of work that the quashing of eight charters by legal process would have presented. Such a process inevitably would have been slow, costly, and unsure. The board preferred to proceed in Parliament where its purposes could be accomplished efficiently by the passage of a single law.

The Board of Trade expected substantial support from diverse groups for its plan to extinguish the private colonies by statute. The board itself had influence and presumably spoke for powerful commercial interests. At the highest level of policy, a strong case could be made that the security of the empire made colonial consolidation a necessity. On both sides of the Atlantic individuals with American experience urged the passage of the legislation. Though these men may have been acting in the public interest, they also hoped to profit personally from the alteration of the American jurisdictions. Edward Randolph headed the list. Robert Quary, a judge of vice admiralty in Pennsylvania, hoped to gain from the demise of the proprietor. Joseph Dudley looked forward to being governor of a combined Massachusetts, Rhode Island, and Connecticut. Jeremiah Bass argued against the Jersey proprietors and expected to be governor. The Earl of Cornbury had large designs for an expanded colony of New York. To these varied interests, the Church of England added its powerful voice.

In 1701, the government chartered the Society for the Propagation of the Gospel. The Society began to make inquiries concerning the state of the Church in America. The same men who had poured hostile reports into the Board of Trade then began to furnish the Society with evidence that equated religious nonconformity with the existence of the private colonies.

Late in 1700, the Board of Trade began considering the Reunification Bill. Randolph returned to London and furnished the latest evidence of illegal activities. In March 1701, the board memorialized the king. They led off with a comprehensive indictment. The private colonies had not complied with the Navigation Act of 1696, had passed laws repugnant to the laws of England, had refused to send their laws to England for Privy Council review and had blocked judicial appeals to the council, had harbored illegal traders and pirates, received contraband goods, refused to pay customs, illegally manipulated the value of coins, and had set up manufacturing industries. They strove to throw off all controls and to become independent. The board requested the king to use Parliamentary authority to "introduce such a regulation of trade and such an administration of government as shall make them duly subservient to England."

In April 1701, a bill was introduced into the House of Lords which extinguished all charter-given powers of government in the private colonies. The Board of Trade retained Randolph to argue for the bill. While the Lords began to consider the bill, Randolph submitted specific evidence to the House of Commons to prepare the way there. The bill had two readings in the Lords, but before final action could be taken, William III dissolved the Parliament and left for the Irish campaign.

In 1702, proposals were made to support a more moderate bill that would have recalled to the crown the colonial powers to collect customs duties and to deal with defense and admiralty matters. The Board of Trade refused to approve the proposal. When the House of Lords asked the board for a list of colonial abuses and "proper remedies," it responded with some new evidence and a recommendation that the Lords proceed along the lines of the previous session. William III died in March, and once again the Parliament was dissolved.

Three years later the Privy Council asked the Board of Trade for a new indictment of the private colonies, and the board complied. In 1706, a bill was introduced into Commons which would have taken away the charter-given powers to govern in Rhode Island and Connecticut. The bill was stopped after its first reading. In 1708, the House of Lords again asked for "charges against the proprietary governments," but the request generated no new legislation. In 1712, the government again considered action, but Queen Anne's death and the ensuing political realignment frustrated the attempt. A Commons' committee considered the matter briefly in 1714 without result. The next year an Indian war in South Carolina brought an appeal from the colonists themselves. They petitioned the Board of Trade and Parliament, asking to be made a royal colony. Following this appeal, a new bill royalizing all of the private colonies was introduced in the House of Commons. It, too, failed.

The Reunification Bills were the natural outgrowth of the trend of imperial policy after 1660—a trend toward uniformity, consolidation, and centralized control. Such a bill would have become the capstone of the imperial structure. Supported as they were by substantial interests, the question comes, why did they fail? In part, as has been mentioned, fortuitous factors such as the death of William and Anne, explain the failure. Often the Parliament could give only intermittent and rather casual attention to American affairs. For example, the session of 1701 was the scene of violent political strife that brought on the attempted impeachment of four members of the House of Lords. But the failure of the bills was not due solely to coincidence.

In the context of the debate over the charters, the argument concerning defense could be made either way. It could be, and was, argued that consolidation would create a more efficient provincial military effort. Yet just as logical was the assumption that action against the charters would create colonial resentment and cause a diminished war effort. In any event, William III certainly understood that questions of security would not wait. In 1702, the Board of Trade had informed William that the colonies were defenseless. Knowing that reunification would not come in time to aid him in the impending War of the Spanish Succession, he inquired "what he might do of himself for the defence of his plantations." Beyond such considerations was the fact that the private colonies made very respectable contributions to the cause of imperial security in the Wars of the League of Augsburg and Spanish Succession.

Though the Board of Trade had powerful backers, the colonial interests could also generate political support. Many of the proprietors were forceful men. A man like William Penn always commanded respect. At one time the roster of the Carolina proprietors included four peers of the realm and they had great weight in the legislature. Either directly or through their agents, the colonies entered into the parliamentary process. After the defeat of the bill of 1701, Penn wrote to seven lords thanking them for supporting the cause of property. At the same time he could write intimately to the speaker of the House of Commons: "I cannot forbear thinking myself safe where I have such a friend in the chair." Perhaps Sir Henry Ashurst was most active in the colonial interest. At one time or another he was agent for Massachusetts and Connecticut. Though a garrulous and egotistical old man, he had influence. In May 1701, he was "soliciting the lords day and night" against the Reunification Bill. That bill failed, Ashurst wrote, because of "an interest I made in ye Lords House." Similarly he claimed responsibility for the defeat of the bill of 1706 which "was thrown out at the first reading." Even when his personal opinion of his own merit is discounted, it is clear that Ashurst's advocacy was important. A baronet, he had sat in Parliament for many years. His brother had been Lord Mayor of London and was also a member of Parliament. By marriage he was related to powerful families. The attorney and solicitor general were his personal friends. In 1706, he retained as counsel lawyers of great reputation and substantial influence.

In defending the charters, the colonial proprietors and agents made strong substantive and constitutional arguments. The most comprehensive defense of the charters was made in a pamphlet written by Jeremiah Dummer. He made a strong practical argument for the validity of the charters. When originally granted, the charters were virtually worthless. They had been converted into valuable properties as the result of arduous effort. Dummer cited the physical and financial risks involved in establishing the colonies. The burden of his argument then became that it would be unfair and illegal to deprive the provincial interests of these self-generated property rights. The fact that the various proposals for vacating the charters reserved rights in real property carried no weight with him. He thought that the proprietary and political rights granted by the charters were so intertwined that one could not be canceled without destroying the other. Penn made a similar argument in opposing the bill of 1701. He cited the common aphorism that "power followed property" and concluded that "power is as much our Property as the Soil."

Both Dummer and Penn attacked the Reunification Bills on the ground that they denied due process of law. Penn regarded the attempts to pass the bills as *ex parte* proceedings. Dummer compared them to bills of attainder. He thought it "a severity without a precedent" that the colonists should "UNSUMMONED, UNHEARD, IN ONE DAY be deprived of all their valuable privileges . . ." Though he admitted that Parliament was not bound by the rules of ordinary courts, he cited the example of Ireland where a notice of thirty days was given when imperial legislation affected Irish property. Though admitting that Parliament had the power to abrogate the charters, Dummer pointed to a higher consideration which would restrain the legislators. He wrote that "the question here is not one of *power*, but *right: and shall not the supreme legislative of all the nation do right?* One may say, that what the parliament can't do justly, they can't do at all . . ."[3]

3. Bradley Chapin (ed.), *Provincial America 1600–1763* (New York: The Free Press, 1966), p. 234.

Chapter 10

A Plural
Society

The People

*A*t the time of the Stuart restoration, approximately 72,000 white persons lived in English America. By the turn of the century they numbered 223,000. In the next generation population increased to 765,000 and by 1760 stood at 1,268,000. A very high birth rate in part explains this incredible increase. At the same time, European population broke away from a level statistical plane and rose rapidly. The absence of plagues, the improvement of medical practice, and the use of better farming methods caused England and the continent to burgeon with people. Though mercantilist theory equated a rising population with national wealth, such rapid growth created large problems.

Through most of the colonial period, England had no overall policy for the control of movement within the empire or for immigration into it from foreign countries. In 1740, Parliament required seven years of residence before an alien in the colonies could be naturalized. Left largely to themselves, the individual colonies controlled immigration and set the rules for naturalization. Policy varied from colony to colony and from time to time in a single colony. Policy was pragmatic and based on self-appraisal of local needs. Yet certain broad regional trends are discernible. Most of the New England colonies pursued conservative immigration policies. The large increase of population there was self-generated, so that New England remained more purely English than any other section. To the south, and in Virginia especially, the attitude toward immigration related directly to the need for labor. In the late seventeenth and early eighteenth century the southern colonies encouraged white immigration. They used the headright system extensively. That system paid the cost of the transportation of immigrants by granting land to the person who financed the Atlantic crossing. Later the system of redemptioneers largely replaced the headrights. The redemptioneer was a person whom an agent obtained by fair means or foul and transported to America. The agent then sold the redemptioneer's labor for a term of years. To satisfy the demand for labor, agents in this traffic resorted to kidnaping and a large number of persons began their life in the American south as "kids." The British courts contributed to this human stream by regularly exporting vagabonds and condemned criminals. Though colonial governments protested vigorously, the practice continued.

The original business of settling English America had been done by the English themselves. The first major addition of non-English people came in 1664 when Charles II seized New Netherlands. The conquest furnished him not only Dutch and Swedish subjects but in the city of New Amsterdam, Flemish, French, Danish, Norwegian, German, Portuguese, Italian, and Jewish subjects as well. The Swedes of the Delaware Valley had been absorbed by the Dutch in 1655. Though numbering only 600 then, they maintained an identity and at the first census of 1790 they were counted to the number of 21,000, or 0.07 per cent of the total white population.

When Stuyvesant surrendered, the Dutch were counted at about 8,000. By the end of the colonial period they had increased to 100,000, or 3.4 per cent of the total white population. The Dutch readily intermarried with their English and German neighbors, diluting their stock beyond recognition in the process. Even so, the Dutch left permanent marks on American places, names, and language. The Bowery is from *bouwerij*, which meant farm. Brooklyn is the English corruption of *Breukelen*, Flushing of *Vlissingen*, and Gramercy of *De Kromme Zee*. They gave us kitchen names—cole slaw, cooky, cruller, and waffle. The political boss is Dutch, as are the Halloween spook and the Christmas Santa Claus.

New York provided the first American place of refuge for a fugitive Protestant minority, the French Huguenots. Since 1598 they had been entitled at least legally to toleration. Gradually Louis XIV began persecuting them. Bringing this policy to a climax in 1685 by revoking the Edict of Nantes, he ordered the Huguenot churches burned and expelled their pastors. The congregations he commanded to remain. Some, disobeying, fled in several directions. They went to Switzerland, the Palatinate, Brandenburg, the Netherlands, and England. Others fled overseas to settle among the Dutch and English in New York. Even before the revocation of the edict, they had crossed the Atlantic. In the 1670's they founded New Paltz (*Nouveau Palatinat*), so named for the Rhenish Palatinate, an asylum in the first stage of their exile. By 1688, two hundred Huguenot families had arrived in the province where they founded New Rochelle named for the historic Huguenot stronghold in their native land.

The Huguenots, perhaps to the number of 15,000, settled all along the coast. The largest number came to South Carolina. The proprietors invited them in and they established themselves near Charleston. The hope had been that they would cultivate silk worms, olives, and grapes. They failed in this, but succeeded as rice and indigo planters. Many not only prospered but became opulent. Large numbers settled in the towns, where they entered the professions or developed large mercantile establishments. In many colonies, Huguenots rose to positions of true prominence— for example, Bonneau, Huger, Laurens, and Legare in South Carolina; in New England, Bowdoin, Peabody, Revere, Faneuil; in the middle colonies, Bayard, Boudenot, Jay, DeLancey.

Other French besides the Huguenots became residents in the English colonies. Perhaps a few were adventurers who emigrated from France solely to seek their individual fortunes. More were French Catholics whom the British uprooted from Acadia in 1755 and dispersed among the continental colonies, especially New

York and South Carolina. These people were less hospitably received than the Huguenots. Both New York and South Carolina forced them into indentured service. Whenever possible they escaped, many of them going to more congenial places like Louisiana. By the census of 1790, the French in America numbered 55,000, or 1.7 per cent of the entire white population.

Excepting only the English, the largest national group at the end of the colonial period was German. The census of 1790 recorded 277,000 persons of Germanic origin, which was 8.7 per cent of the total white population. Large numbers of Germans migrated for religious reasons. Germany was a series of principalities loosely organized as the Holy Roman Empire. The Peace of Westphalia of 1648 had established the rule that the religion of the people should be the religion of the prince. The princes professed three religions, namely, the Roman Catholic, the Lutheran, or the Calvinist. Thus a person adhering to any one of these faiths might find himself the object of persecution if his prince was of a different religion. In addition there were substantial numbers of Germans who rejected the three standard religions. These were the Pietists: the United Brethrens and Moravians, the Amish, the Dunkards, the Mennonites, and the Schwenckfelders.

Religious discontent was aggravated by other grievances, especially in the valleys of the Rhine River and its tributaries. Though this was an area of fertile farms and thriving commerce, the princes impoverished the people by levying very high taxes in order to maintain extravagant courts. Furthermore, since the region had strategic significance in the diplomatic schemes of both the Hapsburgs and the Bourbons, the region had been an important theater of operations during the Thirty Years War; it continued to be so during the Wars of Louis XIV. In 1674 he sent troops into the Palatinate to burn and plunder. In 1680 he sent them again. In 1688 he occupied Cologne. As he did so, he sent troops once more into the Palatinate where, through the orders of his ruthless minister, Louvois, he wrought an almost total desolation. During his last war, in the year 1707, he ravaged the Palatinate again.

In the 1670's, William Penn twice visited this area to preach the Quaker doctrine. Thus the Rhenish sectaries knew Penn as a religious leader before he appealed to them as a colonizer. They responded immediately to his promotional pamphlet about Pennsylvania and laid plans for a large migration. They chose as their agent an able lawyer, Francis Daniel Pastorius. A group of Mennonites founded Germantown in the 1680's, and it served as a base for the distribution of later German immigrants. They came in successive and ever larger waves, pouring through the port of Philadelphia. By 1727, Pennsylvania officials became alarmed that the English character of the province would be destroyed. After that they kept careful count; between 1727 and 1779, almost 69,000 Germans arrived through the port.

Other Palatines sought refuge in England in 1708 and 1709 and from there they were shipped to the colonies in groups. About 3,000 came to New York. Under Governor Robert Hunter's neither kind nor expert direction, they attempted to manufacture naval stores along the Hudson. Many of the Palatines moved to the valleys of the Schoharie and Mohawk. Hunter, acting in the interests of land speculators, refused to grant them land. Rather than become permanent tenants, they removed to Pennsylvania. Together with other Germans, the Palatines pushed through the valley of the Shenandoah into Virginia and the back country of North Carolina.

Germans by the thousands began their colonial life in straitened circumstances. Even if they escaped the homeland with some capital, the chances were that they would be fleeced of it. Especially unscrupulous were agents known as newlanders, who were paid so much a head for every person over ten years of age whom they could induce to emigrate. As a result of their activities large numbers of Germans became redemptioneers. Whatever the circumstances in which they began their new life most of the Germans prospered. As farmers they made Pennsylvania a rich, well-managed agricultural province. They also excelled as artisans. William Rittenhauser erected the first paper mill in the colonies. Others became glass makers and weavers. Germans made iron, and the skilled gunsmiths of Lancaster County manufactured the famous pieces that went by the somewhat misleading name, the Kentucky rifle.

As the continental people arrived in ever larger numbers, all parts of the British Isles contributed to the westward migration. In the seventeenth century, the English reduced the South Irish to a kind of colonial status. The King of Great Britain ruled them as the King of Ireland. He governed his subordinate kingdom through a Lord Lieutenant and a Parliament that was subservient to the one that met at Westminster. The Dublin Parliament represented the landlords, the haughty Anglo-Irish aristocracy. This class exploited their tenants without pity and without remorse. English mercantilist policy created economic difficulties. In the time of Charles II, Parliament closed the English market to Irish meat and dairy products. Later, when the Irish had developed a lucrative trade with the colonies, Parliament required the Irish to import these products by way of England. In 1699, Parliament destroyed a thriving Irish woolen industry by forbidding the export of Irish woolen cloth.

Religious persecution aggravated the troubles of the Irish. The king tried to force his Roman Catholic subjects into Anglican conformity. After 1689, Catholics were barred from the Irish legislature. The English Parliament deprived Catholics of the right to vote and excluded them from all civil and military offices. The law regulating the inheritance of land was changed. Unless one son abjured his faith, the estate would be divided among all of the children. Catholic teachers were driven from the schools and forbidden to teach in the privacy of the home. Though officials enforced these laws irregularly, the Irish Catholic labored under heavy civil disabilities.

The Irish had ample reason to leave their native land and they did so by the thousands. They were easily assimilated into the basic English stock. In America they tended to scatter rather than concentrate. They spoke English. In a hostile, predominantly Protestant land many gave up their Catholicism. The census of 1790 showed that most of the Irish had gone to Virginia and North Carolina, though substantial numbers were to be found in Pennsylvania and Maryland. In the aggregate they numbered 116,000, or 3.7 per cent of the white population.

The same sort of distress which moved the South Irish to emigrate also moved the Ulster or Scots-Irish. They descended for the most part from Scots whom King James I in the years 1609–1611 had colonized in Ireland on lands confiscated from Irish rebels. Like the South Irish, they suffered from rapacious landlords and from the economic and ecclesiastical policies of

England. Both groups carried to America an inveterate distrust of England, a distrust and even a hatred that boded no good for English sovereignty on the far side of the Atlantic.

After William and Mary secured their authority in Ireland during the years 1688 to 1691, Scots thronged into the region to take up long leases of land at low rents. As these leases began to expire around the years 1717 and 1718 the tenants learned that they could not renew them except at double or even treble the rent. These difficulties were aggravated by the loss of the English market for Irish livestock and dairy products. The loss of all empire markets for woolen textiles hit Ulster especially hard, for this was an industry that the Scots-Irish had developed extensively. Economic misfortune was embittered by religious discrimination. The Ulstermen were Presbyterians. Narrow English policy forced them to pay tithes to support the Anglican Church. After 1704, like the Catholics, they were excluded from all civil and military offices.

Urged by these accumulated grievances, the Ulster Irish fled beyond the seas. The first considerable number of them arrived in America between 1714 and 1720. In the following decades up to about 1760, the tide flowed in. Then for a while it ebbed only to flow again before 1770. The successive crests corresponded with depressions in the linen industry, which the Ulster Irish had developed as a substitute for the manufacture of woolen textiles. Bad crops as well as industrial depressions stimulated the flow. In 1740 and 1741 famines occurred and the annual number of Ulster emigrants for several years was estimated at 12,000.

An exception to the general rule, the arriving Scots-Irish passed or were pushed rapidly on to the frontier. The first-comers naturally enough went to New England on the assumption that a common Calvinism would assure them of a warm reception. Though Cotton Mather did welcome them because of their religion, there was not room for them in the eastern settlements. New England officials packed them off to the frontier where land was cheap and the danger of Indian raids persistent. From a first settlement at Worcester they spread themselves through all the western parts of the region. Those who arrived later avoided Boston. Many settled in New York along the Hudson. Their first settlement in the valley of the Wallkill spread out and left a mark on the map of New York in the names of the counties of Ulster and Orange. Many more Scots-Irish came to Pennsylvania. They tended to settle west of the Germans and then fan out along the frontier. They spread south and west through the Shenandoah Valley into Virginia and the Carolinas. They also moved northward up the Delaware; then north-westward up the left bank of the Susquehanna. The Cumberland Valley invited them southward again into western Maryland and Virginia. Thus the Scots-Irish held the frontier most of the way from northern and western New England to the Carolinas.

The Ulstermen proved to be a turbulent breed. In Pennsylvania they trespassed on the proprietary domain. They defied Penn's agents and wrested titles from them for nominal sums. They challenged Indian title even more boldly. Indeed, they seemed to revert to the ancestral type of Scots borderer. It was well that this was so, for if the new American border was to be held, the job required talents rather more like those of the men who once had held the Scottish border than those of sedate Quakers who sat at their ease in Philadelphia. Clad in fringed and belted hunting shirt, in fringed breeches and leggings, with moccasins on feet, rifle in hand, and both scalping knife and tomahawk in belt, the Scots-Irish frontiersman cut a barbarous, Indian-like figure. He not only held his ground; he extended it.

According to the census of 1790, the Ulster Irish numbered more than 190,000, or 6 per cent of the white population. The stock furnished its fair share of colonial leaders. From Johnson Hall in the Mohawk Valley, Sir William Johnson conducted England's complex diplomacy with the Iroquois. Others distinguished themselves in war; for example, Richard Montgomery, John Stark, Charles Clinton and his sons, George and James. James Logan played a central role in Pennsylvania politics, but also studied botany to such good effect that Linnaeus named the order *Loganiaceae* in his honor. In the later colonial period, the Scots-Irish supplied many anti-British leaders—Charles Thomson, Thomas McKean, Matthew Thornton, Joseph Reed, John Rutledge.

Second only to the English, the Scots of Scotland showed a willingness to leave the British Isles and come out to America. After the Peace of Utrecht of 1713 they settled in Acadia, which then became New Scotland, or Nova Scotia. In 1736, George Ogelthorpe established a company of warlike Highlanders at New Inverness as an outpost against the Spaniards. About 1729 a settlement of Highlanders began in the Cape Fear River region of North Carolina. Under the auspices of the Scottish governor, Gabriel Johnston, the Cape Fear settlement became the most numerous of the Highlander communities in America. Sir William Johnson settled yet another group of Highlanders on his Mohawk Valley lands in 1773.

Many Highland Scots left their native land for political reasons. After the Glorious Revolution of 1688–1689 they retained an allegiance to the Stuarts that was not only romantic but also courageous. To a degree this spirit was lessened by the Act of 1707, which united Scotland and England into the Kingdom of Great Britain and gave the Scots representation in the English Parliament. The accession of the Hanoverian house seven years later revived the spirit. Contrasted with the Stuarts, George I was not only a foreign prince, but a repulsive one. Under the Earl of Mar, the Highlanders rose against him in 1715. In 1745, in the name of the bonny Stuart prince, Charles Edward, they rose even more formidably against George II. The crown crushed both rebellions and then proceeded to break up the clans. Chiefs were replaced with lairds and the people were reduced to tenants. An act of Parliament banned the traditional highland garb. These repressive measures caused many Highlanders to emigrate.

Many more left Scotland in search of economic opportunity. A beautiful but not a bountiful land, the kingdom had reconciled itself to the loss of population. Dr. Johnson observed to Boswell that a Scot's finest prospect was the highroad to London. The shortage of labor in the colonies and the relatively high wages paid made the prospect of America even better. This natural exodus was augmented by large-scale kidnaping. Supplanted and impecunious chiefs, in cooperation with Aberdeen merchants, seized boys for sale as indentured servants in the labor-hungry market of America. Colonial newspapers regularly advertised "choice parcels" of these "kids." The Scots came in such numbers that by the census of 1790, they were counted at 260,000 or 8.3 per cent of the white population.

The Scots played important roles in the expansion and administration of the empire. John Forbes seized Fort Duquesne in 1758 and under his command fought Highlanders raised by Archibald Montgomery. Fraser's Highlanders fought with Amherst at Louisbourg, and were with Wolfe at Quebec. John Campbell, Earl of Loudon, commanded the forces in North America in 1756–1757. John Stuart was superintendent of Indian affairs for the southern district. Alexander Spotswood, Andrew Hamilton, William Burnet, Cadwallader Colden were colonial governors. Scots also distinguished themselves as educators. James Blair founded the College of William and Mary and was its president for life. William Smith of Aberdeen was the first provost of the University of Pennsylvania. In 1768, the Reverend John Witherspoon crossed the Atlantic to become in due course the most famous of the early presidents of Princeton.

Scots participated vigorously in the debate that led to American independence. Patrick Henry's father had emigrated to Virginia from Aberdeen. Witherspoon, together with Philip Livingston, William Hooper, George Ross, and James Wilson signed the Declaration of Independence. Wilson, a Pennsylvanian, was probably the outstanding lawyer of his day. Conspicuous in vindicating the declaration by force of arms were Generals Alexander MacDougall and Arthur St. Clair. John Paul Jones, his Welsh name notwithstanding, was born at Kirksbean in Kirkcudbrightshire and was the son of a Scottish gardener.

If the estimate is correct that the population of the colonies in 1660 stood at 85,000, the increase of the English during the succeeding one hundred and thirty years is almost miraculous. The census of 1790 counted them to the number of 1,933,416, or 60 per cent of the population. The increase was due partly to the fact that English immigration was proceeding steadily, although it attracted little attention. English people moving about in the empire must have been so frequent as to have been taken for granted. Sailors from the crews of warships, merchant ships, and fishing vessels often deserted. English men, women, and children arriving in large numbers as indentured servants would hardly have attracted the same attention as Germans of that class. In part, Georgia had been projected as an asylum, and after 1732 many debtors and other poor folks arrived there. An act of Parliament of 1718 authorized judges to commute a sentence of death for forgery, burglary, or robbery to transportation to the over-seas plantations. Thus among the English immigrants appeared many of the colorful characters of *The Beggar's Opera*. Engaging enough on the stage, they were less so when encountered on a dark street or on a lonely road at night. Colonial legislatures tried to stop this kind of immigration, but the Privy Council dis-allowed all such bills.

From the opposite end of the social scale came Englishmen with money to invest in land speculation or with real estate inter-ests to supervise from money already invested. A few came over to manage inherited properties. Sir Thomas Fairfax removed to Virginia as the agent of his cousin, Thomas, the sixth Baron Fairfax, the proprietor of 5,000,000 acres in the Northern Neck. In 1735, the noble lord himself came into the province and there settled down at Greenway Court as a wilderness peer.

The English colonial population depended less on peers than on pirates and less on either for its recruitment and growth than it did on its own natural increase. The seventeenth century Eng-lishmen who settled the land were a hardy and prolific breed. They raised big families. Scores of genealogies bear witness that one married couple would often have nine, ten, or a dozen chil-dren. The wife then dying would leave her mourning spouse to console himself by finding another mate with whom to start another family. Influenced by Scripture and prompted without it, the English in colonial America multiplied and replenished the earth. Nor did they encumber it with a mere mass of popula-tion. In spite of the accession of a few ne'er-do-well and criminal elements in the course of the eighteenth century, they remained a people of quality and spirit; and that quality and spirit they bequeathed along with their estates to their children.

By the eighteenth century, a large Negro minority existed alongside the English-European population. Dutch traders had brought the first Negroes to Virginia in 1619. The fact that the wealth of the colonies could be unlocked only by applying labor to the land and other natural resources put a gradually increasing premium on the importation of Negroes. Until the Stuart restora-tion the trade was largely in the hands of foreign factors and the number of Negro laborers grew slowly. After the Restoration, the government gave a high priority to the African trade and chartered the Royal African Companies to develop it. In the 1690's the slave trade began to grow at a very rapid rate.

Early seventeenth century English law did not recognize a slave status and as a result, the first colonial Negroes began their life in America as indentured servants. Negro indentures were more onerous than those of white servants. The terms of service were much longer and when contracts for life service were made there was little to distinguish such a status from slavery. In Virginia, the status of slave apparently evolved slowly. A law of 1662 referred indirectly to permanent service and in the same year the assembly ruled that a child born of a white father and a Negro mother was a slave. The question of the effect of the conversion of a Negro to Christianity caused some momentary twinge of conscience, but legislation passed declaring that the act had no effect on slave status. During the 1660's Maryland followed Virginia's example and permanent, hereditary slavery was legally established in the early plantation colonies. Slavery existed in the Carolinas from the beginning, provisions for its regulation being imbedded in Locke's Fundamental Constitutions. Georgia began with a prohibition against slavery that reflected the idealism of its founders, but the need for labor proved irresistible and Negroes were brought in early.

Slavery in early America was by no means an exclusively southern institution; it existed in every colony. The Dutch West India Company, deeply involved in the slave trade, brought in Negroes to labor on the Hudson Valley estates. The law of New York recognized slavery from the beginning. Slavery in New Jersey also antedated the English occupation and it was maintained there, especially in East Jersey. The enslavement of fellow humans posed an ethical dilemma for the Quakers, but slavery existed in Pennsylvania. The moral protest against the institution was first registered formally by the Quakertown Friends in 1688. The Pennsylvania assembly attempted to reduce the volume of the slave trade by taxing importation heavily and on one occasion it prohibited the trade. Privy Council disallowed the prohibition and also vetoed import taxes when they appeared to be heavy enough to really burden the trade. The effect of the Quaker conscience, plus the flood of British and European labor into the colony, limited the growth of slavery in Pennsylvania. New Englanders involved themselves deeply in the slave trade. Insofar as they needed to salve their consciences, the Yankee traders justified the horrors of the "middle passage" on the ground that the process brought heathen savages into contact with Christianity. By the early eighteenth century, the Africa-to-America trade was one lucrative leg of the triangular trades upon which New England prosperity was to a large degree based. Within New England, the conditions of slavery were less harsh than in other colonies. Religion and more sophisticated labor needs caused New Englanders to permit, even to encourage, rudimentary education for the Negroes. They shared some white institutions, for example civil marriage, and were permitted a greater degree of freedom of movement and association.

All colonies passed special legislation to control their Negro populations. The slave codes varied, their severity being related to the functions and concentration of Negroes in any given colony. The New England codes were most lenient, that of South Carolina most severe. The codes did have certain common features. All of them restricted the movement of slaves to a limited area, usually only in daylight and with the master's written permission. A Negro's crimes were punished with greater severity than a white person's, and even minor crimes might bring the death penalty after repeated convictions. The laws provided for cruel punishments: whipping, branding, mutilation, death by slow burning; and though such sentences were not limited to Negroes, they were more readily applied to them. The codes regulated the Negro's social activity and punished insolence. Usually the process within courts was modified when a Negro was on trial; for example, in South Carolina slaves were tried for serious crimes by two justices of the peace and a panel of four slaveholders. Regardless of the severity of the public law, the larger part of the disciplining of the slaves remained with the master. In the South, at least, the law permitted almost unlimited discretion, and if a slave was killed while being disciplined the law excused the master.

The severity of life generated many acts of Negro resistance and a permanent, pervasive fear of revolt. Most Negro violence consisted of murder or arson that reflected limited aims of revenge: the killing of a master or overseer or the burning of a plantation. Among the plantation colonies, South Carolina experienced the worst revolts. The Cato conspiracy of 1739 was the best organized and most serious. A group of slaves seized a quantity of guns and began a march toward the Florida border. Before they were stopped, about seventy-five persons, white and black, were killed. Formidable risings occurred in New York City and there the Negro's weapon was arson. A riot in 1712 led to twenty-one executions. In 1741, New Yorkers uncovered what appeared to be a major conspiracy involving poor whites and Negroes. In a single night, the city was the scene of numerous fires. An investigation produced evidence, largely in the form of rumor, that there was a plot to destroy the city. Against a frenzied background, over 175 people, mostly Negroes, were brought to trial. Thirty-one Negroes and four whites were hanged or burned before the terror passed.

The Eighteenth Century Colonial Mind

It is a generalization of long standing that religion dominated the seventeenth century and politics the eighteenth. Tested by the American experience of the six decades after 1700, the generalization fails. During those years when the American extended his mental activity beyond mundane matters, his thoughts and words were very apt to be about religion or be colored by it.

The clearly outstanding fact about the colonial religious experience between 1700 and 1760 was the extent to which it was diversified. The two great colonial churches of the seventeenth century had been the Congregational and Anglican. Here and there other denominations had established beachheads before 1700. After 1700, the flood of new sects and denominations flowed in. The diversification of religious life was a natural corollary to the dilution of the original English stock by the non-English island people and the new immigrants from Europe. Religious life was further fractured by the emotional and intellectual experiences provided by the Great Awakening and the Enlightenment.

Just as Philadelphia had been the great American gateway for the non-English people, so it was the main port of entry for the new religions. The Quakers came first and concentrated themselves in the eastern part of the province where they prospered and formed the dominant group in commerce and politics. Behind them came the German Pietists. Whether Mennonite, Moravian, Schwenkfelder, or Dunker, they formed separate settlements and followed a communal life based on their own interpretations of the Bible. Some of the Pietistic groups combined a primitive socialism with mysticism. The Ephrata community furnished an example. Its leader Johann Conrad Beissel, after a varied religious experience, founded the German Seventh Day Baptists, or Dunkers. He lined out the creed of the sect in *Ninety Nine Mystical Sentences, Published for The Schollars of Divine Wisdom.* Number thirteen advised the communicant "At Night-Time, when it is cloudy and dark, turn thy Eye continually towards Son-raising: for when the Sun raiseth, then all wild Beasts hide Themselves in their Holes." Many of these sects have resisted change and maintained their exclusive identity into this century.

The official religion of New Netherlands had been Dutch Reformed. Other European Calvinists, many from Germany, began arriving after 1700. Apparently those of German Reformed persuasion came as family units rather than as congregations. Gradually several tiny communities developed in Pennsylvania, at Falkner's Schwamp, Schip Bach, and Wit Marche. For a number of years John Boehm, though not an ordained pastor, served as their minister. Their desire to proceed in an orderly and churchly way caused them to seek the advice of the ministers of the Dutch Reformed Church at New York. They referred the Pennsylvania Germans to the Classis of Amsterdam. In direct and simple language the appeal to the Classis described the chaotic situation that the multiplicity of sects had produced. They were "living among all sorts of errorists," and further complained, "Good as the land is in which we live, equally sad and unfortunate is our condition respecting spiritual things." The Classis advised Boehm to seek ordination in New York and he complied. The incident of Boehm's ordination established a close and durable relationship between the American branches of the Dutch and German Reformed Churches.

Among the arriving Germans were many Lutherans, As population began to concentrate in settlements, a Lutheran congregation appeared here and there. For a time it appeared that their common heritage as Germans would draw them into some kind of United German-American church. Alarmed by the state of spiritual flux, orthodox Lutherans appealed to church authorities in Europe for assistance. Help came in the person of Henry Muhlenberg who became pastor of the church at Philadelphia in 1742. In a long career, Muhlenberg rose into the first rank of colonial ecclesiastical leaders. A strong preacher and effective administrator, he brought order and unity to the Lutheran Church. Muhlenberg called together the first synod of his church in 1748 and it adopted a common form of worship.

Even before the great influx of Scots and Scots-Irish, Presbyterian Churches had been established in many colonies. Many of them resulted from the labor of an Ulster missionary, Francis Makemie, whose mission took him from Barbados to Boston. In 1706, Makemie took a step toward Presbyterian union by forming the Presbytery of Philadelphia. In time it grew into the Synod of Philadelphia, which included the churches of Pennsylvania, Maryland, New Jersey, and New York. Early Scots migration to South Carolina led to the creation of a southern Presbytery, that of James Island. In 1729 the widely dispersed churches of New England combined as the Presbytery of Londonderry. A measure of doctrinal unity was given to the church by the passage of the Adopting Act by the Synod of Philadelphia. The act was a skillful compromise between liberal and conservative factions. The dispute centered on the specific question of whether or not a minister needed formally to subscribe to the Westminster Confession when called by a congregation. The act adopted the confession but made it possible for a minister to take exception to parts of it. The act prevented rigid uniformity and gave a considerable degree of freedom to individual Presbyteries. Thus the Presbyterian Church had been founded and given form before its membership was multiplied by the mass migrations of the middle eighteenth century.

The precise origins of the Baptist Church in America are confused by the chaotic religious life in early Rhode Island and the diversity of belief among those labeled Baptist. Several Baptist Churches did thrive in the Rhode Island towns, but elsewhere in New England they were continuously harassed by Congregational authorities. They persisted in spite of persecution and by the early eighteenth century were granted toleration. Most newly arriving Baptists sought out the proprietary colonies where policies of toleration prevailed. In both of the Carolinas, Baptist churches were established early. But for the Baptists, as for other dissenters, Pennsylvania became the main refuge. There, around 1707, they formed the Philadelphia Association. Confronted with a wide variety of opinion within the church, the association in 1742 adopted the essentially conservative and Calvinist London Confession.

The mere description of the many religions that were in America or came to America in the early eighteenth century may imply that the Americans of the time were deeply religious. The evidence leads to a contrary conclusion. Perhaps one must discount, in all ages, the complaints of the clergy that the men of their times are depraved. Yet it is clear that the general spiritual state, not only of America, but of England and Europe as well, was at a low level. Contemporary sermons and pamphlets emphasize the backsliding, immoral, un-Christian, depraved state of society. A reiterated theme was that the faith and purpose of the fathers had been forgotten. Though several colonies had established churches, the majority of the people belonged to no church. The times were ripe for new religious experiences and wholesale conversions.

Between 1720 and 1750 the colonies experienced a series of explosive religious revivals that together have been called the Great Awakening. Though the revivals varied with the personalities of the individual evangelists, they had many things in common. Most of the revival preachers were itinerants, and as such they threatened the stability of established congregations. All of them demanded direct evidence of an individual's experience of conversion. Powerful and emotional orators, they created a psychological atmosphere in which such evidence, real or fancied, came readily enough. The revival preachers were out to save souls and a common man's soul weighed as heavily in the final balance as the soul of the aristocrat. For the first time in the American experience, a potent religious appeal was made to all of the people. The Great Awakening was the first mass democratic experience of the American people and like all such experiences it was convulsive.

The revivals may be described on a regional basis, or as aspects of denominational development, or biographically. Viewing the revivals as a whole, George Whitefield stands out as the most influential man. America first felt his fervor in the summer of 1739, and his several tours carried his message to all colonial sections and to most colonial sects. Yet before Whitefield came from England, the Middle Colonies and New England had experienced home-grown revivals. The first revival was preached in the Dutch Reformed parishes of New Jersey by Theodore J. Frelinghuysen in the early 1720's. A second revival and one with broader influence emanated from the Scots-Irish Presbyterians. The American nursery of Presbyterian evangelism was the Log College, which had been founded by William Tennent, at Neshaminy, Pennsylvania. The Log College became an evangelical seminary that produced the pastors who intensified the revival started by Frelinghuysen and provided "New Light" ministers for the Scots-Irish as they swept into the Valley of Virginia.

The quickening spirit of revival came to New England in the early 1730's and its agent was Jonathan Edwards. Amazingly precocious as a child, Edwards built a towering intellect on the base of his huge mental capacity. In his *Personal Narrative*, Edwards described how difficult it had been for him to accept "God's sovereignty" as expressed in the Calvinist doctrine of predestination. While still a youth he experienced what he described as "a calm sweet abstraction of soul from all the concerns of this world." In his mind the old Puritan covenant of grace became a vividly horrible hell from which man was saved by the majesty and grace of God. And this he preached, producing in the process the best known of all revivalist sermons, *Sinners in The Hands of An Angry God*. Taking as his text Deuteronomy 32:35, "Their foot shall slide in due time," he carried his theme with forceful rhetoric and rich imagery. "That world of misery, that lake of burning brimstone, is extended abroad under you. There is the dreadful pit of the glowing flames of the wrath of God; there is hell's wide gaping mouth open; and you have nothing to stand upon, nor anything to take hold of; there is nothing between you and hell but air; it is only the power and mere pleasure of God that holds you up." But this is small comfort, for "The God that holds you over the pit of hell, much as one holds a spider, or some lothsome insect over the fire, abhors you and is dreadfully provoked." Then the preacher brought the imminence of infinite catastrophe home to the listener and urged them to join the multitudes flocking to Christ.

Southern colonists experienced a series of revivals between 1740 and 1770. The first Scots-Irish Presbyterians to settle in Virginia had been orthodox, but the scattered nature of their communities made regular church life difficult. Whitefield preached in Virginia in 1739 and after that the revival among the Presbyterians began. In the face of opposition from conservative Presbyterians, the Anglican establishment and the government of Virginia, young Samuel Davies established himself as the leader of the "New Light" Presbyterians. From a base in Hanover, he preached effectively along an extended circuit in neighboring counties until called to be president of the College of New Jersey (Princeton). The revivals came to a fervid extreme among the Separate Baptists, especially in North Carolina. Stripped of form, the religious experience became pure emotion. Most of the Separate Baptist preachers were uneducated laymen. They preached violently to rough, illiterate, largely lower-class congregations. The results were equally violent, as stomping, shouting, gesticulating converts came forth to accept baptism.

In the beginning most ministers welcomed the revivals as a quickening of spiritual sense. Before long the crude emotionalism aroused by the new preachers alienated many. Foremost among the critics was Charles Chauncey of Boston's First Church. He used both his pulpit and the press to attack and ridicule the "Enthusiasts." In a published letter to an Edinburgh minister he described the evangelists: "They place their Religion so much in the *Heat* and *Fervour* of their *Passions*, that they too much neglect their *Reason* and *Judgment* . . ." They preached with the "*greatest Vehemence.*"

> If this has its intended Effect upon *one* or *two weak Women*, the Shrieks catch from one to Another 'till a great Part of the Congregation is affected: and some are in the Thought, that it may be too common for those *Zealous* in *the new Way to cry out themselves*, on purpose to move others, and bring forward *a general Scream. Visions* now become common, and *Trances* also, the

Subjects of which were in their own Conceit transported from Earth to Heaven, where they saw and heard most glorious things; conversed with *Christ* and *Holy Angels*; had opened to them the *Book of Life*, and were permitted to read the names of persons there, and the like.[1]

Many evangelists, not content to deliver a positive message, turned to sharp criticism. Whitefield described Harvard and Yale as being covered with "a darkness that can be felt." The revivalists preached in any church open to them and sometimes openly attacked the host minister as unregenerate. Gilbert Tennent indicted all of the clergy who opposed the revivals in a sermon entitled *The Danger of an Unconverted Ministry*. Describing them as "Old-Pharisee-Teachers," he said "They have not the Courage, or Honesty, to thrust the Nail of Terror into sleeping Souls." Such invective, when combined with inevitable doctrinal differences, drove wedges into churches. Frelinghuysen's preaching split the Dutch Reformed Church. Whitefield, Edwards, and others produced complex fissures in New England Congregationalism. The revival among the Presbyterians divided them into Old Side and New Light congregations. Evangelism widened the breach between Regular and Separatist Baptists.

Attempts to measure the effect of the Great Awakening by counting the persons converted fail. That the conversions were numerous there can be no doubt; that they were durable is less clear. One result of the revivals is apparent. By splitting the churches they accelerated the widening diversity of faiths that the migrations of new peoples had started. Though several colonies attempted to restrain the movement towards diversity and maintain policies of uniformity, in the end all yielded and practical religious toleration prevailed. Legal toleration had come to England with the passage of the Toleration Act of 1689. The question whether or not the law extended to the colonies was agitated on several occasions. It figured in the case of Francis Makemie, whom Lord Cornbury of New York had charged with preaching without a license. Though Makemie claimed that the

1. *A Letter from a Gentleman in Boston to Mr. George Wishart, One of the Ministers of Edinburgh, Concerning the State of Religion in New-England* (Edinburgh, 1742).

law was in force, his counsel won an acquittal by basing his defense on a New York statute. Church authorities in Virginia attempted to root out the New Light Presbyterians by arguing that the Toleration Act did not extend to them. Evangelist Samuel Davies successfully contested this view and ultimately got from the governor a promise that the act did extend to the New Lights. The Great Awakening accelerated the trend toward religious freedom.

The revivals agitated men's emotions, derogated the worth of the individual, and focused attention on salvation and life after death. As the Great Awakening occurred, the contrary force of the Enlightenment came to America emphasizing reason, the worth of the individual, and the problems of this world. The new rationalism produced a variety of results in religion. In the mid-eighteenth century it led only a very few through to Deism. Benjamin Franklin is a good example. Raised a Presbyterian, he found the sermons to be "either polemic arguments, or explications of the peculiar doctrines of our sect, and were all to me very dry, uninteresting, and unedifying . . ." In 1728, he formulated a personal creed, "Articles of Belief and Acts of Religion." He stated his first principle; "I believe there is one supreme, most perfect Being, Author of and Father of the Gods themselves."[2] He thought the many Gods might or might not be immortal. Franklin chose to praise and adore "that particular wise and good God, who is the author of our System." He proposed to pay that God homage by leading a virtuous, and thus a happy, life.

More significant than the creation of an occasional deist was the impact of the Enlightenment on the thought of leading ministers. Among the English philosophers, Sir Isaac Newton and John Locke had the greatest influence in America. Newton's *Principia* and *Optics* explained natural phenomena as the working of rational and orderly rules. In the *Essay Concerning Human Understanding*, Locke rejected the idea of innate or inborn characteristics and explained the development of intelligence as a series of reactions to perceptions of the environment. In his *Second Treatise of Civil Government*, Locke based a theory of gov-

2. H. Shelton Smith, Robert T. Handy, and Lefferts A. Loetscher (eds.), *American Christianity, An Historical Interpretation* (New York: Charles Scribner's Sons, 1960), I, 395.

ernment on natural rights. Such ideas permeated America slowly. Some of them became part of the mental equipment of ministers who retained an orthodox Calvinist theology. Cotton Mather furnishes an example. Late in life he wrote *Manuductio ad Ministerium* (Advice to Young Ministers). The first part of the book is standard Calvinism. In places it is even evangelical, as, for instance, where he urges the young men to the "Early Anticipation of Mortality." Yet later in the book he advocated the study of natural or experimental philosophy and described Newton as "*our Perpetual Dictator.*" Another orthodox Calvinist, John Wise of Ipswich, defended the decentralized policy of the Congregational Churches in *A Vindication of the Government of New England Churches.* The remarkable thing about his argument is that he based it primarily on natural right rather than on theological precedents. Mather and Wise represent Congregationalism at a time of transition and their works show the continuing capacity of Puritanism to assimilate new ideas.

In the mid-eighteenth century, Enlightenment ideas led some of the Congregational ministers to a more liberal theology. Outstanding among them were Charles Chauncey and Jonathan Mayhew. Chauncey stripped emotion from his sermons and preached in a dispassionate and rational manner. Mayhew was a forceful preacher who, when the occasion demanded, used his pulpit to apply Enlightenment ideas to current problems. In 1750 he preached his most famous sermon, a *Discourse Concerning Unlimited Submission.* He argued that a people owed no obedience to a bad king because neither divine right nor the doctrine of passive obedience was founded in human reason. Though Mayhew and Chauncey differed in many particulars, they came to stand for certain basic ideas. For them the work of the experimental scientists revealed an orderly world that was the work of a rational God. They rejected the doctrine of absolute predestination and, though recognizing God's sovereignity in the matter of salvation, believed that the choices of an individual between good and evil did affect his fate. In the pattern of their thought the individual regained dignity and God became beneficent. Mayhew and Chauncey helped prepare the way for humanitarianism and Unitarianism.

Though the churches continued to influence schools, the

primary purpose of colonial education was to maintain social standards and transmit those standards to the younger generations. The colonists held to this purpose in the face of the constant and real danger that a new environment would overcome the traditional society. The word *education* immediately suggests a school. Yet anyone who imagines the majority of colonial children seated at desks in school buildings is wide of the mark. The universal agency of instruction was the family, and within it the boy learned the basic skills of his father. If possible the child learned to read at home or, at the minimum level, he put to memory simple prayers and articles of faith of the family's church. That the family should have been responsible for such rudimentary education seems natural enough. But colonial governments did not leave the obligation on a casual basis. Beginning with the seventeenth-century Massachusetts statutes, public authorities made family responsibility for moral and practical teaching a matter of enforceable law.

The assumption that the family would provide education was not limited to New England. In Virginia, for example, public authority intervened only when the family unit failed to educate or when the family simply did not exist. Compulsory legislation in Virginia dealt with the children of the poor, illegitimate children, orphans, and mulatto children born of white mothers. Far from being altruistic, the laws aimed to prevent such distressed children from becoming charges against tax revenues. Virginia law ordered such children to be bound by indentures as apprentices under the jurisdiction of the justices of the peace. The indentures put the master *in loco parentis* and required him to feed and clothe the apprentice, to raise him up in a Christian manner, to teach the youth his trade, and in many cases to teach him to read and write. The arrangement continued until the apprentices reached their majority, eighteen years of age for girls, twenty-one years for boys, and as old as thirty-one years for mulattos. There is evidence that the courts reviewed how well the master discharged his duties. In one case a tailor was fined for continuously using his apprentice as a manual laborer. All colonies used the apprentice system which, together with the family, was the chief agency of instruction in colonial America.

During the eighteenth century, education beyond the family

showed great diversity. Massachusetts and Connecticut continued to maintain more and better schools than other colonies. Among the first settlers there had been a large number of college graduates. They laid a broad foundation for public education with legislation that was renewed regularly. The Puritans built compact communities on the political base of the township. The statutes assigned responsibility for education to the towns and in virtually all of them elementary schools were established. As the two Puritan colonies expanded to the west, new townships found it difficult to finance schools. There the moving schools came into being, with teachers spending a part of the year in several villages. The early laws had required the more populous towns to maintain grammar schools, and though not all did, such secondary schools were numerous and, in some instances, of high quality.

The failure of the southern colonies to establish school systems points up several generalizations about colonial education. Everywhere there was a direct ratio between density of population and availability and quality of schools. Plantation agriculture dispersed the population widely over large areas of land, thus making the establishment of schools difficult. The intellectual characteristics of a dominant religion also affected the schools. In the South, the Anglican Church proved not to be a vigorous advocate of education. The relationship between schools and religion is further illustrated by the experience of newly arriving immigrants. Several such groups moved onto the frontiers where one would not expect education to be emphasized. Wherever the Baptists went it was not emphasized, but Moravians and Presbyterians did establish good schools in North Carolina and western Virginia. In addition to considerations of population and religion, colonial experience proved it to be difficult to generate interest in education unless at least a substantial minority of a community is already educated. In sharp contrast to early New England, few southern settlers were educated. Hugh Jones, an Anglican clergyman, described Virginians as intelligent and alert. Their chief concern was their plantations, and they wanted education to be brief, to the point, and practical. Lacking a system of education the planters of means engaged tutors, sometimes from the North, but more often from among the indentured servants. Some boys went north to school and a few were sent to England. Several endowed schools were established, but they did not prosper.

In the colonial cities a great variety of schools developed. With the exception of New York, there were good grammar schools in each of the seaboard cities. Private schools reflected the wide-ranging demand for practical and fashionable education. Such schools usually consisted of a single teacher offering instruction in one subject. Whether the interest was in fencing, navigation, bookkeeping, French, or dancing, instruction was available. Most common were writing schools, the masters of which guaranteed that their particular method would produce results in a short time. Many city schools accepted boarders from the country, and "finishing schools" for young ladies operated in several cities. The concentration of apprentices in the cities made it feasible to create schools in which the masters could meet their obligations to teach them to read and write. Night schools came into being to serve this need. The Society for the Propagation of the Gospel in Foreign Parts established charity schools for poor children and reading schools for free Negroes.

Before 1760 six colleges had been founded. Virginians had shown sporadic interest in a college, but nothing happened until an Anglican Commissary, James Blair, made a sustained effort that led to the chartering of William and Mary in 1693. Connecticut had supported Harvard College from its early days and had sent its sons to be educated there. The desire to have its own college was strengthened by concern about Harvard's growing liberalism. Local pride and orthodox Puritanism led to the creation of the Collegiate School at Saybrook in 1701. Fifteen years later the school moved to New Haven and changed its name to honor an English benefactor, Elihu Yale. Princeton was a product of the dispute between Old Side and New Light Presbyterians in the Middle Colonies. The Old Sides preferred and even required that their ministers have degrees from European universities. The New Light also wanted an educated ministry, but thought that they could be trained as well or better in colonial schools. William Tennent founded the first New Light school, the Log College. In 1746 this branch of the church founded the College of New Jersey, which became Princeton. King's College (Columbia) was chartered in 1754 after a bitter fight between the DeLanceys and William Livingston over the question of the religious affiliation of the college. It began as a nominally Anglican institution. The rapid growth of Philadelphia made it a natural seat for a college. In two pamphlets written in 1749 and 1751, Benjamin Franklin drew attention to the need. The first step was taken in 1751 with the opening of an Academy. Four years later the Penns issued a charter for the College of Philadelphia and on that base the University of Pennsylvania was built.

Though in many ways the colonial colleges were constructed closely after English models, they differed in one important respect. The English and European colleges were communities of self-governing scholars; the American colleges were governed by lay boards of trustees which employed the faculty and administration. Professors Hofstadter and Metzger have analyzed the cause and effect of external government of colonial colleges.[3] The autonomy of European scholars was rooted in the principles of the medieval guilds and the privileges of the Roman Catholic clergy. Most Protestants resented clerical privilege. The Calvinists, especially, admitted lay members to the government of their churches. It was natural that they should apply the same principle to the government of their colleges. The colonial colleges were created under difficult circumstances by community effort. Having invested its time and resources, the community controlled the institutions. Because the colleges were dependent upon the community for support, they were not likely to be critical of their governing boards. A further reason for lay government was that the faculties were weak. Most instruction was given by young tutors who regarded it as temporary work to be done while they prepared themselves for the ministry. The one powerful figure at the college was the president. In a very direct way, he ran the institution and stood responsible for its relations with the community.

Though the colleges continued to center study on classical subjects, the judgment that "neither in basic philosophy, method nor content did the American educational system make any effec-

3. Richard Hofstadter and Walter P. Metzger, *The Development of Academic Freedom in the United States* (New York: Columbia University Press, 1955), pp. 114–151.

tive advances during the hundred years before the Revolution,"[4] is exaggerated. Those responsible for collegiate studies never assumed that education was limited to required subjects. In his advice to college students, Cotton Mather recommended wide reading in poetry, natural or experimental philosophy, mathematics, astronomy, geography, and ancient and modern history. Though the colleges remained denominational, there is much evidence that they were becoming more secular as the eighteenth century advanced. Whatever the sectarian affiliation, a competition for students and a need to attract funds caused all colleges to adopt policies of freedom relative to the students' religion. The religious parts of the curriculum became less narrow and doctrinaire. Harvard set the pace, beginning in 1708 with the presidency of John Leverett. Significantly Leverett was not a minister, and Professor Morison wrote of him that he "founded the liberal tradition of Harvard University." The tenure of two professors of divinity, the Edward Wiggelsworths, father and son, stretched from 1722 to 1794. Neither man was dogmatic and both presented various sides of knotty theological arguments in an objective manner. The rigid orthodoxy of Yale hardened under the presidency of Thomas Clap, but yielded after 1746 to a spirit of freer inquiry under Ezra Stiles. William and Mary was Anglican and latitudinarian from the beginning. Of the colonial colleges founded later, King's College had a slight Anglican connection and the College of Philadelphia was nonsectarian.

The most significant additions to the curriculum during the eighteenth century were science and mathematics. A Harvard tutor, Thomas Robie, began as early as 1708 to offer work in physics and astronomy. In 1728 Thomas Hollis endowed a chair of mathematics and natural philosophy. A distinguished scientist, John Winthrop, became its second incumbent. In Philadelphia, Provost William Smith installed a curriculum with a substantial scientific content. Other subjects were taught on a private basis with the sanction of the college—for example, French at Harvard. Either formally or informally, the political theories of the Enlightenment were taught. Harvard master's degree candidates argued in the affirmative the question, "Does civil government

4. Leonard W. Labaree, *Conservatism in Early American History* (Ithaca: Cornell University Press, 1959), p. 91.

originate from compact?" five times between 1743 and 1763. The list of these *Quaestiones* remain as evidence of the breadth of interest among the academics. Between 1700 and 1760 religious questions continued to appear with greatest frequency. During those six decades 124 candidates discussed questions relating to the Scriptures, to church and theology. Another forty-nine chose topics in philosophy and ethics that could be distinguished quite clearly from theology. Six questions related to law and thirty-seven to politics and economics. The scholars concerned themselves, among many other things, with paper money, the relative value of commerce and agriculture, the principles of mercantilism, the nature of royal power, the efficacy of capital punishment, the right of resistance to unjust government. Perhaps the man was a wit who argued negatively to the question, "Would the advice of Paul to Timothy 'to use a little wine' bring him under the power of the tavern-keepers?" Though the eleven questions relating to science contained an affirmative approach to alchemy, others dealt with electricity, theories of light, astronomy, and physics. The thirty-three questions in the category of medicine and physiology dealt for the most part with then current theories and practices. One scholar, however, chose to argue that Adam did not have an umbilical cord.

Chapter 11

The Form
and Process of
Colonial Politics

Political Principles

*F*rom their own practice, from precedent and philosophy, the colonists drew their most deeply held political belief, that of the supremacy of law. The idea and definition of a higher law came from many sources: theology, classical philosophy, English history, the common law, and the scientific and political ideas of the Enlightenment.

The Bible enshrines the concept of a higher, divine law, and Christian churches have made such law the base of their theology and polity. The learned clergy of New England applied the doctrine of a supreme law, not only to their churches, but directly and forcefully to civil government and politics. Though in their forays into the realm of natural law they used the Bible as their ultimate authority, they also drew heavily on Cicero, Pufendorf, Locke, and the examples of English history. Though the New England ministers would occasionally use the pulpit on Sunday for political purposes, they were given a more obvious opportunity to speak about government in the annual election sermons. In yet another area, the acrimonious disputes over the true nature of church government produced a literature that used both lay and theological sources in the course of argument. The influence of the literature produced by the New England clergy extended far beyond the boundaries of Connecticut and Massachusetts. The election sermons were published and the polemics about church government often appeared as pamphlets. In sermon and pamphlet the ministers argued that the law of God and the law of nature were the same; they held that all just government had its origins in covenant, compact, or contract, through which the people expressed the ultimate sovereignty of God; they announced that governments that violated the natural law or its specific instrument, the covenant, should be resisted.

The multiple equation of the law of God with the law of nature and of those laws with man's rational being and true liberty was a constantly reiterated theme. "God having made Man a Rational Creature, hath (as it were) Twisted Law into the very Frame & Constitution of his Soul," said Timothy Cutler in his election sermon of 1717. Nathaniel Appleton described law as "founded upon the Nature and Relation of Things . . . Immovable as the Mountains and Immutable as God himself!" John Barnard put it most succinctly, "This Voice of Nature is the Voice of God. Thus 'tis that *vox populi est vox Dei.*"

The idea of a covenant or contract as the foundation of any organized society had deep Puritan roots. Early in the eighteenth century, John Wise of Ipswich lined out the idea. Wise had been involved in the bitter controversy that swirled around the issue of centralized authority in the Congregational churches. In a famous pamphlet, *A Vindication of New-England Churches*, Wise argued the case for the covenant-based, decentralized local church. In startling fashion he based his argument primarily on political philosophy rather than theology. At the start, he announced that "I shall disclose several principles of natural knowledge; plainly discovering the law of nature . . . and in this essay I shall principally take baron *Pufendorf* as my chief guide and spokesman." Describing the origins of government, Wise envisioned men in a state of nature "all naturally free and equal." In creating government, they voluntarily and mutually covenant together "to bring themselves into a politick body." They then decide on a form of government and enter into further covenants that describe the duties and powers of those who are to govern.

The right to resist unjust government flows naturally enough from concepts of higher law. Yet the ministers rarely stated a right of direct resistance. They could, and did, point to the examples of Charles I and James II and argue that by their actions against the higher law those kings became "traytors and rebels." But to glory in past revolutions was one matter; to advocate, even theoretically, present or future revolts was quite another. As social conservatives they had no desire to preach a doctrine that might be used to justify a movement of levelers. What was one to do then if a government violated the constitution? The most common advice was to ignore the government and obey the law of God. Such a passive view was unacceptable to Jonathan Mayhew. In *A Discourse Concerning Unlimited Submission and Nonresistance to the Higher Powers*, he defended the right of violent resistance. If a king violated the fundamental law "to resist the prince, even to dethroning him, is not criminal, but a reasonable way of vindicating their liberties and just rights . . ." Concluding, Mayhew urged his parishioners "to be *free* and to be *loyal*." He left them with the "standing *memento* that *Britons* will not be *slaves* . . ."

Lawyers and publicists, without seeking far, found a controlling concept of higher law imbedded in the common law. The great legal commentators—Bracton, John Fortescue, Mathew Hale, and Edward Coke—showed them the way. Coke had the greatest influence. His opinions, especially in Bonham's Case and Calvin's Case, and *The Institutes* provided the precepts, and his bold advocacy of the superiority of the common law against the pretensions of James I and Charles I provided the example. From the thorny pages of *The Institutes* the attorneys learned much of their law. In the process they learned that *lex* was *rex* rather than the other way around. They learned especially the significance of Magna Carta. According to Coke, the charter was much more than a contract between John and the barons. He emphasized the twenty-ninth article, which could be read to mean that Englishmen's rights could only be abridged by a due process of law. Under the mantle of due process, Coke included the great procedural rights—for example, jury trial and freedom from all except legislative taxation. Coke noted the many times that Parliament had re-enacted Magna Carta and concluded that its principles permeated and controlled ordinary law.

For the colonist, whether he was objecting to royal, proprietary, or parliamentary authority, it was a good thing to be able to include in the arsenal of his argument a document so ancient and honored as Magna Carta. They claimed that the charter, together with the common law and the basic statutes of Parliament, had crossed the ocean with them. This was a moot point, one denied by most English lawyers. This issue came into sharp focus in Maryland in the context of disputes between the Calvert governors and the people. The elder Daniel Dulany became the advocate who claimed the common law for Americans. In a series of maneuvers Dulany and the Maryland assembly attempted to limit the proprietors and their judges by arguing that the common and statute law of England was in force in the colony. In one crisis, the law committee of the assembly compiled a catalog of precedents showing that English law had been used in the province. Dulany attached this gloss: "It would be a great absurdity to advance that we are entitled to all the Rights and Liberties of British Subjects and that we Can't have the Benefits of the Laws by which those Rights and Liberties are Reserved." In 1728, Dulany stated his views in the pamphlet, *The Rights of the Inhabitants of Maryland to the Benefit of the English Laws.*

The colonists drew many precedents for the supremacy of law from seventeenth century English history. The appeal was natural because America had been settled to a large degree by persons who had suffered or believed they were about to suffer at the hands of the Stuart kings. Parliament's resistance to those kings had furnished many dramatic incidents and two climactic events, the execution of Charles I and the overthrow of James II. The colonists viewed the latter event as "that late happy revolution." The execution of Charles provided the example of the ultimate consequences of a royal attempt to rule above the law, and colonial orators often made his ghost walk. The occasion for Jonathan Mayhew's polemic, *A Discourse Concerning Unlimited Submission,* was the celebration of the centennial of

Charles's execution. Mayhew described resistance to Charles as "a most righteous and glorious stand made in defense of the natural and legal rights of the people." He portrayed Charles as "really a man black with guilt and *laden with iniquity!*" Even in the act of praising good kings, Americans always made it clear that they were ultimately regicides. The wages for violating the higher law was death.

Contemporary and ancient philosophy fortified the colonists' commitment to a higher law. Sir Isaac Newton's idea of a physical universe regulated by natural laws and John Locke's justification of the Glorious Revolution had great influence. Yet it would be wrong to overemphasize that influence because the philosophical sources of colonial political thought were very diversified. The educated knew Cicero and from *De Legibis* and *De Republica* learned that "True Law is right reason, harmonious with nature, diffused among all, constant, eternal." But the modern philosophers had the greater effect.

By the eighteenth century, the idea of a political state based on and consistent with natural law contained two essential common denominators: that without government men lived in a state of nature and that governments were created by covenants, compacts, or contracts that individuals entered into voluntarily. These ideas came in upon the colonists from many directions. Samuel Pufendorf, in *The Law of Nature and of Nations*, made such concepts central to his argument. In *The Principles of Natural Law*, the Italian-Swiss Jean-Jacques Burlamqui made a concise and forceful equation between natural law and liberty. Educated colonists, especially the lawyers, read these books. They also read Hooker, Harrington, Hoadly, Grotius, Beccaria. Thus John Locke's *Second Treatise of Civil Government* appeared as part of a generally accepted pattern of ideas. Locke had great influence in the colonies because he had written in the context of a famous event in English history, because his work had become a Whig canon and had enjoyed great vogue in England, and because he emphasized the protection of property rights.

Mid-eighteenth century colonists agreed fairly well on the form of government that was most consistent with natural law. They thought about forms of government as alternatives among the classical forms of absolute monarchy, aristocracy, or democracy. They rejected the first and last out of hand; absolute monarchy and democracy would inevitably degenerate into tyranny. They believed in good kings and limited monarchy, more specifically, in mixed government. In the *Spirit of the Laws*, Baron Montesquieu made the most thorough statement of mixed· government with its doctrines of separation of powers and checks and balances. But Montesquieu's work had its greatest influence during the Revolution when the states and the nation made their constitutions.

A seventeenth century English philosopher, James Harrington, had advanced a pattern of mixed government in *Oceana*. Because Harrington wrote during the Civil Wars, he assigned the executive function to a magistrate rather than to a king. The aristocracy originated positive law and the people approved or rejected it. Though Harrington had a fairly large number of readers in the colonies, their view of mixed government differed substantially from his. For them, political society consisted of three estates: Royalty was one estate, exercising its public authority through an hereditary king; a bicameral legislature accommodated the interests of the second and third estates, the aristocracy and the people. Permeating and limiting all were independent judges, sworn to interpret the law and render judgment impartially. Such a system well served the root eighteenth-century principle that government should preserve and protect liberty and property. When property was the issue—for example, in a question of taxes—compromise was essential between the houses of the legislature. Neither would permit legislation that would destroy its own interest. Presumably both would combine to block a royal invasion of property rights. Each estate would be jealous of its liberty and would prevent subversion by jealously watching the activity of the other estates.

The man most responsible for spreading this highly practical view of mixed government has been little honored and barely remembered. Henry St. John, Lord Bolingbroke, had stood high in the councils of Queen Anne. He had been anti-Hanoverian and fled the country to support the Stuart pretender at the accession of George I. Though he later returned to England, he spent a large part of his life in France. Bolingbroke was a prolific writer, the bulk of his work consisting of deistic philosophy and extended comments on politics. Two of his works, *The Idea of a Patriot King* and *A Dissertation upon Parties*, influenced the men who would later make the Revolution and build the republic. Both John Adams and Thomas Jefferson left clear evidence of their close reading of his works. Bolingbroke argued for limited monarchy and mixed government. Adams' marginal notes in *A Dissertation Upon Parties* indicate how positively he responded to Bolingbroke's ideas. Democracies and absolute monarchies "do not degenerate into tyranny, they are tyranny in their very institution." But the English constitution admitted the three estates to government, and it "is by this mixture of monarchical, aristocratical, and democratical power, blended together in one system, and by these three estates balancing one another, that our free constitution of government hath been preserved so long inviolate."

Colony Government and Politics

Colonial governments were not organized into neat compartments of executive, judicial, and legislative authority. By the eighteenth century all colonial governors, except in Rhode Island and Connecticut, were appointed. Maryland and Pennsylvania retained proprietary governors; the remaining nine colonies had royal agents as governors. Whether royal or proprietary, the governors had much in common. Both represented an external authority much resented by the colonists. The governor derived his powers from his commission, which, according to Thomas Pownall, who was a colonial governor, "becomes the known, established constitution of that province . . . whose laws, courts, and whole frame of legislature and judicature, are founded on it: It is the charter of that province." Under the commission the governor exercised vice-regal powers: as the source of justice he could create courts and appoint judges; with his council and assembly he could make law; as the executive he appointed officials and enforced whatever English law applied to the dominion as well as the laws made in the colony.

The story of the governors' attempts to use their powers is one of primary frustration. As an executive office the governor had powers that related to all parts of the establishment: civil, military, naval, and religious. The law enforcement and fiscal officers—the attorney general and sheriffs, the auditor general and collectors of the quit rents—were responsible to him. An extensive patronage should have given the governor considerable power, and sometimes it did. But in practice, the power inherent in the control of the civil list was worn away. Often the king or proprietor insisted that he should appoint the chief officers. In most of his actions, including many appointments, the governor needed to have the consent of his council. The assembly also limited his executive power. Though the governor commanded the militia and held a commission as vice admiral, the assembly limited his freedom because they passed the militia law and controlled finances. Among his many other duties, the governor's instructions ordered him to maintain high standards in the Anglican church, but in practice he had little ecclesiastical authority because the vestries and parishes appointed their own ministers. With rare exceptions, the governors failed either to be effective agents for the English government or forceful executive agents for the colonies.

Though all branches of government shared the judicial function, English royal and feudal precedent made the governor the source of justice. His commission gave him the power to "erect, constitute and establish" courts and to appoint the judges and justices. In practice, the assemblies created the ordinary system of colonial courts. The governor did retain the special jurisdictions of chancery and vice admiralty and, with his council, was the supreme court. In the earlier stages of colonization this court had broad original jurisdiction, but in time the high court heard few first instance criminal cases and limited its civil jurisdiction to cases involving substantial sums. As the highest court of appeals on the American side of the Atlantic, the governor and council heard those cases that would have been decided finally by the three common law courts at Westminster.

The governor's commission gave him "full power and authority to make, constitute and ordain laws" with the consent of the council and assembly. By the eighteenth century, no governor exercised the legislative power implicit in this statement. He could not initiate legislation. He could sit with the council but could not vote. His legislative power was limited to the veto and the right to summon, prorogue, and dissolve the assembly. All of the colonies except Pennsylvania developed bicameral legislatures. The council formed the upper house and tended to be a conservative body with a stable membership. In all colonies except Massachusetts and the corporate colonies, the king or proprietor appointed the councilors upon the recommendation of the governors. In the council the external and local interest were both represented and the council often held the balance of power between the governor and assembly.

Every colony in British North America had an elected assembly. These legislatures shaped themselves after the obvious model of the House of Commons, adopting parliamentary forms of organization and procedure. They claimed the full privileges of Commons and jealously guarded those rights against intrusions by the governors and the population at large.* Clearly the assemblies were the agencies of government within which the interests of the colonists were represented and where colony policy was defined. Much less clear is the answer to the question of whose interests were represented within the assemblies. Historians have studied the colonial suffrage for years and today are disagreed as to how democratic the colonial assemblies were. All colonies required the voter to be possessed of property, the English forty-shilling freehold or an equivalent appearing as the most common standard. Detailed studies of Massachusetts and Virginia have indicated that property was so widely distributed that 80 to 95 per cent of the white adult population had the right to vote. From these facts it has been concluded that "middle class democracy," characterized by popular participation in politics and considerable social mobility, prevailed in the colonies.

Any broad generalization about colonial politics is hazardous, for the outstanding fact about those politics was diversity. Modern terminology is misleading when applied to early American politics. The very concept of party was negative, implying a group of persons working for their own interest and against the common welfare. In describing such groups, the colonists used the word *faction*. The area of action for the provincial governments was limited and this restricted the range of politics. The

* The claim of privilege is dealt with in Chapter 12.

colonial governments left virtually the whole problem of social welfare to be solved by private agencies or local government. The very fact that they were colonial governments further restricted the areas within which basic political decisions might be made. The colony might be deeply divided about matters of defense, but the central government made the ultimate decisions about war and peace and conducted external relations. In many other fields of government action such as land disposal, currency policy, and economic regulation, the colonial politicians found room for dispute; but even as they argued, they did so under the eye of a central government that had an interest in the issues and might easily negate the policy of a successful party.

The older historians of the colonies interpreted political action as an irresistible march toward democracy. By so placing their emphasis, they concentrated on the political contests between the colonists and the external authority of crown, Parliament, and the proprietors. In this view, the colonies represented democracy; the external authorities stood for tyranny. Though this reading of colonial politics was oversimplified, the largest part of political controversy did involve the external authority and colonial attempts to limit it. Other interpretations of colonial politics have emphasized class or sectional conflict. The economically distressed or newly arrived religious groups moved onto the frontier, where, as debtors, they demanded cheap money, easy access to land, a tough Indian policy, and a tax structure that would fall upon wealth. The politics of Pennsylvania and New York have been presented as a struggle between a privileged elite and unfranchised masses. Though this view does not square with what is known about the widespread right to vote, class issues did agitate politics. For example, the chronically short money supply provided a persistent political issue. The debtors favored an inflated paper money, whereas the merchant creditors favored controlled expansion of the currency.

The most recent view of colonial politics is that the use of the word *democracy* is misleading. However broad the suffrage may have been, politics was a contest between rival groups within the upper classes. In some colonies the voters tended to line up behind individuals and families. The revolt of Jacob Leisler in New York had divided the colony into two hostile factions and when the bitter memories of Leisler's time had faded, the voters fell into parties led by the great DeLancey and Livingston families. In Rhode Island, Samuel Ward led a party that contended sharply with the adherents of Stephen Hopkins. The Wentworths dominated New Hampshire politics. Merchant groups tended to coalesce into parties. In Massachusetts they weakened the Puritan oligarchy and in South Carolina they opposed the great planters. In Maryland and Pennsylvania the proprietary interest provided a natural base for party. In those colonies, "country parties" opposed those who gathered on the side of the proprietor. In Pennsylvania the country party was labeled Quaker even though many of its leaders were not of that faith. In Connecticut, religion furnished the party labels, the colony dividing into New Lights and Old Lights who fought over such nonspiritual matters as western land policy. New Jersey divided into parties along the old line separating East and West Jersey. After Bacon's Rebellion, Virginia did not separate into clear-cut parties. The great families provided the leadership, which the small planters appear to have accepted.

Certainly it was natural for the upper class families to strive for political leadership. Such power added honor to great family names. But there were more practical things to be gained than prestige. By controlling colony government, the great families were in a position to define colony policy toward external authority, either proprietary or royal, and in the process defend their interests as best as they could. From positions of power they could dispense or influence the dispensation of patronage. Because of the fee system, colonial offices had an intrinsic value and beyond that worth, control of the judicial and administrative machinery guaranteed the maintenance of a safe social order. As the dominant group in the legislature, the upper class families controlled the basic policies that affected their interests as planters or merchants. In a society in which land not only represented durable wealth, but also a chief opportunity for speculative gain, they were in a position to help shape land disposal policy and to profit from grants.

The roots of the American two-party system are not in the colonial period. Provincial politics were a rude facsimile of English politics. Individuals and factions shifted around the figures of power—royal and proprietary agents, and the leaders of family coalitions. Policy remained relatively static, reflecting settled values that were stated in the words "liberty and property." Liberty found its definition primarily in the context of resistance to the external authority, and by liberty the colonists meant the traditional procedural rights of Englishmen. The defense of property was by no means limited to the upper classes because the wide distribution of land and the promise of a chance to rise in society gave a majority of the people a stake in its preservation.

Such a conservative political system failed to serve the interests of all colonists. When groups wanting real change for themselves failed to realize their aims through normal politics, they used physical violence. From the seventeenth century the colonists inherited a legacy of violence used to accomplish public purposes. The rebellions of Bacon, Leisler, and Coode formed the major elements of the legacy. The land riots in New Jersey, the New York antirent riots, the action of the Paxton Boys in Pennsylvania, and the rising of the regulators in both Carolinas extended the violent tradition into the eighteenth century. This use of force to attempt to change policy can be and has been interpeted as class or sectional conflict. But it would be wrong to view the aims of these rioters as revolutionary. The western rebels demanded a hard Indian policy, recognition of land titles, and at least reasonably honest government. The land rioters wanted ownership rather than tenancy. Those who moved outside of the system of normal politics and appealed to force did not want to destroy existing society. They just wanted to share the advantages enjoyed by the majority.

Structure of Local Government

The sources of power within the colonial jurisdictions were both external and internal. The external authority, descending from the crown, was exercised by Privy Council, royal governors, and proprietors. The internal authority proceeded upward from the colonial communities. At the level of local government, the external authority to appoint officials and promulgate rules mixed with the internal right to elect officials and enact law. The two forces amalgamated to produce the American institutions of local government, which then in the colonies and ever since in the states have at once showed many common features as well as great variety.

Slow travel and poor communications guaranteed that the largest volume of governing would be done at the local level. Colonial law assumed the integrity of the family and assigned to it large responsibilities for the control of morals, labor, education, and the care of the sick and poor. The colonists accomplished much within the limits of the neighborhood by mutual family self-help. Within the neighborhood the churches admonished the wayward and helped those in distress.

The basic units of government beyond the family and neighborhood were the township and parish. As befitted the "Old Dominion," Virginia shaped the parish closely after the English model. In addition to the supervision of church affairs, the Virginia parish exercised substantial powers of civil government. The powers of the parish were exercised by the vestry, which by the eighteenth century had become a nonelective, self-perpetuating body. In civil matters, the vestrymen administered the poor law, reviewed and registered private land boundaries, and punished immoral conduct. In Maryland and South Carolina the parish vestries were elected bodies. The Maryland parish never developed much civil power, but in South Carolina it became the most important agency of local government. There the parish became the unit for representation in the assembly—in effect, the election district. The colony levied its taxes on the parish and it was the unit of law enforcement, a function discharged by the constable. It also maintained the roads.

New England developed the most widely used basic agency of American local government, the township. Though it is possible to see certain parallels between the township and the Anglo-Saxon tun and the medieval English free village, it cannot be proved that the founders of New England regarded these ancient forms as models. In Massachusetts, the general court created the towns and retained the right to supervise and impose standard rules. In physical design, the town did bear a striking resemblance to the old English village. The families held house lots in the village and worked fields on its perimeter. The town withheld from the general division lands to be used in common as pasture and wood lots. The land and the people formed a community of cohesive integrity, the town holding what amounted to a first option to buy land in order to prevent the intrusion of unwanted strangers.

The agency for discussion and action was the meeting where an elected moderator presided. Though a distinction was made between proprietors, who had rights in the commons, and newcomers, all were members of the meeting with the right to vote. The meeting had an extremely broad jurisdiction which brought the smallest matters of public concern before it for debate. The meeting entrusted the business of day-to-day governing of the town to a board of elected selectmen. Something of the range of their activities is indicated by a partial list of the jobs undertaken by the Boston selectmen:

> Licensing ordinaries or "victualling houses," ordering the erection of buildings and "yard parles"; authorizing the construction of "salt peter" houses and limekilns; directing the building and repair of bridges and wharves; superintending the paving of streets and the making of sewers; abating nuisances; removing obstructions from ways and landings, and appointing overseers of landing places; establishing ferries; enacting fire ordinances requiring ladders and engines to be provided and regulating the construction and inspection of chimneys; licensing brewers and fixing the price of beer; approving persons applying to the county court for license to still strong waters and retail the same; admitting apprentices "to follow their calling"; directing the constables watch; employing teachers and prescribing regulations for the public schools; controlling almshouses; letting the public printing; quarantining vessels; providing dinners for school visitors and town officers; defining the duties of the sexton; and registering the "middle price" of bread under the "assize of bread."[1]

Massachusetts law made the selectmen overseers of the poor and they also were to "set idle and disorderly persons to work; to bind out poor children as apprentices; provide a town stock of arms and ammunition and levy a tax for the same; relieve idiots

1. George E. Howard, *An Introduction to the Local Constitutional History of the United States* (Baltimore: The Johns Hopkins Publication Agency, 1889), pp. 180–182.

and insane persons; take the census." Where the problem existed, they regulated disputes between colonists and Indians. The selectmen also assessed all taxes, audited the accounts of the constable and treasurer, let contracts for public works, admitted newcomers, authorized the sale of real estate, and regulated the use of common lands.

A mere listing of town officials who held office under the selectmen provides a panorama of town life. In addition to a town clerk or recorder, the selectmen appointed the following:

> Hog reeves, water bailiffs, cow keepers, fence viewers, town drummers and teachers of town drummers, constables, tithing men, perambulators, town treasurers and recorders, ringers and yokers of swine, pound-keepers, sealers of weights and measurers of corn and of boards, corders of wood and overseers of wood corders, overseers of chimneys and chimneysweepers, overseers of almhouses, gaugers, viewers, surveyors of casks of tar, firewards, and informers of offenders against the license laws.[2]

There were also sealers of leather, inspectors of brick-makers, cullers of fish, inspectors of hides for transportation, measurers of grain, boards, and salt, packers of flesh, preservers of deer, deer reeves, school wardens, school teachers, truckmasters, brewers, rebukers of boys, sizers of meadows, persons to keep dogs out of church, scavengers, lot layers, judges of delinquents at town meetings, commissioners to carry town votes to the county seat, town fishers, grubbers and doctors, commissioners for equalization of assessment, jurymen, and town cannoneers.

Though the English county had origins in the Anglo-Saxon shire, its functions and officers were defined after the Norman Conquest. The Norman and Angevin kings used the county as their agency for control of local affairs. It was an instrument of the royal prerogative. Bishop Stubbs organized the functions of the county courts under the following rubrics: judicial, police, military, and fiscal. The court also elected the knights of the shire who attended Parliament. The court initiated petitions to the crown and put into effect the king's response to those petitions. The sheriff acted as the chief officer of the crown and he

2. Howard, *op. cit.*, pp. 97–98.

exercised virtual vice-regal power. In the fourteenth century the Norman county court and the office of sheriff declined in power. To a large degree the functions of the court and sheriff were taken over by the courts of quarter sessions. Within this new court, the justices of the peace met to render judgment and see to the administrative business of the county.

Colonial local government began in great diversity and then moved to shape itself after English models. The process of change continued, and several colonies went beyond those English models to create county governments in the forms that were to be adopted by and endure in most of the American states. In the beginning the colonies had made little distinction between central and local government. Indeed, little needed to be made because the body politic and the neighborhood were in fact one and the same. Massachusetts furnishes a good example of the evolution. At first, the governor, assistants, and general court discharged all public functions. When the community grew and spread out the court created new townships. As the towns multiplied and were located in more remote areas, the general court created the county as a large intermediate agency between the central government and the towns. The main agency of the county was its court, which had a broad civil jurisdiction, a limited criminal one, and general supervisory powers over the towns. The elected magistrate and his assistants made up the court. When they returned to their homes, they discharged functions in the town roughly equivalent to those of the justice of the peace. After Massachusetts was royalized by the charter of 1691, county government changed so that it resembled the English form. In the reorganized counties the key figure was the justice of the peace. Gathered together, the justices of a county formed two new courts, the quarter sessions, where crimes were tried and administrative work done. A separate tribunal, the inferior court of common pleas had the equity and civil jurisdiction. Within the township the single justice tried criminal cases that did not involve corporal or capital punishment and civil cases in which less than forty shillings were at stake.

The county derived its main revenue from fees and fines, but it also levied the country rate that was used for both colony and county purposes. The court levied the rate on a complex base of assessment. Every adult male, who was defined as one sixteen years old or older, paid a poll tax of twenty pennies. The rate also taxed real and personal property at a ratio of one penny per twenty shillings of value. Common laborers paid an income tax that varied with the length of time they worked each year. Businessmen were taxed in proportion to an estimate of their income. The country rate became a fixed standard for taxation. When an emergency created the need for additional revenue, the legislature voted more than one rate. The county also became the basic militia district. When the trained bands of the townships assembled on a county basis they became a regiment commanded by a sergeant-major.

By far the largest volume of work done by the quarter court was administrative:

> [The justices] could exercise probate and grant letters of administration; construct bridges, lay out highways, and fine town road surveyors for neglect of duty; admit freemen of the jurisdiction, subject to the approval of the general court; appoint commissioners to solemnize marriages; license clerks of the writs, retailers of liquors, and keepers of ordinaries and coffee houses; appoint "tryers of malt" and surveyors, gaugers, and searchers of tar in seaport towns; abate common nuisances; order the town treasurer to pay accounts for entertainment of strangers lying sick in the respective towns of the county, and press lodgings for such when necessary; prevent the landing within the shire of persons visited with infectious diseases; count the votes for county treasurer; audit the accounts of the treasurer and sheriff; provide for the erection of prisons; appoint masters of houses of correction and prescribe rules for their government; and order indigent persons to be relieved by their relatives, should the latter be found able to support them.[3]

In the South, Virginia furnished the model of county government. Plantation agriculture dispersed the population widely and made infeasible units of government based on small geographic areas. As in New England, the county had judicial, administrative, fiscal, and military responsibilities. It also served as the election district and unit for representation in the house of burgesses.

The familiar pattern of local government, equipped with

3. Howard, *op. cit.*, pp. 331–332.

sheriff, justices of the peace, and quarter sessions, appeared in New York and Pennsylvania. There the counties had the traditional powers in relation to justice, the militia, finance, administration, and representation. Although they used English models, these two colonies experimented with new forms of county government. New York created the board of supervisors and Pennsylvania used a system of commissions. Unlike the justices of the peace, both the supervisors and commissioners were elected officials. Originally the boards and commissions limited their activity to fiscal affairs, the levying and collecting of taxes, and supervision of county expenditures. In time they branched out and took over many of the administrative functions that the justices of the peace had discharged in quarter sessions. Pennsylvania and New York thus developed forms that went beyond the English model and set the pattern for town-county government that has endured in the United States.

Of the various concentrations of colonial population, some two dozen may be designated as cities. The criterion for labeling such areas cities was not numbers, for with the exception of the seaboard cities of Boston, New York, Philadelphia, and Charleston, the "cities" were little more than expanded villages. The city was defined legally as an area of concentrated population which possessed the rights of an incorporated borough. The act of chartering boroughs in England had been a part of the royal prerogative. In the colonies the governor and council normally issued the charters. The assemblies created a few cities and regardless of how they were created, passed laws regulating the jurisdiction and powers of city governments.

From the beginning, the promoters of colonization, royal officials, and the colonists themselves encouraged the development of cities. They identified the city with commerce and industry, which they desired to stimulate. Some efforts were made, both imperially and locally, to designate certain cities as staple ports with exclusive rights in the trade of specified commodities. Whether or not a staple was created, the city was a place where trade concentrated in narrow channels—thus simplifying control. From the colonists' viewpoint, the city created an opportunity to monopolize valuable trade and to control the quality of goods produced. As a center of quickened economic activity, the colonial city stood as a symbol of that important American principle that has equated a rising standard of living with the creation and use of material things.

With the exception of New England, where the cities retained the township form of government, the colonial city resembled the English borough. As a jurisdiction, the city was either a "democratic" or a "close" corporation. The majority of corporations were "close." In such cities admission to its freedom was jealously guarded and the council was a self-perpetuating board. In the "democratic" corporation, it was easier to become a freeman. In New York City early in the eighteenth century the right could be purchased cheaply. The freemen elected the council in the "democratic" corporation. With the status of freeman came the right to vote, but more importantly, the right to share in the economic privileges of the city, to engage in trade and the craft industries.

The power and jurisdiction of the city closely resembled that of the county. In some cases, Albany, for example, city and county government were united. The city officials, consisted of the mayor, recorder, aldermen, and common council. When they all sat together, they acted as the legislature of the city, passing its ordinances and bylaws. As in the county, the judicial part of the government did the bulk of the business. In most cities the mayor, recorder, and aldermen either were justices of the peace or exercised their authority. The mayor's court, a direct descendant of the ancient courts baron and leet, had a limited civil and criminal jurisdiction. As in the county, the larger part of the court's work was administrative, dealing with security, health, and economic well-being.

The mayor and aldermen regulated the night watch, originally a military guard, which gradually assumed a general police function. They decided where streets would be laid out, when they should be paved, and if and how they should be cleaned. They provided at least a rudimentary fire protection. But the largest area of concern was economic and here the city fathers hewed to lines of policy that were medieval in character. Through ordinances and "assizes" they enforced a just price and maintained a level of quality. They looked out for light loaves of bread, watered milk, short cords of wood, and adulterated liquor. The control of the liquor trade was no mean task when one contemplates the fact that New York City had a liquor outlet for every fifty-five residents. They regulated the trades, following generally the old rule of "one man, one trade." They protected the valuable city monopolies of markets and fairs. The latter were trouble, for in addition to merchants and prospective buyers, the pitchmen, hawkers, gamblers, and whores came to fleece the innocent or unwary.

The list of ordinances in effect in New York City in 1701 illustrates the range of urban problems:

(1) For the observation of the Lord's Day.
(2) Concerning strangers.
(3) Concerning freemen.
(4) Concerning keeping the streets clean.
(5) Concerning retailers of liquor.
(6) Surveyors of the Citty.
(7) To prevent fire.
(8) Concerning negroes.
(9) Concerning Engrossers and Forestallers of the Markett.
(10) Assize of Bread.
(11) No timber, etc., to lye in the streets.
(12) Concerning Swine.
(13) Regulations concerning Carmen.
(14) Officers to be observant in the Execution of these Laws.
(15) Concerning Negroes and Indian Slaves.
(16) Common Council not to be absent on summons.
(17) Gaugers, Packers, and Cullers.
(18) Weights and Measures to be sealed.
(19) Masters of Vessels to give an account of their passengers.
(20) Concerning Bucketts.
(21) Packers Marke of beefe and porke.
(22) Freemen to be Inrolled.
(23) Apprentices to be bound before the Mayor, etc.
(24) Ordinances for paving, etc.
(25) Laws for the Dock and Slips, etc.
(26) Oath of freemen.
(27) Regulation for the Markett.
(28) Against Firing Guns.

(29) Relating to Apprentices.
(30) Who are deemed Freemen.
(31) Freemen to be made by Mayor and Aldermen.
(32) To prevent Fire.
(33) Against Hawkers.
(34) Against Emptying Odours in the Streets.
(35) About Carmen.
(36) Killing cattle in slaughter house only.
(37) Keeping the Streets Clean.
(38) Swine prohibited in the Out Ward.[4]

The colonial city began as an expanded neighborhood with a homogeneous population possessed of common interests. In the neighborhood "city," individual householders performed the public works. They mounted the watch, built and cleaned the streets. The rise of a truly urban community resulted directly from increased size. As the population grew it became heterogeneous and lost its sense of common purpose. The tradition of individual service declined and the cities began to pay for their services. As the cities grew they faced "certain imperatives which demanded an answer": water supply, fire protection, garbage disposal, more regular police protection. By the middle of the eighteenth century the colonial cities of larger population had evolved into communities exhibiting all of the tensions and vitality of American urban life. Yet, as the pace of city life increased and became more complex, urban government retained the ancient, often archaic, forms of city government that had come down from the Middle Ages.

4. Ernest S. Griffith, *History of American City Government, the Colonial Period* (New York: Oxford University Press, 1938), pp. 119–120. My description of city government is based on this fine book.

Chapter 12

The Eighteenth
Century Empire

"Salutary Neglect"?

*O*ne of those convenient, but inaccurate, historical generalizations is that of salutary neglect. According to the concept, the escalating struggle with France, which began in 1689 and continued to 1763, forced English officials to abandon their efforts to enforce their law in America. If there was such a thing as salutary neglect it did not begin in 1689. The most thorough efforts to reform the imperial system came in the 1690's and the mercantilist-inspired attacks on the private colonies were not abandoned until 1715. Nor did the accession of the House of Hanover to the English throne in 1714 bring any change to basic colonial policy. The Whigs, coming to power with George I, had occasion to outline their economic policy in the context of a debate over a proposed commercial treaty with France; in opposing the treaty, they advanced a theory of orthodox mercantilism.

Though they were committed to conservative economic policy, the Whigs abandoned the strenuous effort to improve the system of imperial law enforcement. That they did so was due in no small measure to the nature of the problems created by the kings they served. The first two Hanoverians were German princes who retained their continental interests and power. As foreigners they were intensely disliked by many Englishmen and especially by those who supported the cause of the exiled Stuarts. Those "kings across the water," when backed by a foreign power, posed a real threat to the Hanoverian succession. In the name of the pretenders, Scotland rose twice, once in 1715 and again in 1745.

The years between the Treaty of Utrecht (1713) and the outbreak of the War of the Austrian Succession (1740) were not a time of peace in Europe. Through those years international relations were volatile, and the fact that England had German kings further complicated her diplomacy. Sweden and Spain had been hurt at Utrecht and, under Charles XII, Sweden launched aggressions that threatened Hanoverian interests. Spain sought to recoup at the expense of Austria, a traditional English ally. As chief minister of George I, the Earl of Stanhope was primarily concerned with continental diplomacy, and after a long and difficult course of negotiation, he produced a series of treaties that guaranteed English interests and restored peace. Stanhope's successor, Robert Walpole, based his political supremacy on a policy of peace. Yet, it was no small task to remain disengaged at a time when the European powers fought the War of the Polish Succession and maneuvered around the complex issue of the Pragmatic Sanction and the Austrian Succession.

The Hanoverian succession pointed up a serious unresolved problem created by the constitutional settlement of 1689. Parliament had established its ultimate supremacy by deposing James II, installing William and Mary, and settling the succession on the Hanoverians. But these makings and unmakings of kings were extraordinary acts that left unanswered questions of how the government was to function from day to day. Such questions were further complicated by the fact that the first two Hanoverians were foreigners with little understanding of English political processes. After 1715, English politicians found the answer to the problem of operating government in the complex but practical cabinet or ministerial system. Between 1715 and 1742 there were two ministries—Lord Stanhope's, which lasted until 1721, and Sir

Robert Walpole's. After 1742, Henry Pelham and Thomas Pelham-Holles, Duke of Newcastle, dominated English politics. In Newcastle's second ministry William Pitt controlled policy as Secretary of State. What these men came to understand was that stable policy depended upon their ability to gather around themselves a ministry that had the confidence of the king in his closet and could command a majority in the House of Commons. Such a system put a large premium on political acumen and technique. Thus, almost regardless of issues, the main business of a first minister was politics. Such a system forced the politicians to avoid sweeping change and heroic measures. Under such a system, American affairs came to the center of the parliamentary stage only when forced there by English economic groups that had political power. Thus the political system virtually guaranteed that changes in colonial policy would be sporadic and would come only when English interests with sufficient political power to affect the stability of a ministry made demands.

Responsibility for American affairs was not clearly fixed in any one place. Under the ministerial system the lines of authority in the colonial administrative system became even more confused. In theory the colonies remained his majesty's dominions and in fact formal decisions were still registered in the Privy Council. Parliament concerned itself much more regularly with colonial matters, especially when defense or general trade matters were at issue. The Treasury, Admiralty, and law officers continued to be involved. The largest amount of confusion was created by the relationship between the Secretary of State for the Southern Department and the Board of Trade.

In the years following its creation (1695) the Board of Trade had enjoyed the prestige of a committee of the Privy Council. As such it had direct access to the monarch because the king, William III, for example, actually sat in council. After 1714, the Privy Council did its business as a committee of the whole, and the king did not attend. In effect the board became an administrative agency reporting to a committee of the Privy Council. More important than the change of the board's relationship with the council was its submission to the Secretary of State for the Southern Department. Through the ministry this secretary assumed executive authority for colonial affairs. All dominion matters affecting diplomacy, defense, or general economic policy were referred immediately to him by the board. In time, the secretary came to control all correspondence with the colonies, referring what matters he chose to the board. As a politician, the secretary was interested in the colonial civil list and dispensed the patronage. Thus the Board of Trade became a place where reports were prepared when questions were referred to it by the Privy Council, the Secretary of State, or either House of Parliament. For a few years after 1749, the prestige of the board revived under the presidency of Lord Halifax. As president he demanded a seat in Privy Council and executive rank equivalent to the secretaries of state. Though these were denied, he was made a member of the cabinet in 1757. The demands of Halifax illuminated the central problem of colonial administration, the need for centralization and clear assignment of responsibility for colonial policy and administration. Such reform did not come until 1768, when an American secretary of full cabinet rank was finally appointed. Pitt saw the creation of this office as the signal for extraordinary measures against America, and he was right.

In the hands of the Whig ministries the colonial system after 1715 remained basically what it had been in 1700. Thoroughly committed to a closed mercantilist system, the ministers were content to make an occasional adjustment in policy or administration. The change of pace from Edward Randolph's day is demonstrated in the area of the royal colonies. He had aggressively pursued the private colonies. During the period of Whig supremacy the question of royalization was raised in relation to four colonies. In both North and South Carolina proprietary government literally collapsed. Crown officials established royal government in these colonies only when there was absolutely no other alternative; they did so almost reluctantly. An opportunity to royalize Pennsylvania was not taken. Maryland, which had been made a royal colony in 1691, was restored to the proprietor in 1715.

The static nature of policy is made clear in the statutes of Parliament, the decisions and judgments of the Privy Council as it reviewed legislation and heard appeals, and in the instructions to the governors prepared by the Board of Trade and the Secretary of State. Excepting the problem of imperial defense, most of the actions taken represent a policy of muddling along, of patching and repairing complex policy and an unwieldy system. Yet, in the mass of detail one can detect policies, which, if effectively implemented, would threaten substantial colonial interests. Several of these sensitive points lay in the area of the colonial economy: land disposal and tenure, money supply, and the triangular trades. Others were constitutional and legal; for example, the powers of the assemblies and the jurisdiction of the colonial courts.

In the royal colonies, rules regarding land tenure and disposal evolved out of the fixed legal concept that all ungranted land was the property of the king. Parliament never intruded and land policy was defined in the instructions given to the royal governors. The crown permitted individuals to hold by free and common socage. By this tenure ultimate title remained permanently with the king, the tenant agreeing to pay an annual quitrent, which varied from one to ten shillings per hundred acres. The usual requirement was that the rents be paid in sterling, though sometimes proclamation money (foreign coin at fixed rates) was accepted. Cumulatively the quitrents represented the best hope of the crown to raise an independent revenue in America. Unlike customs duties the rents were not subject to parliamentary adjustment, nor were the revenues realized open to appropriation by the colonial assemblies.

The policy of land disposal was shaped primarily by the desire to increase quitrent revenues. In order to achieve this the crown instructed the governors not to make large grants of land. The general rules came to be that patents could be issued only in areas where a survey had actually been made. A common denominator for size of grants was one hundred acres for a family plus fifty acres for each servant—whether black or white—man, woman, or child. The instructions to several governors suggested one thousand acres as a maximum grant. To further prevent speculation, rules established late in the colonial period required that three of every fifty arable acres be cultivated, that there be at least three cattle on every fifty barren acres and that in stony or rocky land at least one man for each hundred acres be employed in mining. Other rules attempted to prevent engrossment of river valley land by requiring that for each linear measure of land along the river the patent should extend four measures into the country.

In all its aspects the land system worked very poorly. With land so abundant the colonists could not understand the need for rents. Quitrent collections never realized more than a fraction of potential revenues. The governors were constantly admonished to perfect the rent rolls and collect the arrears. The policy of restricting grants also failed. The governors themselves and those who supported them often speculated in land on a grand scale. The speculators, then, as they would throughout American history, proved to be an ingenious group. To avoid restrictions they used dummy entry men, with title changing hands at a later date. Some governors issued patents to unsurveyed land with the number of acres left blank. Such unspecified land could be held for long periods of time. The policies of quitrent and restricted grant ran counter to very real American instincts and interests. The ordinary farmer, as well as the great planter and speculator, resented the rents. Men of substance, the colonial leaders, needed the opportunity to invest in large land grants. The planter, for example, needed to be assured of an adequate supply of new land because tobacco rapidly exhausted the soil. The successful planter or merchant, who represented the emerging capitalist class, needed a place to invest surplus earnings. Because British policy limited trading opportunities and manufacturing, the chief investment opportunity open to the provincial capitalist was speculation in western land. Whenever the time would come that the English land policy could be enforced, a real grievance would exist.

A chronic colonial economic problem was a short supply of money. The shortage was a consequence of English mercantilist theory, which in its most simple form saw colonies as producers of raw materials that were to be exchanged for British manufactured goods. The mercantilist held it as axiomatic that a trade that drained gold and silver from England was a bad trade. In the English-colonial trade the question of the export to America of English specie was academic, because the balance of trade ran heavily against the colonies. At a more sophisticated level, the mercantilist went beyond the balance of trade concept to an understanding that a plentiful colonial money supply would facilitate the development of American commerce and manufacturing.

For these reasons all of the agencies of imperial administration cooperated to keep money in the colonies in short supply.

However primitive the colonial economy was supposed to be, some medium of exchange was essential. From very early times all colonies used commodity money, usually a staple of the area, such as grain in the northern provinces or tobacco in the south. Such a money had obvious disadvantages when compared to gold and silver. Though the colonies kept their accounts in pounds and shillings sterling, they saw little such money. The specie that circulated was foreign and mostly Spanish. In the late seventeenth century, extraordinary amounts of foreign coin came into the colonial economy when Americans opened their ports to pirates. But that windfall was short lived and the ordinary supply of foreign specie was earned in the provisions-for-sugar trade with the foreign West Indies. Whatever its source, most foreign coin stayed in the colonies but a short time and then went to England to redress the trade balance. In order to attract and hold foreign money, the colonists, either by private contracts or public acts, assigned artificially high values to it. For example, a Spanish piece of eight might be assigned a value 50 to 75 per cent higher than its weight as metal warranted.

Since the supply of coin was never sufficient to meet the needs either of commerce or public finance, the colonies used a wide variety of paper money. Several types of private or commercial paper were used as money. Promissory notes of individuals circulated, as did bills of exchange drawn upon assets held by mercantile houses. Private persons formed banks by pledging all of their property to secure interest-bearing notes, which circulated as money. Of much greater significance were the paper issues of the colonial governments. The colonial treasurers created temporary money by issuing notes to pay public debts and bills of credit to obtain short-term loans. The legislatures issued more permanent forms of paper money. For example, Virginia issued notes against inventories stored in public warehouses. The most common public paper money was issued directly by the assemblies with future taxes pledged for security. Some colonies established land banks, and by such schemes the government issued money as loans with private mortgages as security.

Several factors explain the various attempts to increase the colonial money supply. There was a real need to expand the medium of exchange, which a growing economy demanded, and the extraordinary expenses of war created further demands. The assemblies also manipulated the volume and value of money to implement public policy: policies ranging from these designed to attract foreign coin in order to stimulate business to frankly inflationary attempts to raise prices or relieve debtors. Whatever the justification, English officials opposed all efforts to expand the colonial money supply. In part the negative British attitude can be explained as an attempt to protect creditors, but the mercantilist also saw enlarged money supply as either a catalyst for or symptom of inappropriate colonial industrial and commercial growth.

The first general act to regulate the colonial money supply came in 1703 in the form of a royal proclamation. It established what came to be known as proclamation money by setting a standard of value that equated a Spanish piece of eight to six shillings. Other standard foreign coins were then related to this ratio. Though the proclamation overvalued foreign coin by one third, its intent was to deny to the colonies the right to regulate the value of specie. Since the proclamation did not have the same force as a statute, Parliament enacted its provisions into law five years later in An Act for Ascertaining the Rates of Foreign Silver Coins. The imperial government also took a consistently negative attitude toward colonial paper money. The rules evolved out of specific instructions to governors: no paper money was to be made legal tender; all issues had to contain provisions for redemption at a specified time and by a specific form of taxation; the governor's consent to such issues was to be withheld until the law had been reviewed by the Privy Council. Parliament gave these restrictions the force of a statute by passing an act in 1751. It was limited to the New England colonies that had offended most by issuing large amounts of paper money. Reacting to a specific case, Parliament also outlawed private land banks. Such a bank had been created on a large scale in Massachusetts. Parliament destroyed the bank in 1741 by extending the Bubble Act to the colonies. By that act no corporation could be established without Parliamentary approval.

The system of monetary controls worked poorly. The colonists continued to overvalue foreign coin in private transactions or by rating money in relation to ounces of silver rather than shillings. The assemblies again and again forced the governors to give their assent to paper money bills, especially in time of war when it could be argued that it was the only means available to meet expenses. Yet money remained in short supply. Should the time come that the system of controls could be made fully effective, thus retarding normal growth and denying local control of economic policy, a substantial grievance would be created.

The Caribbean sugar trade was vital to many interests within the empire. Specialized to a very high degree, the West Indian plantations depended on external supplies of work animals, fish, grains, meat, and lumber. Ireland and the northern continental colonies drove a large and lucrative trade in these commodities. For New England and the Middle Colonies the provisions trade to the West Indies was the indispensable leg of the triangular trades. In the Indies trade they exchanged their natural produce for goods or money that served as returns with which they could buy English manufactured goods. During the eighteenth century, Virginia also came to have a large stake in the trade as the planters began to grow grain for export. To a considerable extent the standard of living and the prosperity of the continental colonies depended on this sugar-provisions trade.

In the second decade of the century, the British West Indian planters felt the pressure of heavy competition from the French islands. Direct trade with the French West Indies had been made illegal by a treaty ratified in 1686. In spite of it, a large, clandestine, inter-island trade developed. English island factors imported the products of the French islands and, describing them as English, exported sugar and molasses to England, Ireland, and the North American colonies. French competition had a disastrous effect on British West Indian interests. The price of provisions soared; French sugar undersold British by 50 per cent; French molasses, barred from the home country to protect the brandy industry from rum competition, sold at very low prices.

To arrest their economic decline, the British planters tried to force through Parliament legislation that would give them protection in empire markets. As members of the commercial nobility they had political power and they brought it to bear. In the Parliamentary session of 1731 they introduced a bill to bar the produce of the foreign West Indies from the empire. The bill passed in Commons but the session ended before the Lords could act. The same process was repeated in 1732. Both Houses of Parliament held extensive hearings at which the planters, colonial agents, and English merchants presented their cases. The debates showed how very complex economic regulation had become. Some chose to see the bill as of primary importance in the context of England's relations with France. Those arguing for the bill on these grounds made the point that the economic decline of the British islands made them militarily weak, easy prey for the French in the event of another war. Others took the other side to argue that if the English North American colonies did not supply the French islands with provisions, then France would be forced to develop Louisiana and Canada to guarantee a supply. A larger part of the debate turned on questions of the interests of groups within the empire. That the planter group was being hurt was beyond question. Was it possible to strike a balance, or would aid to the Indies do irreparable harm to the continental colonies? The colonial merchants argued that unless they could vent their surplus in the foreign Indies, they would not be able to buy English manufactured goods. Counter to this, the mercantilists argued that the demand for lumber in the foreign Indies was destroying the king's forests in America and that stopping the trade would force Americans to produce naval stores as returns for manufactured goods.

In the session of 1732, the British planters prevailed and the Molasses Act passed. Their victory was complete in the prohibition of the Irish-Indies trade. Perhaps as a compromise, the act applied very high duties, rather than prohibition, to the import of foreign molasses and sugar into the North American colonies. Colonel Martin Bladen, speaking for the Board of Trade, told the House of Commons that though the duties did not amount to absolute prohibition "he owned that he meant them as something that should come very near it." To a degree the British planters succeeded. They monopolized the Irish market, and by another law passed in 1734 they drove up the price of their products in the English market. In America they failed to realize their purpose.

No other English law was so widely evaded by smuggling or corruption as the Molasses Act. Captains would secretly unload away from main ports and later declare to the customs collectors that they had come back without a cargo. In fact, they seldom needed to do this because the collectors regularly let the molasses through to New England distilleries after levying only a fraction of the taxes due. Bribes and even most of the duties collected went into the pockets of the customs agents. But if the time would come when a law such as the Molasses Act could be enforced, another real grievance would have been created.

The Problem of Law Enforcement

The central problem of the first empire was one of law enforcement. The matter was considerably confused because of a lack of clarity as to what law was in force in the colonies. Basic colonial law came from two sources, the charters and the commissions and instructions to the governors. Beyond such fundamental law, it was clear that acts of Parliament that legislated for the colonies specifically—for example, the Navigation Acts—were in force. For themselves, the colonists claimed that their law should be compounded of those parts of the common and statute law that fit their circumstances and the legislation produced by the American assemblies. Though agitated in many jurisdictions, the question of whether or not the colonies had a right to the common and statute law was most thoroughly debated in Maryland. There, as a means to limit the proprietor's power, the elder Daniel Dulany argued that the colonists did have that right in the pamphlet, *The Right of the Inhabitants of Maryland to the Benefit of the English Laws*. But the rules that emerged went largely against Dulany. Though very complex and not without contradiction, the rules came to be as follows: the common law as such did not extend to the dominions; statutes passed before the settlement of the colonies were in force if they were declaratory of the common law; statutes passed after the settlement applied only if the colonies were named specifically. In spite of these rules, the colonies appropriated and used the principle of the common and statute law. British officials viewed the law produced by the colonial assemblies as being rules produced by inferior corporations, a view which was not acceptable to the colonies.

The creation and administration of such a complex law created trouble on both sides of the Atlantic, in London at the Privy Council and in America in the office of royal governor. The council had the best opportunity to set out the rules for a national and reasonably uniform body of colonial law. Acting as a supreme court for each of the colonies, the judgments of the highest dominion courts came to the council on appeal. It also reviewed colonial legislation, disallowing or nullifying acts that were repugnant to the English law. The council never established uniform rules for appeals, and practice varied from colony to colony. For example, Massachusetts denied the right of appeal in cases involving real property. Connecticut tried to prevent any appeals from its highest courts, whereas Rhode Island permitted a virtual flood of appeals. There was disagreement in several colonies as to the minimum sum necessary to warrant appeals. Hearings on appeals were often extensive and sometimes involved learned English lawyers. Yet, when a decision had been reached the council merely issued a terse order confirming or correcting the judgment given in the provincial courts. Had the council written opinions in support of its orders, it would have created an invaluable body of precedent for the guidance of colonial lawyers and judges. In addition to the appeals, the council reviewed more than 8,500 acts of colonial assemblies. Though it approved almost 95 per cent of these laws, the colonists resented the process. At best, procedure was very slow and necessary legislation was sometimes held in a state of suspension for years. The council nullified many laws on grounds that were purely technical. It also often failed to appreciate that American conditions could create legitimate reasons for deviation from English legislative standards.

The royal governors were the visible agents of the prerogative in the colonies. Their commissions and instructions gave them very broad powers in all areas of government, executive, judicial, and legislative. The governor summoned, adjourned, and dissolved the assembly. Armed with a veto power, he was the first in the administrative hierarchy to test new colonial laws by British standards. His commission ordered him to consent to no law that was not "agreeable unto the laws and statutes of Our Realm of England." With the council he formed the supreme court of the colony, and the creation of lesser courts and the appointment of judges was assigned to him. In his executive capacity he commanded the militia and had large powers in relation to the established church. Most importantly, the whole of the police power was his and it was his responsibility to enforce the law as stated in his commission and instructions, in the many statutes of Parliament, and in the laws of the assembly. To accomplish this task he had a broad power of patronage, which should have made possible control of civil officers at all levels of government.

The system of strong executive government for the colonies rested on the assumption that the provincial assemblies would cooperate with the governors. They did not cooperate. By the eighteenth century they claimed many of the powers and privileges of the House of Commons and, in conducting their business, followed the procedures of Parliament. At the opening of a session, they set out their privileges in the speaker's petition. They demanded freedom of speech and freedom from arrest, the latter being no mere academic matter in an age when imprisonment for debt was common. Following the leading English case of *Goodwyn v. Fortescue* they received their own election returns and determined who would be seated as members. This privilege effectively prevented executive interference in elections. Among the privilege of Commons was the right of members to be free from molestation. Interpreting this broadly the assemblies used their power to publish for contempt very freely. In the process of protecting their self-defined dignity, they trampled on individual rights. Though offenders usually got off with a sharp reprimand and a fine after they had prayed for a pardon at the bar of the assembly, they were sometimes imprisoned. When confined by the order of the assembly, the prisoner was denied the writ of habeas corpus. There is a case on record in which the members of an assembly were proceeding solemnly into the hall to open their session when a cat jumped on a startled bystander. He knocked the cat away onto the shoulder of a member. One reads the record breathlessly, wondering whether the assembly would cite the cat or the man for contempt; it proceeded against the man. It was with such strong-minded legislatures as these that the royal and proprietary governors needed to deal if they were to carry out their commissions and obey their instructions.

The battles between the governors and their assemblies were facsimiles of the seventeenth-century struggle between the Stuarts and Parliament. The assemblies claimed an exclusive right to initiate legislation and made the claim good at least in relation to money bills. The instruction ordered the governors to obtain a permanent revenue from the assemblies. In every continental colony they failed to get such legislation. The governor opened a typical assembly session with a request for funds. Then a grudging process of bargaining began with the assembly demanding approval of their bills in return for specific appropriations. Usually the governor violated his instructions and accepted the specific grants. His alternative was to have no revenue at all, and, especially in time of war, he justified his conduct to the central government on the ground of an absolute need for funds. The assemblies not only controlled the raising of money, but also supervised the way in which the governor spent it. They did this by specifying in detail the purposes of their appropriations, by demanding a rigid accounting, and by appointing commissioners to oversee the expenditure of funds.

Symbolic of the governors' weakness was the refusal of several assemblies to give him a permanent salary. They preferred to grant annual salaries, often describing the money that they did vote as gifts or grants. Sometimes they offered gifts, in fact bribes, that were larger than the salary demanded. In 1703 the Board of Trade wrote new instructions on salaries and they became standard for the rest of the colonial period. The board ordered the governor to demand from his first assembly a permanent revenue bill that would pay his salary and meet the costs of the civil list. The instructions forbade him to accept any gift or present from the assembly. No colony granted the permanent revenue, and in at least four the salary question provided the issue for perennial and bitter disputes. The governors' power existed mostly on paper, and the assemblies made them dependents.

If the central problem of the first empire was that of law enforcement, the key to the solution was an independent revenue to support royal government. When, after 1765, the Grenville and Townshend administries undertook to provide such a revenue by direct Parliamentary taxation they created the great grievance of the Revolution.

The Empire at War, 1689–1763

Since Elizabeth's time, English statesmen had based the nation's diplomacy on two main principles: the maintenance of the European power balance and the expansion of commercial and colonial opportunity. From the accession of William and Mary to the conclusion of the Seven Years' War, these two aims of foreign policy were usually in harmony. The fact of French military power plus the promise that she would become a great commercial nation dictated an English policy of hostility to France. The Spanish empire remained largely intact and the English desire to trade within it projected the Anglo-Spanish conflict into the eighteenth century.

After 1650, Louis XIV committed France to an aggressive military and diplomatic policy that sought to gain for the nation her "natural" boundaries of the Alps, the Pyrenees, and the Rhine. Before 1678 he fought the War of Devolution and the Dutch War and in them made real progress toward his goal. Through the next decade he made it clear that he had not been satisfied, and most of Europe entered the League of Augsburg to oppose him. The Dutch had suffered heavily and feared worse. William of Orange had become the leader of the fight against France, and in 1689 the Glorious Revolution made him the King of England. He brought the nation into the Grand Alliance and the War of the League of Augsburg. The French threat to the Low Countries would have been cause enough for England to go to war. But she had other reasons, for under Louis' great finance minister Colbert, France had adopted a thorough-going policy of mercantilism. She had built a great navy and had thrown the immense power of the French state behind existing or newly created trading companies.

During the first year of the war, Louis chose to concentrate his effort in the Germanies rather than to throw down a challenge to the English and Dutch at sea. The war continued as it began, as primarily a European military conflict. In 1690 the French fleet did win a victory over the sea powers at Beachy Head, but this was reversed by a French defeat by the English and Dutch at La Hogue. For William III it was primarily a European war and in it the armies of the alliance did what had not been done before—they stopped French continental expansion.

The war in America was a little one, disconnected from the larger strategic considerations of the European struggle. Though small in course and consequence, the first intercolonial war exhibited the factors that would be common to all: the ineffectiveness of hastily assembled militia units; the complexities of Indian diplomacy and the savage horror that the use of the tribes brought to war; the difficulty of obtaining English aid; and the problems of coordinating English-colonial efforts.

The war began in America with Indian raids on the Maine frontier, and Sir Edmund Andros fought a difficult campaign against the Jesuit-agitated Abneki. The collapse of the Dominion of New England ended the artificial northern union and the colonies returned to their particular ways. Massachusetts, Connecticut, New Hampshire, and New York bore the brunt of the war and found effective cooperation most difficult. The situation in New York was compounded by the bitter conflict between Jacob Leisler, who had established a government by armed revolt, and the city of Albany. The war continued as it began and consisted largely of sporadic but ferocious French and Indian attacks on isolated frontier villages. French attacks in the first year of the war forced a general withdrawal along the northeastern frontier of Maine. In 1689 Count Frontenac came out again as governor of Canada. In 1690 he challenged the Iroquois and also sacked Schenectady, New York, Salmon Falls in New Hampshire, and Falmouth, Maine.

The intensification of raiding by Frontenac brought forth ambitious colonial plans for counterattack. Throughout the Anglo-French conflict one fact stood out: France held Canada, indeed all of her American possessions, with a thinly spread population. A major, concerted attack must drive France from North America. The first attempt to strike at a major French position came out of Massachusetts. Under Sir William Phips a joint public-private expedition went against Port Royal in Acadia. Phips won an easy victory and an important one that helped secure the Maine frontier and the fishery. After frustrating delays,

Leisler assembled a congress of the northern colonies at New York. From it came an ambitious plan of a two-pronged assault on Canada. The routes of battle were obvious and would become classic in subsequent wars: a land campaign based in New York along the Hudson-Champlain-Lake George line against Montreal, and an amphibious assault from New England against Quebec by way of the St. Lawrence.

Though colonial strategy was clear, the obstacles to execution were large. The land march was through difficult terrain with ambush an ever-present possibility; the logistics of supplying even a small army in the wilderness were complex. In 1690, Fitz-John Winthrop led the colonial force north. Smallpox and bad meat complicated his task. Though the force got into Canada and perpetrated a small massacre, the expedition failed. Phips gathered 2,300 men for the attack on Quebec. Here the difficulties were the cost of putting together an adequate naval force out of limited colonial resources, the difficulty of navigating the St. Lawrence, and the easily defended location of Quebec. Though Phips made it to Quebec his feeble attack failed. After these campaigns, the war settled down to border raids that occurred with sufficient frequency to keep the outlying villages in terror. By the time a force could be gathered and sent to the scene, the enemy disappeared. The colonists attempted to protect the frontier with small ranger forces and garrison towns, but the French and Indians continued to raid.

The peace made at Ryswick in 1697 restricted Louis XIV in Europe and by its terms Acadia was restored to France. It was clear that the peace was merely a truce. Through the next several years, the diplomats worried over the succession to the Spanish throne, because with the death of Charles II, the direct Hapsburg succession would be interrupted. The Bourbons had a candidate in the grandson of Louis XIV. Though the diplomats tried to find a solution to the Spanish problem in the Partition Treaties of 1698 and 1700, in the end Louis declared for his grandson and brought on the War of the Spanish Succession. The threat of France and Spain combined under the house of Bourbon drove Austria and the Sea Powers together. The English and Dutch had clear-cut war aims: to prevent an actual union of France and Spain; to prevent the extension of French influence in the

Spanish Netherlands; to limit French naval power in the Mediterranean; to prevent any further growth of French commerce in the Spanish-American trade.

For England the war began when Louis XIV declared James III to be king of England. Under the Duke of Marlborough the allied armies won a series of stunning victories in the Germanies and the Low Countries. Because the allies backed Hapsburg Carlos III as king of Spain, the peninsula became a major theater of war. The Methuen Treaty (1704) created a durable Anglo-Portuguese alliance. Marlborough concentrated the fleet around the peninsula and it seized Gibraltar in 1704 and Port Mahon on Minorca in 1708. As a result of her involvement there, England became the dominant Mediterranean power.

During the first four years of the war in America, the French raided along the northern borders, especially in Maine. When the governor of Massachusetts, Joseph Dudley, raised a force adequate to protect that area, the Canadian commander, Vaudreuil, moved the attack into the Connecticut Valley, perpetrating there in 1704 the massacre of the settlers at Deerfield. During the last half of the war, the colonies again attempted attacks on Canada. Dudley sent a force against Acadia in 1707 but it failed dismally. In 1708, Samuel Vetch wrote a pamphlet, *Canada Surveyed*, in which he urged the expulsion of the French. Responding to his argument, the English government planned assaults against Montreal and Quebec. In the first instance the campaigns aborted because the regular troops were sent to Spain. But in 1710 Port Royal was again seized. For 1711, England planned major Canadian campaigns and was able to send 5,000 regular troops for the attack. The Boston-based expedition floundered from the beginning. The colonies were hard-pressed to supply such a large force. After long delays the expedition departed, only to lose ten ships in a storm in the Gulf of St. Lawrence. The English commanders then abandoned the campaign.

The American war left the issues between England and France largely unresolved. England won the War of the Spanish Succession on the European continent and in the Mediterranean. At Utrecht she registered great gains. The kingdoms of France and Spain would never be united. Louis XIV withdrew his support of the Stuart pretenders to the English throne. The Spanish

Netherlands were transferred to England's ally, Austria. England retained Minorca and Gibraltar, thus guaranteeing her dominant Mediterranean position. Spain awarded England the *asiento* contract, the right to supply Spanish-America with Negro slaves. France surrendered St. Christopher's in the Caribbean and New Foundland, Acadia (Nova Scotia) and Hudson's Bay in North America. Beyond all else the war established one incontestable fact: England's supremacy at sea.

The thirty years after Utrecht was a time of tension and shifting alliance in Europe. Russia emerged from the Great Northern War (1700–1721) as a Baltic power and a potential menace to Britain's supply of naval stores. The rise of Prussia agitated the Germanies, where England's Hanoverian kings had a continuing interest. Spain, seeking to recoup her losses at Utrecht, did not fall easily into the orbit of French policy. The uncertainties of a tenuous peace led to a triple alliance among the British, Dutch, and French in 1717. Glossing over the issues that remained unresolved between Britain and France, it guaranteed the general peace of Europe for fifteen years. In 1718 Spain seized Sicily, and Britain, having landed an Austrian army in Italy, smashed the Spanish fleet at Cape Passaro. In 1721, Robert Walpole became first minister to George I and he consistently pursued a policy of peace. He maintained the *entente* with France and prevented Anglo-Spanish incidents from becoming war.

The North America zones of friction and points of confrontation between the English colonists and the empires of France and Spain became more definite. The boundaries of northern New England remained in dispute, and raiding continued. English traders and settlers pressed west along the Mohawk, into central Pennsylvania, and into the valley of Virginia. The French countered by building forts at critical points along the fur-trading routes. Antoine Cadillac had constructed Fort Detroit in 1701. In 1726 the trading post at Niagara became a fort. The English protected trade and the advancing line of settlement with a fort at Oswego. Both the English and French were moving rapidly into the territory of the great Iroquois confederation. Though based in New York, the Five Nations had extensive land claims along the whole northwestern and central frontier. The

Iroquois had remained neutral during the last war, and both the French and British worked assiduously to extend their influence among the tribes against the time when the conflict would be resumed.

South Carolina was the base for English expansion in the south and Charles Town the depot for the Indian trade. From the earliest days the Carolina traders had pressed aggressively into the Spanish province of Guale (Georgia) and had forced the withdrawal of the mission frontier into Florida. They also pushed west into the lands of the Cherokee, Chickasaw, Creeks, and Choctaw. When the French arrived in the lower Mississippi Valley they found the Carolina traders already active in the area. Before 1700 both England and France had large plans for extending their empires into the Mississippi Valley. Iberville established a base at Mobile in 1702 and another at New Orleans in 1718. In 1717, the French pushed into the Gulf plains area and built Fort Toulouse on the Tallapoosa River. The English strove to maintain and extend their Carolina-based trade in the same region. The success of either nation depended on its Indian diplomacy. Generally the English held the Cherokee and Chickasaw to their side, while the French depended upon a durable alliance with the Choctaw. The Creeks shifted their loyalty and often played an independent role in the confused intrigue of frontier diplomacy. The normal condition of life was war. One Carolinian wrote, "It is a very great discouragement to the settlers of our Southern Frontiers to be always obliged to hold the plough in one hand and the sword in the other." Whatever the conditions of European diplomacy, by 1740 French and English in America were locked in a struggle for a huge belt of territory extending southward from the Gulf of St. Lawrence to the Gulf of Mexico. Both colonists and British officials feared French encirclement. It was this fear more than hostility to Spain that defined policy for the disputed Carolina-Florida border.

In 1721, the Carolinians attempted to push their boundary south to the Altamaha River, about half way between the Savannah River and St. Augustine. They built Fort King George on the Altamaha and held the flimsy fortification for six years. Through the1720's there were many proposals for the settlement of Georgia. All of the plans projected a colony that would be a buffer for Carolina, one consisting of planned, compact communities to be inhabited by the distressed persons of Great Britain and Europe. The colony of Georgia evolved out of the many-sided interests of a group of philanthropists who worked to further the ideals of an Anglican rector, the Reverend Dr. Thomas Bray. The founder of the Society for the Propagation of Gospel in Foreign Parts, Bray was interested in Negro education, prison reform, libraries for Anglican ministers in the colonies, colonies for the unemployed and frontier missions. Among Bray's associates was a parliamentary reformer, James Ogelthorpe. Though Bray died in 1730, Ogelthorpe and others obtained the charter for Georgia in 1732.

From the beginning, philanthropic and security considerations combined to make Georgia an unsual venture. The charter entrusted the administration of the colony to a board of trustees for twenty-one years, at which time it was to become a royal colony. The charter restricted land grants and controlled the inheritance of land in an attempt to guarantee that the colony would consist of numerous small farmers who would be fighters against Spain and France. A charter ban on Negro slavery and rum reflected the idealism of the founders. During the proprietary period, the government of Georgia was both unique and ineffective. The trustees, in part to avoid Board of Trade control, did not appoint a governor. Ogelthorpe made three Atlantic crossings, acting in Georgia as an agent or attorney for the trustees and administering the colony as a quasi-municipal corporation. The founding and early settlement of Georgia received great publicity in the English press, and Parliament regularly supported it with subsidies. In spite of the effort, the colony was little more than a tenuously held string of scattered outposts during the last two intercolonial wars.

As the Indian traders defined the areas of friction along the interior frontier of North America, the old issue of trade with Spanish America produced a series of incidents and then war. After Utrecht, the British government assigned to the South Sea Company the *asiento* and the right to send the annual ship with general merchandise to Spanish America. The system worked badly. The Spaniards complained about the number and quality of slaves and accused the company of vastly exceeding its general trading rights. Individual captains continued to conduct an interloping trade with the islands and Central America. The Spanish tried to keep the company within limits and drive out the illegal traders with the ships of the *guarda costa*. Many of the coast guard were private vessels, and they applied rigorous rules of contraband that resulted in the condemnation of many British ships. Claims for monetary damages mounted and Walpole attempted to adjust these by diplomacy. The opposition to Walpole's government gradually grew, and the charge that he sacrificed Britain's maritime rights played on old emotions. In 1739 he negotiated the Convention of Pardo, which would have provided for settlement of claims by arbitration. William Pitt, speaking for the opposition, condemned the convention as "insecure, unsatisfactory, dishonourable." Reducing an old theme of policy to an aphorism, he said; "when trade is at stake it is your last retrenchment; you must defend it, or perish." The maritime interests rallied to the cry of "No Search!" and Walpole's policy of peace collapsed. Later that year Britain and Spain were at war —the War of Jenkin's Ear, so named after an English captain who was the alleged victim of Spanish atrocities.

The war began with British attacks in the Caribbean. Within a month of the outbreak of hostilities, Admiral Vernon took Porto Bello; then the offense failed at Cartagena in 1741 and Santiago de Cuba in 1742. The Anglo-Spanish conflict became part of a larger war in 1740, that of the Austrian Succession, when Frederick the Great invaded Austrian Silesia. Britain made only a desultory effort in the continental war, but during its course put down the last of the risings for the Stuarts "the '45". In North America the usual alarms ran along the Indian frontiers, and the French and British involved themselves yet more deeply in the convolutions of Indian diplomacy. There was little action, although the French did force a slight English withdrawal north of Albany. On the southern frontier Ogelthorpe led two expeditions against St. Augustine—with no success.

The governor of Massachusetts, Sir William Shirley, initiated the great act of the American war. After the loss of Newfoundland, the French had built a great fortress at Louisbourg on Cape Breton. From this bastion, France agitated the Indians on the northeastern frontier and let loose privateers to harass English fishermen. In 1745, Shirley appealed to the shipping and fishing interests and proposed an assault on Louisbourg. All of the New England and some of the middle colonies cooperated. William Pepperell, a successful businessman, was put in command of a force of 4,300 men. A British fleet came up from the West Indies and after an extended siege Louisbourg surrendered. But this splendid triumph was wiped out by the Treaty of Aix-la-Chapelle. Except for some exchange of territory in the Germanies and in Italy, the diplomats based the peace on the principle of *status quo ante bellum*. Louisbourg was handed back to France in return for the restoration of British territory in India.

In America, the War of the Austrian Succession had settled nothing. The French continued to push south from the St. Lawrence and the eastern Great Lakes. Fur traders and land speculators extended the English interest westward from Pennsylvania and Ohio. Virginians formed the Ohio Company and sent Christopher Gist to explore the area of its grant, a huge tract along the Ohio stretching between the Monongahela and Kanawha Rivers. In 1749 the French countered by sending Celeron de Bienville into the Ohio by way of Lake Chautauqua and the Allegheny River. Along his route Bienville buried lead plates that proclaimed the area to be French. They also strengthened their position in the St. Lawrence-Ontario region by building Fort Rouille at Toronto and La Presentation on the site of Ogdensburg. Reports kept coming back from the frontier that the French were about to extend their forts into the Ohio Valley.

The French activity caused great concern, and New York assumed the initiative in an attempt to improve relations with the Iroquois, who were disenchanted with English military weakness and land policies. In 1754, James DeLancey, the acting governor of New York, called a general conference at Albany to consider the problems of the frontier. Seven colonies sent representatives to the Albany Congress. The first item on the agenda was relations with the Iroquois, but extensive parleying produced no definite Indian commitment. What had long been apparent was the need for common policy in dealing with defense and Indian relations. Benjamin Franklin, a delegate from Pennsylvania, brought with him a plan for limited colonial union. The plan of union provided for a president-general to be appointed and paid by the crown.

The colonial assemblies were to elect a grand council in which individual colonies would be represented in proportion to their fiscal contributions. The united colonies were to be concerned with defense, Indian relations, and new western settlements. Though passed by the congress, neither the colonies nor the central government approved the plan. Simultaneously the Board of Trade considered a centralized plan of defense and Indian relations, but before it could be perfected, the war had begun.

War came in the Ohio Valley. In their push south into the valley the French had built fortifications at Presque Isle, on Lake Erie, at LeBoeuf on French Creek, and at Venango on the Alleghany. Governor Robert Dinwiddie of Virginia assumed the initiative, sending a young officer, George Washington, to warn the French that they were intruding upon Virginia territory. Washington had conversations at Venango and LeBoeuf, and though the French agents said that they needed to refer the matter to the governor at Quebec, they made it clear that they intended to stay. The next year, 1754, Dinwiddie sent Washington to build a fort at the source of the Ohio. An advance company of carpenters found that the French had pre-empted the place. Informed of the fact, Washington threw together Fort Necessity and awaited an attack. When it came, he was forced to surrender, the French permitting him to return to Virginia.

In the fall of 1754, the news from western Pennsylvania forced the ministry at London to the decision to send regular troops to America for the campaign of 1755. They chose Edward Braddock to command the expedition. He was to sieze Fort Duquesne and go on to destroy Niagara. In addition he was to plan attacks in Nova Scotia and against Crown Point. In Virginia, Braddock mustered 2,000 men. After long delays he began the difficult march into Pennsylvania, laboriously constructing a road as he proceeded. The French with Indian allies came out to meet him. Braddock's disastrous defeat resulted from his insistence that the British fight in regular order. The French and Indians, fighting from concealed positions, cut the battalions to pieces. Braddock suffered a mortal wound and the remnants of his army retreated to Virginia. During this first year of as yet undeclared war, a Massachusetts force won a minor victory in Nova Scotia by seizing Fort Beauséjour. Sir William Johnson moved against

Crown Point, but contented himself with building Forts Edward and William Henry. The French countered by moving south from Crown Point and constructing Fort Ticonderoga. Governor Shirley was to have attacked Niagara, but all that came of it was a strengthening of the post at Oswego.

Late in 1755, Great Britain declared war. As they did so, the continental powers realigned themselves radically. The issue of Prussian power in the Germanies caused Austria and France to reassess their positions. Having done so, they dropped their centuries-old animosity and formed an alliance into which Catherine the Great brought Russia. Britain, in part to protect the Hanoverian interest, then allied herself with Prussia, thus completing the Diplomatic Revolution. Frederick of Prussia opened the Seven Years War by invading Saxony and then, in a brilliant series of campaigns against vastly superior numbers, turned the allies back at Rossbach, Leuthen, and Zorndorf. In spite of these triumphs, the allies kept heavy pressure on Prussia and Frederick barely survived. Britain committed no major armies to the continental war, but supported Prussia with subsidies.

In the spring of 1757, William Pitt became Secretary of State for the Southern Department. He held office for several months, was dismissed, but returned to power and greatness that summer. An imperious man and a great orator, Pitt had the confidence of the English people. He had self-confidence, too, and an overall plan that sought to annihilate French naval and commercial power once and for all. Pitt galvanized the nation, strengthened the army, vastly increased the fleet, and concentrated on the American war. But Pitt's leadership could have no effect on the campaigns of 1757, and the chronicle of defeat lengthened. Lord Loudon led 15,000 against Louisbourg but, lacking local naval superiority, never really engaged the enemy. Montcalm moved down the lake chain with a huge Indian host and captured Fort William Henry. The ministry recalled Loudon and gave the overall command to James Abercrombie. Under him the tale of defeat extended into 1758. He attempted a frontal assault on Ticonderoga and suffered a crushing defeat.

In 1758, Pitt's work and policy began to pay off. Jeffrey Amherst besieged Louisbourg and after his success there he was made commander-in-chief. John Bradstreet took Fort Frontenac, and John Forbes led 6,000 men westward through Pennsylvania to the seizure of Fort Duquesne. For 1759, Pitt proposed to clear Lake Ontario and invade Canada along the line of the St. Lawrence and Lake Champlain. John Prideaux and Sir William Johnson took Niagara. In the face of 11,500 men led by Amherst, the French abandoned Ticonderoga and destroyed Crown Point. The French line had been shattered and they had withdrawn to the St. Lawrence. James Wolfe, a young general who had proved himself in the continental war and at Louisbourg led the greatest amphibious force that Britain had ever assembled against Quebec. Wolfe gained the Plains of Abraham outside of the city and engaged the armies of France under Montcalm. Wolfe won the fight but was mortally wounded in the process. The following year Amherst completed the conquest of Canada with a victory at Montreal.

By 1760, British seapower had triumphed everywhere. The French had lost their Caribbean islands; Britain dominated the West African coast; Clive had beaten the French in India. In that year of victory, George III ascended the throne of Great Britain bringing with him as his most trusted minister, the Earl of Bute. The new king and Bute desired to end the war and this assured them of Pitt's animosity. France opened negotiations for peace in 1761 and the discussions dragged on for a year. The greater part of Bute's ministry wanted peace. They argued that Britain could no longer bear the cost of war and they feared a new alliance between France and Spain. What they feared became a fact in the summer of 1761 when the two Bourbon kings signed the third family compact. When it was reasonably certain that Spain and France would unite, Pitt urged that Britain should immediately attack Spain. When he failed to carry his point, Pitt resigned from the ministry.

Britain declared war on Spain in January 1762 and soon added Cuba and Manila to the list of conquests. Negotiations with France continued and were marked by lengthy haggling over the West Indies and the North Atlantic fishery. Ultimately Bute and the French foreign minister, Choiseul, produced a preliminary treaty. Pitt delivered a tremendous indictment of the treaty in the House of Commons. He argued that it gave away too much and that leaving France in the West Indies and the fishery guaranteed the resurgence of French naval power. In spite of Pitt's argument, the Commons approved the treaty by a huge majority. The Treaty of Paris did give back much to the Bourbons. Cuba and Manila were restored to Spain and France received her sugar islands back and was guaranteed a place in the North Atlantic fishery. Yet the treaty measured the magnitude of the British victory. It gave her India, Canada, and Florida, and all of eastern North America became British. Great Britain had humiliated France and pushed Spain further along her rapidly declining path. In 1763, Great Britain stood in an absolutely pre-eminent position in commerce and colonies. The first empire was at its zenith. So circumstanced, British statesmen turned to the task of reorganizing the empire—and in the process destroyed it.

Bibliography

Chapter 1: Opportunity for Empire

For English backgrounds, see Conyers Read, *The Tudors* (New York: Holt, 1936), and John B. Black, *The Reign of Elizabeth, 1558–1603* (Oxford: Clarendon Press, 1959). Wallace Notestein, *The English People on the Eve of Colonization, 1603–1630* (New York: Harper & Row, 1954), is the first volume in the new American Nation Series. A valuable standard work is Ephraim Lipson, *The Economic History of England* (3 vols., London: Adam & Charles Black, 1949). The electric careers of Drake and the sea dogs have attracted many authors. One of the better books is James A. Williamson, *The Age of Drake* (London: Adam & Charles Black, 1938). *The Cambridge History of the British Empire* is written from the imperial point of view. The relevant volume is J. Holland Rose, *et al. The Old Empire from the Beginnings to 1783* (Cambridge: Cambridge University Press, 1929): Chapter 2, J. A. Williamson, "England and the Opening of the Atlantic"; Chapter 4, J. Holland Rose, "The Spirit of Adventure."

The classic primary source is Richard Hakluyt, *The Principal Navigations, Voyages, Traffiques and Discoveries of the English Nation.* . . . The most accessible edition is in the Everyman Library (8 vols., London: Dent, 1926–1928). Hakluyt's *Discourse Concerning Westerne Planting* is conveniently reprinted in Bradley Chapin, *Provincial America* (New York: The Free Press, 1966).

Chapter 2: The Early Settlements

Colonial history provides many examples of conflicts of interpretation. The largest disagreement has arisen from the intrinsic difficulty of finding a unity in or imposing a synthesis upon the data. The first school of colonial historians elaborated the theme of national origins and found in our first past a chronicle of progress toward a democratic society. Around 1900, a major revision began. The revisionist or imperial school insisted that early American history be regarded as an aspect of the larger history of the first British empire. The national historians viewed the development of the colonies from the western shore of the Atlantic and referred to British policies and statesmen largely to castigate them as barriers to progress. The imperial historians, looking out from London, emphasized the attempts to fit the diverse parts into a unified empire. The national historians saw the imperial system, and especially the system of economic controls, as conservative, exploitive, and bad. The imperial historians have emphasized the benefits derived by the colonies from their status as units within a powerful empire. The classic of the nationalist school is George Bancroft, *History of the United States, from the Discovery of the American Continent* (10 vols., Boston: Little, Brown, 1834–1875). The greatest of the imperial historians was Charles M. Andrews, the dean of the last generation of colonial historians. The first three volumes of his *The Colonial Period of American History* (4 vols., New Haven: Yale University Press, 1934–1938) are a detailed authoritative account of the founding of the colonies.

Herbert L. Osgood wrote the most extensive general colonial history by a single author, *The American Colonies in the Seventeenth Century* (3 vols., New York: Macmillan, 1904–1907) and *The American Colonies in the Eighteenth Century* (4 vols., New York: Columbia University Press, 1924–1925). Osgood's work is the most detailed analysis of colonial development and is especially valuable for political history and political institutions. Another useful general work is Edward Channing, *History of the United States* (New York: Macmillan, 1905–1925). Though there are detailed accounts of the founding of each colony, only more general works are cited here. James T. Adams, *The Founding of New England* (Boston: Atlantic Monthly Press, 1921). Wesley F. Craven, *The Southern Colonies in the Seventeenth Century, 1607–1689* (Baton Rouge: Louisiana State University Press, 1949). Thomas J. Wertenbaker, *The Founding of American Civilization*, a trilogy of which *The Old South* (New York: Scribner's, 1942) and *The Puritan Oligarchy* (New York: Scribner's, 1947) are relevant here.

J. Franklin Jameson was the general editor of *Original Narratives of Early American History* (19 vols., New York: Scribner's, 1906–1917); especially useful are Lyon G. Tyler (ed.), *Narratives of Early Virginia;* William T. Davis (ed.), *Bradford's History of Plymouth Plantation;* James K. Hosmer (ed.), *Winthrop's Jour-*

nal; Clayton C. Hall (ed.), *Narratives of Early Maryland.* William Bradford, *Of Plymouth Plantation,* is especially recommended; it has been reprinted many times.

Chapter 3: The Expansion of New England

Standard accounts are in Andrews, *Colonial Period,* and Osgood, *Seventeenth Century.* Clinton Rossiter, *Seedtime of The Republic: The Origin of the American Tradition of Political Liberty* (New York: Harcourt, Brace, 1953), contains good, brief accounts of Thomas Hooker and Roger Williams. Hooker has had one biographer, George L. Walker, *Thomas Hooker* (New York: Dodd, Mead, 1891). Williams has had many biographers, of whom the better ones are Samuel H. Brockunier, *The Irrepressible Democrat: Roger Williams* (New York: Ronald, 1940), and Ola E. Winslow, *Master Roger Williams: A Biography* (New York: Macmillan, 1957). There are substantial accounts of the New England Confederation in Osgood and in J. T. Adams, *Founding of New England.* See also Alden T. Vaughn, *New England Frontier: Puritans and Indians, 1620–1675* (Boston: Little, Brown, 1965).

Chapter 4: The English on the First Frontier

The physical conditions on the first frontier are set out best in the accounts written by the colonists. See again the relevant volumes of Jameson's *Original Narratives.* Also good is Ellen G. Semple, *American History and its Geographic Conditions* (Boston: Houghton, Mifflin, 1933). Thomas J. Wertenbaker, *The First Americans, 1607–1690* (New York: Macmillan, 1927), is in *History of American Life,* a pioneering series that emphasizes social and economic history.

A standard series of economic histories was sponsored by the Carnegie Institute and they remain valuable works of reference: Percy W. Bidwell and John I. Falconer, *History of Agriculture in the Northern United States, 1620–1860* (Washington: Carnegie Institute, 1925); Lewis C. Gray, *History of Agriculture in the Southern United States to 1860* (2 vols., Washington: Carnegie Institute, 1933); Victor S. Clark, *History of Manufacturing in the United States, 1607–1914* (2 vols., Washington: Carnegie Institute, 1916–1928). Emory R. Johnson, *et al., History of Domestic and Foreign Commerce of the United States* (2 vols., Washington: Carnegie Institute, 1915). Another standard work is John R. Commons, *et al., History of Labour in the United States* (4 vols., New York: Macmillan, 1918–1935). The system of indentured servitude is treated at length in Abbott E. Smith,

Colonists in Bondage: White Servitude and Convict Labor in America, 1607–1776 (Chapel Hill: University of North Carolina Press, 1947), and Marcus W. Jernegan, *Laboring and Dependent Classes in Colonial America, 1607–1776* (Chicago: University of Chicago Press, 1931). Old, but still valuable are Philip A. Bruce, *Economic History of Virginia in the Seventeenth Century* (2 vols., New York: Macmillan, 1896), and William B. Weeden, *Economic and Social History of New England, 1620–1789* (2 vols., Boston: Houghton Mifflin, 1890).

The development of early political institutions may be traced in Osgood. Rossiter, *Seedtime of the Republic* is again useful. Louise P. Kellogg, *The American Colonial Charter*, which is volume one, *Report for 1903*, The American Historical Association, is the standard monograph on the subject. See also Andrew C. McLaughlin, *The Foundations of American Constitutionalism* (New York: New York University Press, 1932).

The history and especially the influence of the Puritans has generated much dispute. In the 1930's it became fashionable to portray the Puritans as narrow-minded, crass bigots. A major revision has been accomplished by Professors Samuel Eliot Morison and Kenneth B. Murdock and their students. In *The Puritan Pronaos* (New York: New York University Press, 1936) and reissued in 1956 as *The Intellectual Life of Colonial New England*, Morison judged the Puritan accomplishment by seventeenth-century standards and by so doing substantially modified attitudes toward them. Morison's *Builders of the Bay Colony* (Boston: Houghton Mifflin, 1930, reissued 1958) contains perceptive, readable biographies of Puritan leaders. Perry Miller, who was one of our most accomplished intellectual historians, found the theme of his work in Puritan ideas. The books relevant here are *Orthodoxy in Massachusetts, 1630–1650* (Cambridge: Harvard University Press, 1933, reissued by Beacon Press, 1959) and *The New England Mind: The Seventeenth Century* (New York: Macmillan, 1939). Other recent contributions to our understanding of the Puritans are Sumner Powell, *Puritan Village: The Formation of a New England Town* (Middletown: Wesleyan University Press, 1963), and Edmund S. Morgan, *The Puritan Family: Essays on Religious and Domestic Relations in Seventeenth-Century New England* (Boston: The Trustees of the Public Library, 1944).

The best literary history of the colonial period is Moses C. Tyler, *A History of American Literature* (New York: G. P. Putnam's 1878, reprinted Ithaca: Cornell University Press, 1949). *The Colonial Mind, 1620–1800*, which is volume one of Vernon L. Parrington, *Main Currents in American Thought* (New York: Harcourt, Brace & World, 1927 and reissued 1954) is written with a vigorous liberal bias.

Many of the basic documents of the colonial churches are in H. Shelton Smith *et al.*, (eds.), *American Christianity, An Historical Interpretation with Representative Documents* (New York: Scribner's, 1960). Perry Miller and Thomas A. Johnson (eds.), *The Puritans* (New York: American Book Co., 1938; reprinted in 2 vols., New York: Harper & Row, 1963) offers a rich variety of Puritan writing. Chapin, *Provincial America*, reprints the charter of Maryland, *New England's First Fruits*, and a substantial selection from early New England political documents.

Chapter 5: The Origins of the Empire

The question of the nature of the imperial constitution has been of more than ordinary importance because to a substantial degree after 1760 the colonists based their resistance and ultimately their revolt on interpretations of that constitution. Then, and for the historian since, the majority opinion has been that after the Glorious Revolution, supreme power in the empire and over the dominions lay with Parliament. This view is set out extensively in Robert Schuyler, *Parliament and The British Empire* (New York: Columbia University Press, 1929). In 1775, John Adams, James Wilson, and Thomas Jefferson rejected Parliamentary authority and argued that the sole tie binding the dominions to the realm was allegiance owed the king. Two modern historians have argued that this view was not polemical but an accurate reading of the Constitution: Charles H. McIlwain, *The American Revolution: A Constitutional Interpretation* (New York: Macmillan, 1923; reissued Ithaca: Cornell University Press, 1958), and Julius Goebel, Jr., "Matrix of Empire," which is the introduction to Joseph H. Smith, *Appeals to the Privy Council from the American Plantations* (New York: Columbia University Press, 1950). Two excellent, brief works are A. Berriedale Keith, *A Constitutional History of the First Empire* (Oxford: Clarendon, 1930), and Hugh E. Egerton, *A Short History of British Colonial Policy* (London: Methuen, 1897). Chapter 7 of the Cambridge History, *The Old Empire*, is J. A. Williamson, "The Beginnings of an Imperial Policy, 1649–1660." Lipson, *Economic History* is good on the precedents for a mercantilist policy. George L. Beer, *The Origins of the British Colonial System, 1578–1660* (New York: Macmillan, 1922) was one of the pioneering works of the revisionist school. Beer's work comes near to being an apology for imperialism.

An extensive collection of primary materials covering most topics in early American history is Merrill Jensen (ed.), *American Colonial Documents to 1776* (London: Oxford University Press, 1955).

Chapter 6: Charles II: Imperial Definition and Expansion

For post-Restoration English politics, see George N. Clark, *The Later Stuarts, 1660–1714* (Oxford: Clarendon, 1934). The best book on the colonial aspects of English mercantilism is Lawrence A. Harper, *The English Navigation Laws: A Seventeenth-Century Experiment in Social Engineering* (New York: Columbia University Press, 1929). George L. Beer, *The Old Colonial System, 1660–1754* (2 vols., New York: Macmillan, 1912) covers only the period to 1688. Chapters 8 and 9 of the Cambridge History, *The Old Empire*, are J. A. Williamson, "The Colonies after the Restoration, 1660–1713," and C. M. Andrews, "The Acts of Trade." Lipson, *Economic History*, continues to be useful.

The settlement of the post-Restoration colonies is described in the appropriate volumes of Andrews and Osgood. More detailed studies are: Edwin B. Bronner, *William Penn's "Holy Experiment": The Founding of Pennsylvania, 1681–1701* (New York: Columbia University Press, 1962); John E. Pomfret, *The Province of West New Jersey, 1609–1702: A History of the Origins of an American Colony* (Princeton: Princeton University Press, 1956) and *The Province of East New Jersey, 1609–1702: The Rebellious Proprietary* (Princeton: Princeton University Press, 1962); for New York, Alexander C. Flick (ed.), *History of the State of New York* (10 vols., New York: Columbia University Press, 1933–1937). On the Carolinas, again, Wesley F. Craven, *Southern Colonies in the Seventeenth Century*.

Chapter 7: American Politics, Imperial and Domestic, 1660–1685

The most detailed general account is Osgood, *American Colonies in the Seventeenth Century*. Thomas J. Wertenbaker describes the weakening of conservative Puritanism after the Stuart restoration in Chapters 9 and 10 of *The Puritan Oligarchy* (New York: Scribner's, 1947 and reprinted by Grosset & Dunlap). Michael G. Hall, *Edward Randolph and the American Colonies, 1676–1703* (Chapel Hill: University of North Carolina Press, 1960) is a fine study of England's most active American agent. For Bacon's Rebellion, Thomas J. Wertenbaker, *Torchbearer of the Revolution* (Princeton: Princeton University Press, 1940) and Wilcomb E. Washburn, *The Governor and the Rebel* (Chapel Hill: University of North Carolina Press, 1957). Wertenbaker portrays Bacon as a democrat resisting oppression; Washburn justifies Berkely. For primary material, Jameson, *Original Narratives*, Charles M. Andrews (ed.), *Narratives of the Insurrections, 1675–1690* (New

York: Scribner's, 1915). Chapin, *Provincial America* reprints the text of the New York Charter of Liberties.

Chapter 8: The Rise and Fall of the Dominion of New England

The standard study is Viola M. Barnes, *The Dominion of New England* (New Haven: Yale University Press, 1923). See also, Kenneth B. Murdock, *Increase Mather, the Foremost American Puritan* (Cambridge: Harvard University Press, 1925), and again Wertenbaker, *The Puritan Oligarchy*. On Leisler and New York, Jerome R. Reich, *Leisler's Rebellion: A Study of Democracy in New York, 1664–1720* (Chicago: University of Chicago Press, 1953) and Lawrence H. Leder, *Robert Livingston, 1654–1728, and the Politics of Colonial New York* (Chapel Hill: University of North Carolina Press, 1961). Chapin, *Provincial America*, reprints "The Declaration of the Gentlemen, Merchants, and Inhabitants of Boston."

Chapter 9: The Empire at the End of the First Century

George H. Guttridge, *The Colonial Policy of William III, in America and The West Indies* (Cambridge University Press, 1922). Oliver M. Dickerson, *American Colonial Government, 1696–1765* (Cleveland: Arthur H. Clark, 1912) is a study of the Board of Trade. See again, Kellogg, *American Colonial Charters*, which is the best treatment of the attack on the private colonies. Hall's *Randolph* is relevant here. On the admiralty courts, Helen J. Crump, *Colonial Admiralty Jurisdiction in The Seventeenth Century* (London: Longmans, Green, 1931) and Charles M. Andrews' introduction to Dorothy Towle (ed.), *Records of The Vice-Admiralty Court of Rhode Island, 1716–1752* (Washington: American Historical Association, 1936).

Chapter 10: A Plural Society

On the origins and distribution of population, Evarts B. Greene and Virginia D. Harrington, *American Population before the Federal Census of 1790* (New York: Columbia University Press, 1932). For immigration, Carl Wittke, *We Who Built America: The Saga of the Immigrant* (New York: Prentice-Hall, 1939) and Marcus L. Hansen, *The Atlantic Migration, 1607–1860* (Cambridge: Harvard University Press, 1940 and reprinted New York: Harper & Row, 1961). For the Negro in colonial America, John H. Franklin, *From Slavery to Freedom, A History of American*

Negroes (New York: Knopf, 1947). There are monographs on every immigrant group. For a select bibliography see Louis B. Wright, *The Cultural Life of the American Colonies, 1607–1763* (New York: Harper & Row, 1957). Wright's book is useful for all subjects treated in this chapter.

An essay on colonial education is Bernard Bailyn, *Education in the Forming of American Society, Needs and Opportunities for Study* (Chapel Hill: University of North Carolina Press, 1960; reprinted New York: Vintage Books). The bibliography is extensive. Richard Hofstadter and Walter P. Metzger, *The Development of Academic Freedom in the United States* (New York: Columbia University Press, 1955) has an excellent analysis of the institutional origins of American colleges. Carl C. Bridenbaugh, *Cities in Revolt: Urban Life in America, 1743–1776* (New York: Knopf, 1955) contains a substantial description of city schools. Also generally useful is James T. Adams, *Provincial Society, 1690–1763* (New York: Macmillan, 1927), as are Parrington's *Colonial Mind* and Tyler's *History of American Literature*. Leonard W. Labaree, *Conservatism in Early American History* (New York: New York University Press, 1948; reprinted Ithaca. Cornell University Press, 1959) is a series of interesting essays.

On the diversification of religion, see William W. Sweet, *Religion in Colonial America* (New York: Scribner's 1942). For up-to-date references to books dealing with individual churches see the bibliography in H. Shelton Smith, *American Christianity*. More specialized books are Edwin S. Gaustad, *The Great Awakening in New England* (New York: Harper & Row, 1957); Wesley Gewehr, *The Great Awakening in Virginia, 1740–1790* (Durham: Duke University Press, 1930); Perry Miller, *The New England Mind: From Colony to Province* (Cambridge: Harvard University Press, 1953) and *Jonathan Edwards* (New York: W. Sloane Associates, 1949).

Chapter 11: The Form and Process of Colonial Politics

Though a large part of the books about colonial America deal with government and politics, there is no single volume on the subject. One goes again to Osgood's volumes for the most detailed account of politics by a single author. The first two volumes of Channing's *History of the United States* present the same material in more compact form. The earlier volumes of Bancroft are useful, as are volumes one and two of Richard Hildreth, *The History of the United States* (New York: Harper & Row, 1860). Among the older histories, Hildreth's work deserves a larger audience than it apparently has.

A good modern work on colonial politics is Clinton Rossiter, *Seed-*

time of the Republic. Chapter 1 describes "Colonial Government and the Rise of Liberty." The second part of the book analyzes the political thought of eighteenth-century colonists John Wise, Jonathan Mayhew, Richard Bland, and Benjamin Franklin. Parrington's *Colonial Mind* and Tyler's *History of American Literature* are again useful. Edward Corwin, *The "Higher Law" Background of American Constitutional Law* (reprinted Ithaca: Cornell University Press, 1955) is a succinct description of the development of natural law. The political ideas of the ministers are described in Alice M. Baldwin, *The New England Clergy and the American Revolution* (Durham: Duke University Press, 1928). The title is somewhat misleading; the first four chapters are about eighteenth-century ministers' political ideas.

Informative books dealing with specific subjects in colonial government on an all-colony, comparative basis are Mary P. Clarke, *Parliamentary Privilege in the American Colonies* (New Haven: Yale University Press, 1943); Evarts B. Greene, *The Provincial Governor in the English Colonies of North America* (New York: Longman's Green, 1898); Leonard W. Labaree, *Royal Government in America* (New Haven: Yale University Press, 1930); A. E. McKinley, *The Suffrage Franchise in the Thirteen English Colonies in America* (Philadelphia: University of Pennsylvania, 1905). Cortland F. Bishop's, *History of Elections in the American Colonies* (New York: Columbia College, 1893) deals with procedures rather than political issues.

George E. Howard offers basic coverage of local government in *An Introduction to the Local Constitutional History of the United States* (Baltimore: The Johns Hopkins Publication Agency, 1889). The best analysis of city government is *History of American City Government, the Colonial Period* by Ernest S. Griffith (New York: Oxford University Press, 1938). I have relied heavily on Howard and Griffith, and the lists of officers and functions set out in the chapter are taken from their books.

The subject of colonial politics has attracted many historians, especially in recent years. Opinion about the nature of those politics is currently in a state of flux. An excellent summary and criticism is Jack P. Greene, "Changing Interpretations of Early American Politics," which is in Ray A. Billington (ed.), *The Reinterpretation of Early American History, Essays in honor of John Edwin Pomfret* (San Marino: The Huntington Library, 1966). The first group of historians of the subject, of whom George Bancroft is the symbol, saw colonial politics progressing inevitably toward democratic forms. The "progressive" historians rudely jolted this view. The first to offer a new view was Charles H. Lincoln in *The Revolutionary Movement in Pennsylvania* (Philadelphia: University of Pennsylvania, 1901) and Carl L. Becker in *History of Political Parties in the Province of New York, 1760–1776*

(Madison: University of Wisconsin Press, 1909). Becker reduced the late colonial political conflict in New York to the pervasive aphorism that "who should rule at home" was as much the issue as "home rule." Most historians followed this lead and projected backward through the eighteenth century an interpretation of colonial politics that ranged debtor against creditor, lower class against upper. Robert E. Brown has explicitly challenged this view in *Middle Class Democracy and the Revolution in Massachusetts, 1691–1780* (Ithaca: Cornell University Press, 1955) and Robert and B. Katherine Brown, *Virginia 1705–1786: Democracy or Aristocracy?* (East Lansing: Michigan State University Press, 1964). The Browns argue that land ownership was so widespread that property qualifications for the right to vote were easily met and that a democratic political process resulted. In turn, they have been challenged, and for the criticism see Greene's essay cited above. Before and since the Browns' books, detailed studies have shown the great diversity of colonial politics. Greene's essay analyzes these books. A highly readable account of southern politics is Charles S. Sydnor, *Gentlemen Freeholders: Political Practices in Washington's Virginia* (Chapel Hill: University of North Carolina Press, 1952).

Chapter 12: The Eighteenth Century Empire

On the colonies and their administration, see the Cambridge History, *The Old Empire*, Chapter 13, Cecil Headlam, "The Development of the Colonies under the First Georges, 1711–1755," and Charles M. Andrews, "The Government of the Empire, 1660–1763." The standard accounts of the governors in America are Evarts B. Greene, *The Provincial Governor in the English Colonies of North America* and Leonard W. Labaree, *Royal Government in America, A Study of the British Colonial System Before 178?*. For the colonial assemblies see again Mary P. Clarke, *Parliamentary Privilege in the American Colonies*.

For the underlying dilemmas created by the mercantile system in regard to land, trade, money, and manufactures, see Chapters 9 and 10 of Louis M. Hacker, *The Triumph of American Capitalism* (New York: Simon and Schuster, 1940, reprinted New York: McGraw-Hill, 1965) and Curtis P. Nettels, *The Money Supply in the American Colonies before 1720* (Madison: University of Wisconsin Press, 1934). Chapters 1 and 2 of Bernhard Knollenberg, *Origins of the American Revolution: 1759–1766* (New York: Macmillan, 1960) describe the operation of British policy in the late colonial period.

The monumental, modern work dealing with the late colonial period is Lawrence H. Gipson, *The British Empire before the American*

Revolution (13 vols., Caldwell, Idaho: Caxton and New York: Knopf, 1936–1967). The bibliography of the intercolonial wars is immense. Osgood's *American Colonies* contains detailed accounts, as do Chapters, 10, 11, 12, 15, 16, 17, and 18 of the Cambridge History, *The Old Empire*. The classic is Francis Parkman, *France and England in North America* (Boston: Little, Brown, 1865–1892). The volumes relevant here are *Count Frontenac and New France; A Half-Century of Conflict; Montcalm and Wolfe.* Parkman has been abridged by Samuel E. Morrison (ed.), *The Parkman Reader: From the Works of Francis Parkman* (Boston: Little, Brown, 1955). A succinct account of the wars is Howard Peckham, *The Colonial Wars, 1689–1762* (Chicago: University of Chicago Press, 1964). See also Verner W. Crane, *The Southern Frontier, 1670–1732* (Ann Arbor: University of Michigan Press, 1929, reissued, 1956). Alfred T. Mahan, *The Influence of Sea Power upon History, 1660–1783* is a classic. Originally published in 1890, there is a convenient paperback edition (New York: Sagamore Press, 1957).

For the founding of Georgia, James E. Caldwell, *The Early Settlement of Georgia* (Athens: University of Georgia Press, 1948); E. Merton Coulter, *A Short History of Georgia* (Chapel Hill: University of North Carolina Press, 1933).

Index

Index